COMPREHENDING POWER IN
CHRISTIAN SOCIAL ETHICS

American Academy of Religion
Academy Series

edited by
Susan Thistlethwaite

Number 93

COMPREHENDING POWER IN
CHRISTIAN SOCIAL ETHICS

by
Christine Firer Hinze

Christine Firer Hinze

COMPREHENDING POWER IN CHRISTIAN SOCIAL ETHICS

Scholars Press
Atlanta, Georgia

COMPREHENDING POWER IN CHRISTIAN SOCIAL ETHICS

by
Christine Firer Hinze

Library of Congress Cataloging in Publication Data
Hinze, Christine Firer.
    Comprehending power in Christian social ethics / Christine Firer
Hinze.
        p.   cm. — (American Academy of Religion academy series ; no.
93)
    Includes bibliographical references.
    ISBN 0-7885-0167-4 (cloth : alk. paper). — ISBN 0-7885-0168-2
(paper : alk. paper)
    1. Power (Christian theology) 2. Christian ethics. 3. Power
(Social sciences) 4. Social ethics. I. Series
BJ1278.P68H56   1995
241—dc20
                                                95-41245
                                                CIP

Printed in the United States of America
on acid-free paper

TABLE OF CONTENTS

ACKNOWLEDGEMENTS

Writing is a profound exercise in collaborative efficacy. While it is impossible to name all the persons whose kind assistance has enabled me to pursue and complete this project, I want to take this opportunity to publicly acknowledge some of them. First, I am grateful for the support, challenge, and wisdom shared with me by the professors I have been privileged to study with at Catholic University of America and the University of Chicago Divinity School. Charles E. Curran, James M. Gustafson, and my dissertation director, Robin W. Lovin, deserve special thanks. I am grateful for the institutional and moral support the administration, faculty, and staff of St. Norbert College so generously provided at the dissertation-writing stage of the project, and that I have received from the Department of Theology of Marquette University during the revision and preparation of this manuscript. At critical points, Ginny Richards, Cindi Vian, and Bradford Hinze provided wonderful editorial and technical assistance.

Innumerable words and deeds of kindness, patience, and help from family members, child care providers, friends, and colleagues must remain unmentioned here. For what each of you have done, I am grateful.

My deepest love and appreciation go to my parents, Donald Paul Firer and Rosemary Kendrick Firer, and siblings, Donna Marie, Jane Elizabeth, Paul Jude, and Margaret Mary; to my husband, Bradford E. Hinze, and our sons, Paul Thomas and Karl Joseph. To you, dear family members, this work is lovingly dedicated.

INTRODUCTION

Power's significance in social and political relations is universally acknowledged. Yet scholarly attempts to precisely define, situate, or evaluate socio-political power have occasioned seemingly endless debate.[1] Some theorists describe power primarily as domination; others view it as a communal resource by which collective action is effected.[2] "Pluralists" find power dispersed widely through social systems, while "elite theorists" and Marxists aver that power clots at the tops of such systems, where dominant minorities manipulate public life, frequently without the consent or

---

[1] The focus of this book is *socio-political* power. "Social" here refers to interactions extending beyond the face-to-face interpersonal relations of friends and family. "Political" signals particular attention to the traditional areas of politics, public interactions among citizens and government.

[2] Power is understood primarily as superordination or domination by Robert Dahl, C. Wright Mills, Steven Lukes, Thomas Wartenberg, and a host of others. Talcott Parsons, Hannah Arendt, and others form a minority who contend that power is basically transformative efficacy. See, e.g., Robert Dahl, *Who Governs? Democracy and Power in an American City* (New Haven, CT: Yale University Press, 1961); Steven Lukes, *Power: A Radical View* (London: Macmillan, 1974); C. Wright Mills, *The Power Elite* (New York: Oxford University Press, 1956); Thomas Wartenberg, *The Forms Of Power* (Philadelphia: Temple University Press, 1990); Hannah Arendt, "On Violence," in *Crises of the Republic* (New York: Harcourt Brace Jovanovich, 1969); Talcott Parsons, "On the Concept of Political Power," in *Sociological Theory in Modern Society* (New York: The Free Press, 1967).

even the awareness of the majority.[3] As for normative assessments
of power, disagreements persist among those who deem power a
social good which institutions ought to foster, and those who regard
it as at best a necessary evil, which legal and political structures
must limit and control.[4]

Christian social ethicists face a complex task in coming to grips
with the issue of power. Whenever an ethicist makes evaluations
and advances prescriptions bearing upon socio-political life, some
understanding of power is brought into play. In formulating a
theory of power, the Christian ethicist must attend to conflicting
claims of social scientists and philosophers, and at the same time
seek a view that coheres with particular religious affirmations about
God, human nature, and human destiny. No social ethic can avoid
incorporating descriptive and normative assumptions about power.
The notion of power employed in Christian social ethics,
accordingly, ought to be deliberately chosen and grounded in
defensible judgments about human agency, sociality, and the

---

[3]Representatives of these positions include, of the pluralist view, Robert
Dahl; of the elite or power structure approach, C. Wright Mills; of Marxist
and post-Marxist views of hegemony and oppression, so-called critical
theorists such as those associated with the early Frankfurt School (Theodor
Adorno, Max Horkheimer, others.), and later, Jürgen Habermas. See, e.g,
Raymond Geuss, *The Idea of a Critical Theory: Habermas and the Frankfurt
School* (Cambridge: Cambridge University Press, 1981).

[4]Thinkers who judge power negatively and advocate its limitation
highlight power's propensity for becoming oppressive. See, e.g., José
Comblin, *The Church and the National Security State* (Maryknoll, NY: Orbis
Books, 1979), esp. 68-70, 96-98. See also, Geuss, *The Idea of a Critical
Theory*, and William Connolly, *The Terms of Political Discourse*, 2nd ed.
(Lexington, MA: Heath Publishing Co., 1974), esp. ch. 3. The maximization
of power as a social good is promoted by those who regard power as
indispensable for communal survival and flourishing. See, e.g., Talcott
Parsons, *Politics and Social Structure* (New York: The Free Press, 1969);
Hannah Arendt, *The Human Condition* (Chicago: The University of Chicago
Press, 1958); and practitioners such as Saul Alinsky, *Rules for Radicals* (New
York: Harper Vintage Books, 1970).

purposes and possibilities of civil community as these are seen through the lens of a communal commitment to the Gospel.

Its undeniable significance, its disputed definition, and its contested prescriptive status all argue for the importance to ethicists of a clear and coherent theory of socio-political power. Yet, compared with the volume of social theoretical writing that deals explicitly with the theme, only a small number of recent Christian ethical works have given the notion of power sustained, direct attention.[5] Over the past decade, a few works in theology and many in allied disciplines have analyzed notions of power.[6] However, literature in Christian social ethics which investigates the social theoretical discussions on power, and then elucidates ways that theological perspectives might incorporate or modify elements of those secular analyses, remains scarce.

This study responds to the need for systematic reflection upon the notion of power in Christian social ethics by addressing the relation between descriptions of power, understandings of human

---

[5]Two influential exceptions are the writings of Reinhold Niebuhr and Paul Tillich. Niebuhr's treatment of socio-political power, to be considered in Chapter II, is occasional and not thoroughly systematic. Tillich, whose contribution will be analyzed in Chapter IV, takes a more philosophical and systematic approach. See, e.g., Reinhold Niebuhr, *Moral Man and Immoral Society: A Study in Ethics and Politics* (New York: Charles Scribner, 1932), and *The Structure of Nations and Empires* (New York: Charles Scribner's Sons, 1959); Paul Tillich, *Love, Power and Justice: Ontological Analyses and Ethical Applications* (Oxford: Oxford University Press, 1954), and "The Problem of Power," in *The Interpretation of History* (New York: Charles Scribner's Sons, 1936).

[6]See especially, in theology, Anna Case-Winters, *God's Power: Traditional Understandings and Contemporary Challenges* (Louisville, KY: Westminster/John Knox Press, 1990); Kyle A. Pasewark, *A Theology of Power: Being Beyond Domination* (Minneapolis: Fortress Press, 1993); in the social sciences, Seth Kreisberg, *Transforming Power: Domination; Empowerment, and Education* (Albany: State University of New York Press, 1992); Kenneth E. Boulding, *Three Faces of Power* (Newbury Park, CA: Sage Publications, 1989); Wartenberg, *The Forms of Power*.

agency and sociality, and prescriptions for social action and organization, as these are found in selected major works of the last century. First, two general understandings of power, "power-over," and "power-to," will be presented and used to analyze a variety of secular and religious writings.   Second, the relation between descriptive and normative claims in representative theories of power will be examined, with particular reference to two complex interactions: the interaction between descriptions of power and assumptions about the nature of society and human agency, and the interaction between the descriptive theory of power employed and prescriptions regarding socio-political life.   Third, and most important, I will argue that treatments of power accommodating and plausibly integrating power-to and power-over are more adequate than those that do not. Such a comprehensive approach, I will seek to show, better accounts for social experience, and enhances the explanatory, prescriptive, and practical repertoire available to theorists and activists.   Each of these three tasks requires elaboration.

Power: Two Descriptive Models

Ethicists and social theorists typically conceptualize socio-political power with one of two emphases, either as transformative capacity or as superordination.   We can cull from the extensive literature of social and political theory *two ideal typical models*, which elaborate different pictures of power based on distinctive root metaphors.[7] The first model, the one most prevalent in social and

---

[7] I employ the term "ideal type," following Max Weber, to indicate a construct which assembles and organizes elements found in historical experience for the sake of descriptive and explanatory clarity. An ideal type has a certain conceptual purity, but the pure type is rarely, if ever, found in concrete experience. See Max Weber, *The Methodology of the Social Sciences*, E. A. Shils and H. A. Finch, trans. & eds. (New York: The Free Press, 1949), 90.

ethical theory, views socio-political power primarily in terms of *superordination*--power is essentially *control over* decisions, paths of action, and outcomes, but especially over other people. In the second, the root image is that of *effective capacity*--power is primarily people's *ability to* effect their ends. This study will refer to the superordination model as "power--over." Power-over involves any agent's capacity to significantly affect others, especially by eliciting their cooperation, obedience, or acquiescence in furthering ends determined by that agent.[8] There is a coercive dimension to power-over: to some degree, X's effect on Y or procurement of Y's compliance occurs irrespective of Y's choice in the matter. A power-over relation does not extinguish the agency of the subordinate party. Nonetheless, the agency of the ascendant X, advancing ends over or against the subordinate Y, is the focus of this model of power.

A second model locates the heart of social power in the capacity of persons to collaborate in effecting ends. "Power-to" can require that resources be gathered and directed, or that the resistance of others be overcome. Doing so may require the introduction of elements of power-over. However, this model's general description of power as effective agency sets superordination within a broader compass and limits its status to only one possible instrument in the expression of power, rather than identifying it *as* power itself. Power on this view inheres in agency rather than in domination. In contrast to power-over's stress on the agency of the "over" party versus a subordinate other, the power-to model tends to regard the agency of all together as productive of power, locating power as a feature of the entire acting collective rather than in one segment thereof. Whereas the first model emphasizes power's capacity to act *against* or *in spite of* others, the power-to model

---

[8]Power-over can exist whether or not X consciously intends or recognizes such relations with Y.

focuses on power's efficacy as emerging *with* or *because of* others.[9]

Socio-political power viewed from either perspective involves *receptivity* and *relationship*. Both models portray power in terms of activity and initiative, yet each also incorporates a dimension of receptivity. Though rarely to the fore in popular usage, traditional philosophical theories of power--and standard dictionary definitions --affirm that besides being the ability to influence, power also means the capability of being influenced, receptivity to being affected.[10] Receptivity is interpreted differently in the two models, but that it has a role in both is testimony to the further fact that relationships are constitutive of socio-political power. These relationships are never wholly unidirectional. Even in the most oppressive power-over relations the superordinate requires an agent to participate in subjugation, and agents almost by definition retain some ability to

---

[9]These two models, in my estimation, capture the most significant dimensions of the complex phenomenon to which "socio-political power" refers, and configure them in ways consistent with prevalent social and ethical thinking. Our two ideal types are, however, neither logically nor empirically exhaustive. The root meaning of power-to as transformative capacity, for example, could be portrayed in an individualistic rather than a communal manner. Such an individualistic version of power-to may underlie political theories that describe freedom as the individual's right to effect self-chosen ends as long as this does not infringe on others' right to similar freedom--that is, as long as one's "individual power-to" does not become illegitimate "power-over" others. Yet an individualistic construal obscures the relational features of *socio-political* power highlighted by the models used here.

[10]Power may mean, e.g., "(1): ability to act or produce an effect . . . (3): *capacity for being acted upon or undergoing an effect . . . .*" *Webster's Ninth New Collegiate Dictionary* (Springfield, MA: Merriam-Webster Inc., 1983), 922, emphasis supplied. John Silber attends to the philosophical tradition on receptive power, reflected in Plato's equation of power and being, and concludes, "When we recognize that power is the ability to affect or be affected we shall be able to recognize the family resemblances of power in its many forms . . . ." John R. Silber, "The Conceptual Structure of Power: A Review," in D. W. Haward, ed., *Power: Its Forms, Bases, and Uses* (New York: Harper and Row Publishers, 1979), 2.

influence their partners. Likewise, transformative capacity, power-to, is never actualized without the explicit or implicit collaboration of others, who inevitably affect one another."

Illuminating differences obtain between the ways that receptivity and relationality are evaluated within each model. In the power-over model, power is considered the greatest when the superordinate is the least susceptible to being affected by subordinates. Receptivity tends to be either obscured or denigrated when power is viewed as domination. Conversely, the power-to model regards power as most present when all members of an acting body freely participate in the relations of mutual affecting and being-affected (activity and receptivity) that collaboration demands, and when leaders responsively (receptively) tap and coordinate the myriad potentialities of communal members toward the accomplishment of mutually agreed-upon purposes.

The question of whose benefit or interest is served by the exercise of power, and in what such benefit or interest might consist, is left open in the two descriptive models just delineated. Relations of power-over can be destructive of the interests or welfare of the power agent or recipient, or they may advance the well-being of either or both. Likewise, in the case of power-to, agency may be effected to the benefit or to the detriment of all or some of those who make up the acting body, or those affected by them.[12]

---

[11] As we shall see, secular social theorists often consider relationality and receptivity in the context of dialectical control between superordinates and subordinates, or of dynamics of authority and consent. Some Christian ethicists also ponder solidarity and suffering in relation to these, often unexamined, features of power.

[12] By leaving open this question of the interests served by the expression of power in the two models, I intend to signal both recognition of the problem of interests as raised by Marxists, critical theorists and others (e.g., Steven Lukes) as germane to the problematic of power. I also wish to emphasize that power's *descriptive* lineaments are not, in my view, essentially determined by whether or not it serves the best interests of those exercising

In actual practice one inevitably faces questions about what constitutes the good, or benefit, or interest of individuals and groups, and about what sorts of relationships and which ends advance those goods or interests. Addressing such questions brings social theory to the brink of ethical theory. Different theorists' formulations of these issues have much to do with their descriptive and normative assumptions about persons and societies.

Normative Contexts and Implications

Along with demonstrating the presence and operation of these two models of power, the analysis contained in the following chapters will reveal that operating models of power are undergirded by assumptions regarding human agency and society, and, in turn, influence the way in which social injustice is described, and its remedies prescribed. A variety of possible relations between anthropological frameworks and understandings of power, and between theories of power and assessments of social injustice, may be envisaged. A second principal aim of this study is to explore the ways in which selected secular and religious thinkers relate sociological and anthropological assumptions, notions of socio-political power, and social ethical judgments.

To this end, a number of questions will be posed to the materials under consideration. What facts about human personhood are deemed most important in theories emphasizing one or the other model of power? Is there a systematic relationship between basic images of society and understandings of power? For example, does an emphasis upon power-to accompany a sociology that admits the possibility of common public goods, with power-over coming to the fore in theories that picture society in terms of competing and incommensurable interests? How does the

---

it or affected by it. The *ethical* status attributed to particular power relations, on other hand, may be systematically related to whose good or interests are being served in power's exercise.

description of power affect the way the social ethical project is construed? For instance, does an emphasis upon power-to lead to a view of the ethical task as arranging socio-political relations so that power may be harmoniously maximized? Injustice from this perspective might be thought to result from powerlessness, and solutions would focus upon empowerment of the weak. On the other hand, power-over theories must first be examined for their assessment of the normative status of domination, and then for their judgments about its exercise.

Toward a Comprehensive Approach

This brings us to the third and most important task to be pursued here. I will argue that, besides being coherent with undergirding convictions about humanity and society, an adequate descriptive and normative approach to socio-political power must be *comprehensive*, that is, it must account for and conceptually integrate the kinds of interaction and experience each of our two models seeks to capture. More specifically, I hope to show that Christian social ethics is best served by a theory of power comprehends and relates both transformative efficacy--power-to, and superordination--power-over, in a manner consistent with a clearly articulated philosophical and theological horizon.

While neither model of power denies the existence of the characteristic central to the other, the orienting metaphor of each significantly colors the way in which power and its place in social and political processes is described. Certain social and political phenomena are highlighted and others muted when seen from the perspective of each type. The model emphasized will also affect normative judgments regarding power's appropriate uses and ends. This means that a comprehensive approach to power in Christian ethics must be more than a random amalgam of features of the power-to and power-over models. The ethicist must make a case for the descriptive and normative adequacy of the specific way the two notions of power are related. The comprehensive interpretation of socio-power that results will be backed by warrants drawn from the ethicist's religious tradition, from relevant secular measures of reasonableness and practicality, and from the wisdom born of human experience broadly construed.[13]

An explicit case for a comprehensive approach to power in Christian social ethics will be made in the final chapter, but the thesis acts as a guiding thread, and evidence of its validity is marshalled throughout. Theories accenting specific models of power will serve to challenge the coherence and comprehensiveness of alternative positions. What is included and what is omitted, what is obscured and what is stressed will be noted in both power-to and power-over theories. Reasons for such emphases and shadings, and their consequences for ethics will be sought.

Whether a particular theorist offers an adequately comprehensive approach to power will depend on the following: Are both understandings of power accounted for? Are sufficient grounds given for the way power-over and power-to are linked and prioritized? How does this theory of power cohere with orienting sociological and anthropological assumptions, and with resulting normative positions? How effectively does this theory illumine

---

[13]I have in mind the basic sources from which Christian ethics draws, helpfully summarized by Lisa Sowle Cahill as, "the foundational texts or 'scriptures' of the faith community--the Bible; the community's 'tradition' of faith, theology, and practice; philosophical accounts of essential or ideal humanity ('normative' accounts of the human); and descriptions of what actually is and has been the case in human lives and societies ('descriptive' accounts of the human)." *Between the Sexes: Foundations for a Christian Ethics of Sexuality* (Philadelphia: Fortress Press, 1985), 5. Cf. James M. Gustafson, *Protestant and Roman Catholic Ethics: Prospects for Rapprochement* (Chicago: The University of Chicago Press, 1978), 142; Timothy E. O'Connell, *Principles for a Catholic Morality*, revised ed. (San Francisco: HarperSanfrancisco, 1990), 8-10. The seriousness with which this approach takes secular sources for religious ethics bespeaks an underlying theological position best described as a "critical correlation" model. See David Tracy, *Blessed Rage for Order: The New Pluralism in Theology* (New York: Seabury, 1975), ch. 2.

concrete social ethical practice? Since, as we will see, power-over has been the prevalent emphasis in both social and religious theory, part of our evaluative task will be to expose the deficiencies of approaches that give short shrift to the power-to model, and to demonstrate the benefits of integrating that model more fully and explicitly into descriptive an normative analyses of social and political life.

Plan of Study

This work unfolds in five chapters. Chapter One will elucidate the pre-eminence of the power-over conception in modern social theory by way of an analysis of Max Weber's classic formulations on political and social power. Note will also be taken of the profound contribution of Karl Marx to contemporary understandings of domination, especially through his insights into alienation and ideology. Marxian and Weberian influences and interactions with other theoretical strands in more recent works will be briefly considered.

Chapter Two takes up the treatment of power in mainstream Christian social theory and ethics during the middle of the twentieth century. Following remarks on the impact of theological presuppositions on political theory and ethics, a comparative analysis of the treatment of power in the Catholic political thought of Jacques Maritain, and in the Protestant social ethics of Reinhold Niebuhr will be provided. The two authors' positions will be compared with respect to their Christian anthropological and sociological orientations, the relation they perceive between power-to and power-over within the socio-political arena, and the relative comprehensiveness of their respective theories of power. I will show that, with certain qualifications, both Niebuhr and Maritain reflect modern social theory's predilection for identifying power with superordination. In light of this, Christian social ethics can benefit from the study of other strands in social theory which give a more prominent place to the notion of power as transformative agency.

Chapter Three returns to social theory and political philosophy to probe for insights into the power-to conceptualization. Here, voices of dissent against the predominance of power-over will be highlighted, with Hannah Arendt as their chief spokesperson. Different appropriations of power-to will be uncovered in varying contemporary social theoretical approaches, namely, those of Michel Foucault, Anthony Giddens, and certain North American feminists.

Chapter Four investigates recent Christian theological ethicists who incorporate, in varying ways, the model of power as transformative capacity. All these treatments of power, it will be seen, are rooted in specific descriptive and normative visions of the human person and of society, which in turn are grounded in theological affirmations about human nature, history, and destiny. Highlighted will be ontologically grounded theories of power, represented by Paul Tillich and process theologians, along with Christian liberationist theories of Latin American, African American, and North American feminist origins.

The concluding chapter makes a case for a systematically comprehensive approach to power in Christian social ethics. The outlines of a constructive argument for a theology and ethics oriented by power-to will be sketched. Regardless of the model of power they may wish to make central, I shall argue that being comprehensive will require most Christian ethicists to integrate the notion of power as transformative agency more fully and clearly into their thinking. Doing so, I shall contend, will contribute toward a social ethics that is not only more theologically, anthropologically, and sociologically accurate, but one whose conceptual depth and breadth better suit it to the pressing 21st century work of building emancipatory, empowering social and political forms.

CHAPTER I

POWER AS DOMINATION
IN SOCIAL AND POLITICAL THEORY

Introduction

The terminology concerning power employed by contemporary scholars is significantly influenced by social theory and the social sciences, disciplines which take their place along with religious texts and traditions, philosophy, and human experience as sources for Christian ethics. It is important for this project, then, that major streams of social and political thought feeding recent social ethics be considered. By examining significant representative theories of socio-political power, this chapter will serve two purposes. First, the prevalence of what we here call the "power-over" model in modern social and political thought will be illustrated. Second, the relationship between these formulations of power and the anthropological and sociological tenets that accompany them will be probed.[1] Showing how power is treated in two prominent social

---

[1]As Steven Lukes states, "any given conception of power will necessarily incorporate a theory of that to which it is attributed: To identify the power of an individual, or a class, or a social system, one must, consciously or unconsciously, have a theory of the nature . . . of individuals, classes, or social systems." "Power and Authority," *History of Sociological Analysis*, T. Bottomore & R. Nisbet, eds. (New York: Basic Books, 1978), 635.

scientific instances will help illumine the theoretical landscape of contemporary ethical reflection on power, and lay groundwork for the discussion of Christian social ethics in later chapters.

We will begin with a close look at the theory of power found in the writings of Max Weber. His classic formulation of the power as superordination will be analyzed and set in the context of his undergirding assumptions regarding human agency and society. Weber's theory will then be compared and contrasted with the treatment of power by another formidable figure in modern Western social thought, Karl Marx.

Despite important similarities between these original and influential descriptions of socio-political power, Marx and Weber represent two different ways of accommodating a an emphasis on power-over. Max Weber not only studies domination, but this model of power permeates his normative views about politics and social relations. For Marx, the situation is more complex. His theory of the future communist society accords normative priority to social relations in which dominative power is replaced by mutual effective capacity, what we call here power-to. Despite this fact, he merits study as a power-over thinker since, in the political economy of his day (as in our own), that is the form in which power prevails, and in which Marx dissects it. It is as the supreme analyst of dominative power-over that Marx contributes some of his greatest insights to social theory.

Marx will be examined here, then, for his analysis and criticism of the power-over model; Weber, for his analysis and dependence upon this same model. Special attention will be given to the two thinkers' treatments of power as a feature of modern political processes and systems.

Max Weber

Max Weber identified the aim of his interpretive sociology as understanding social action by explaining its development and effects in causal terms.[2] "Action" is behavior to which an individual attaches a meaning, and a social action is one whose intention "has reference to the behavior of another person and which therefore is determined in its course by that behavior."[3] The social scientist, observing such behavior, seeks to accurately interpret the meaning it holds for the actors involved. The goals of Weberian sociology include comprehending the causes of past and present social action, and predicting--to the extent possible given human freedom--the behaviors and outcomes that may be expected in similar future circumstances. Such interpretive understanding is to be pursued by investigators from a carefully preserved position of value-neutrality.[4]

---

[2]Max Weber, "The Interpretive Understanding of Social Action," in H. Feigl & M. Brodbeck, eds., *Readings in the Philosophy of Science* (New York: Appleton-Century-Crofts, 1953), 20. "Causal" here refers to the search for the historical antecedents and conditions for social conduct. Weber believes that discovering these can provide a certain measure of predictive power, but that in the arena of human freedom, one must not expect mechanistic "laws" of social action comparable to what might be approximated in the natural sciences.

[3]Weber quoted in Raymond Aron, *German Sociology*, Mary & Thomas Bottomore, trans. (Glencoe, IL: The Free Press, 1964), 100. See also Weber, "Interpretive Understanding of Social Action," 20-21.

[4]Weber fought to establish social science as a discipline in which the determination of "facts" is kept carefully distinct from judgments of "value" on the part of the investigator. Only in this way, he argued, could science make its proper contribution to ethics and politics. Science can provide accurate information about the possibilities for choice, and, based on previous examples, point out probable consequences of diverse courses of action. In so doing scientific theory genuinely serves ethics and political action, for it increases the freedom of actors by clarifying the ramifications of choice and widening the scope for its exercise. See Max Weber, "Value Judgments in

Weber's stress on intentionality as a central feature of genuine social action makes his an actionist, rather than a structurist, notion of social conduct in general, and of socio-political power in particular.[5] "Intentional" action involves the deliberate combination of means in order to attain an end, or, more broadly, any behavior which is not an instinctive or mechanical reaction.[6] This is not to say that Weber views social life as wholly controlled by conscious intentionality. His frequent reference to the unintended--and often noxious--consequences of deliberately pursued courses of action reflects his recognition that structures also work "behind the backs" of social actors. Weber's treatment of the effects of the historical process of rationalization provide the most important example of this. This combination of a generally actionist perspective and a more structurist understanding of rationalization's unintended

---

the Social Sciences," W. G. Runciman, ed., *Weber: Selections in Translation* (Cambridge: Cambridge University Press, 1978), 86-87. Cf. Stephen L. Esquith, "Politics and Values in Marx and Weber," in R. J. Antonio & R. M. Glassman, eds., *A Weber-Marx Dialogue* (Lawrence, KS: University Press of Kansas, 1985), 308-15.

[5]This distinction is used by Steven Lukes, among others. See Lukes, "Power and Authority"; Steven Lukes, "Power and Structure," *Essays in Social Theory* (New York: Columbia University Press, 1977), 3-29. In another account, M. Bloch, B. Heading, and P. Lawrence distinguish the ontological claims undergirding actionist and structurist theories of power: "Structuralist meta-theory . . . involves an ontological claim that human behavior is totally causally determined by the structures within which men are located. They are the passive 'bearers' of structurally-determined inputs rather than being capable of exercising . . . free will." Embedded in actionist meta-theory is the ontological claim that "humans are qualitatively different from other subjects for science because they are agents who always have the potential . . . to exercise a degree of free will in thought and deed." "Power in Social Theory: A Non-Relative View," in S. C. Brown, ed., *Philosophical Disputes in the Social Sciences* (Sussex, NJ: Harvester and Humanities Press, 1979), 248-49.

[6]Aron, *German Sociology*, 100.

effects produces tensions within Weber's social theory as a whole, and frames his treatment of socio-political power.

An important feature of Weber's method is his practice of accumulating and interpreting historical data, which are then crystallized as historically saturated typologies, or "ideal types."[7] The types are meant to make coherent, and provide insight into, the vagaries of collective human action. Weber's typology of legitimate domination is perhaps the most well-known example of this ideal typical approach.

Power and Rationalization
in Western Capitalist Society

Investigating the process of rationalization in Western society, charting its course, and elucidating its consequences for individual and collective life in the modern period were orienting aims of Max Weber's work.[8] His concern with rationalization and its

---

[7]Guenther Roth, in Max Weber, *Economy and Society*, Guenther Roth & Claus Wittich, eds. (Berkeley: University of California Press, 1968), 1:C. Critics of ideal types charge that their abstraction from the historically concrete makes them irrelevant to practically oriented analysis. See, e.g., Beverly Wildung Harrison, *Making the Connections: Essays in Feminist Social Ethics* (Boston: Beacon Press, 1985), 64-67, n. 33. Roth's terminology reflects Weber's intention that ideal types be abstractions, but abstractions drawing their content from, and serving to clarify, the historical events on which they are based. Weber emphasized that the types neither replace nor fully capture the richness of historical reality, but are selective, heuristic devices meant to help us understand it. Weber, *Ethics and Society*, 1:20-22. See also, Wolfgang J. Mommsen, *The Age of Bureaucracy: Perspectives on the Political Sociology of Max Weber* (Oxford: Basil Blackwell, 1974), 20-21.

[8]Anthony Giddens compares the significance of Weber's concept of "rationalization" to that of "class" in Marx's writings: It is an idea so fundamental to his theory that, in his more important works, he often takes its meaning for granted. *Capitalism and Modern Social Theory* (New York: Cambridge University Press, 1971), 36-37, 83.

empowering and disempowering effects in western society, is the broader context that situates his articulation of power as *Herrschaft*. Weber describes rationalization summarily as a process of "demagicalization" or "disenchantment of the world" in which magical understandings are displaced with ever-more systematically coherent and naturalistically consistent explanations.[9]   As a multidimensional historical process involving the systematic organization of *ideas*, normative *patterns for action* that stress effectiveness, consistency, and calculability, and culturally inculcated *motivations* for thinking and acting in rationalized patterns, rationalization is, in Weber's eyes, the greatest single force for change in the modern world.[10]

Issues pertaining to social power are at the heart of the rationalization process as Weber depicts it.   Rationalization is originally propelled by a liberating movement away from the domineering power of nature and supernature, and toward agents' purposive control over their own actions and destiny.   Indeed, insofar as it involves the collaborative actuation of humans' transformative capacity, it could be said that the positive intent of rationalization is to increase both the dominative control of--power-

---

[9]A thicker description uncovers three interlocking dimensions of this complex historical process. In any social sphere, rationalization refers, first, to abstract reflection about the realm of life in question (e.g., religion, nature, politics) leading to the *systematic organization of ideas* held to be true. These ideas are then linked to *normative patterns for action* geared toward achieving the goals of that societal sphere with the greatest possible effectiveness, consistency, regularity, and calculability. These norms are accompanied by corresponding *motivations* by individuals and groups to adopt a lifestyle (involving both beliefs and obligations) conducive to carrying out the patterns of behavior that the ascendant organization of ideas requires. See Talcott Parsons, introduction, in Max Weber, *The Sociology of Religion* (Boston: Beacon Press, 1964).

[10]Two other forces for dynamic change are traditional and charismatic leadership; of these, the latter shares with rationalization a significant place in the modern world. Mommsen, *The Age of Bureaucracy*, 80-81. See also, Parsons, "Introduction," in Weber, *Sociology of Religion*, lxii.

over--natural and social forces, and the efficacy--power-to--of agents within a social system.

Weber conceives the driving force in this process as the ascendance of means-ends rational (*zweckrational*) action. Social action is *zweckrational* "when the ends, the means, and the secondary results are all rationally taken into account and weighed. This involves rational consideration of alternative means to an end, of the relation between the end and secondary consequences, and finally of the relative importance of different possible ends."[11] Efficiency and control over social and material environments are enhanced to the extent that social action and structure exhibits this kind of rationality.[12] Though not unique to modern western industrial societies, means-ends rationalization has developed to an incomparable degree in them.[13] In economic and social relations, rationalization is expressed through bureaucratic organization, and in political life, through legal-rational domination.

As means-ends rationality takes hold in every area of communal life, however, a surprising reversal occurs. Purposive rationality becomes systematized in bureaucratic structures and procedures that seem to take on a life of their own. Increasingly bureaucratized social organization eventuates, willy nilly, in the subordination of substantive, orienting ends (the domain of normative, "substantive rationality") to the formal means (related to "instrumental rationality") of the bureaucratic machine.[14]

---

[11]Weber, *Economy and Society*, 1:26.

[12]On the types of rationality in Weber's work, see, e.g., Weber, *Economy and Society*, 1: 24-26, 85-86; Mommsen, *The Age of Bureaucracy* 73 n. 1; and Donald N. Levine's helpful analysis, "Rationality and Freedom: Weber and Beyond," *Sociological Inquiry* 51 (1982): 5-25.

[13]Max Weber, *The Protestant Ethic and the Spirit of Capitalism*, Talcott Parsons, trans. (New York: Charles Scribner's Sons, 1958), author's introduction.

[14]"Formal" rationality refers to the methodical ordering of activity according to fixed rules and routines which maximize predictability and minimize the influence of personalities, social status or other special

Bureaucracy, originally developed to extend persons' control over their lives, becomes an end in itself, subordinating its supposed masters to the requirements of the processes that maintain it. Besides holding its participants in thrall to the requirements of formal efficiency, rationalization in the form of bureaucratization has another principal effect: it so entrenches the structures in question that systematic political or social change is extremely difficult.[15] Thus, ironically, rationalization comes to generate consequences exactly the opposite of its original liberating and empowering intent. Weber viewed the irrationality spawned by the historical process of rationalization as the pathos of modern life.[16] His examination of socio-political power both reflects and seeks to address this pathos.

Individual and Society

His use of collective concepts notwithstanding, Max Weber's approach to the study of society never obviates the role of individual agency. Within his interpretive sociology, action exists only as the behavior of one or more individual human beings; social

---

considerations. "Substantive" rationality relates to evaluative standards and the establishment of valid canons for empirical investigation.

[15]Mommsen, *The Age of Bureaucracy*, 80.

[16]More specifically, for Weber, capitalism's superlative attainment of formal rationality is associated with increasing substantive irrationality. Yet Weber saw no way out of this predicament. Marx's communistic solution did not, in Weber's judgment, address the essential problem: how maximum individual freedom was to be preserved. While remaining one of its most probing critics, Weber ultimately defended capitalism because he believed that no other system could provide as much social mobility, or better chances for preserving a degree of individual freedom and creative leadership in an inescapably bureaucratic modern world. See Weber, *Economy and Society*, 1:138; Karl Löwith, *Max Weber and Karl Marx*, T. B. Bottomore and M. J. Mulkay, eds., H. Fantel, trans. (London: Allen & Unwin, 1982), 40-41, 48-49; Mommsen, *The Age of Bureaucracy*, 6.

collectivities such as states, associations, or corporations are ultimately, "*solely* the resultants and modes of organization of the particular acts of individual persons, since these alone can be treated as agents in a course of subjectively understandable action."[17] This individualist focus colors Weber's entire construal of the terms and relations of social interaction. Its impact is plainly seen in his agent-oriented definitions of social action, power, and domination, in his attention to leaders in political life, in his concern about the individual's loss of creativity and mobility under the tyranny of bureaucratic routine, and in his hope in inspired charismatic "heroes" who might overcome bureaucracy's constraints.[18]

Weber's retention of the individual reflects important anthropological and sociological differences between his theory and that of Karl Marx. Marx emphasizes humans as "species-beings" and class structures, while Weber stresses the irreducibility of the individual and the artificial nature of collectivities. While not denying the usefulness of collective concepts for sociological analysis, Weber insists that sociology's task is to interpret accurately, by coming to understand subjectively, the action of the component individuals of any body.[19] For Marx, the individual intentions and motivations behind social action are secondary if not insignificant to the larger structural dynamics at play. These divergent accents have a decided impact on the two thinkers' descriptions of socio-political power.

---

[17]Weber, "Interpretive Understanding of Social Action," 33.

[18]This is not to equate Weber's approach with the atomistic individualism characteristic of some British social theory. My intent is to distinguish Weber both from the strand of German idealism that tends to endow corporate entities with collective personality, and from the collectivism of Marx.

[19]Weber, "Interpretive Understanding of Social Action," 31, 33.

Weber on Socio-Political Power

Max Weber's definition of power is very likely the one most frequently used in the social theoretical literature.[20] Weber's initial definition of *Macht*, power, as "the probability that one actor in a social relation will be in a position to carry out his own will despite resistance, regardless of the basis on which this probability rests," stakes out an intentional and asymmetrical understanding, but does not limit power to species of domination. He swiftly dismisses this definition as "sociologically amorphous," however, in favor of a focus on power in the form of *Herrschaft* or, "authoritarian power of command."[21] Weber defines *Herrschaft* as "the probability that a command with a given specific content will be obeyed by a given group of persons." *Herrschaft* refers to "the situation in which the manifested will (*command*) of the *ruler* or rulers is meant to influence the conduct of one or more others (*the ruled*) and actually does influence it in such a way that their conduct to a socially relevant degree occurs as if the rule had made the content of the command the maxim of their conduct for its very

---

[20]Anthony Giddens, *Central Problems in Social Theory: Action, Structure, and Contradiction in Social Analysis* (Berkeley and Los Angeles: University of California Press, 1979), 256. Giddens, whose theory will be considered in Chapter III, criticizes Weber's definition in two respects relevant to the critique offered here. First, the definition reflects Weber's subjectivist methodological position and leads to a dualism of action and structure that Giddens insists has to be overcome. Second, ". . . considered solely from the point of view of the connection between power and agency, it does not bite deeply enough. For the notion of human action logically implies that of power understood as transformative capacity . . . we have to relate power as a resource drawn upon by agents in the production and reproduction of interaction to the structural characters of society. Neither aspect of power is more 'basic' than the other." Ibid., 256-57.

[21]Weber, *Economy and Society*, 1:53.

own sake."[22] This shift to exclusive focus on *Herrschaft* is a crucial move, for it locks Weber into a vision of socio-political power as superordination, or power-over.

Why does Weber judge the most sociologically significant referent of "power" to be relations of command and obedience, authority manifest in diverse forms and grounded in a variety of motivations? A main reason for this judgment seems to be the difficulty he anticipated in adequately systematizing the more diffuse sorts of encounters associated with other expressions of power.[23] Another is Weber's interest in the role of creative leadership in modern society. Weber's theory of authority uses ideal types that underline the elements he deemed particularly relevant for the future of the liberal societies of the west. Consistent with his

---

[22]Weber, *Economy and Society*, 1:53, 2:946. Many commentators have discussed the difficulty of translating the term, *Herrschaft*. Its meaning seems to lie somewhere between "legitimate authority" and "domination." See, e.g., Guenther Roth in Weber, *Economy and Society*, 1:xciv, 1:61 n. 31; Mommsen, *The Age of Bureaucracy*, 72 n. 1.

[23]Though Weber briefly discusses relations in which power operates outside of fixed authoritative command, he resists any formulation that moves significantly away from the notion of power-over. "Domination in the quite general sense of power, i.e., of the possibility of imposing one's own will upon the behavior of other persons, can emerge in the most diverse forms. . . . [If] one looks upon the claims which the law accords to one person against one or more others as a power to issue commands [for example, the claim of the civil servant over the king by way of a right to salary] . . . one may thereby conceive of the whole system of modern private law as the decentralization of domination in the hands of those to whom the legal rights are accorded. . . . Such a terminology would be rather forced, and, in any case, . . . of not more than provisional value. . . . However, a position ordinarily designated as 'dominating' can emerge from the social relations in a drawing room as well as in the market, from the rostrum of a lecture-hall as well as from the command post of a regiment, from an erotic or charitable relationship as well as from scholarly discussion or athletics. Such a broad definition would, however, render the term 'domination' scientifically useless . . ." *Economy and Society*, 1:942-43.

concerns, Weber placed the question of how leaders are identified, and their rule justified, at the center of his classification of the various types of domination.[24]

Authority, more specifically legitimate authority, is the specification of power-over that most absorbs Weber. Now, two basic elements inhere in any notion of authority: the surrender of private judgment, and the identification of the possessor or exerciser of authority as having a claim to do so. Beyond this commonality, as Steven Lukes has pointed out, authority may be conceptualized in a variety of ways: as authority over belief, whereby the right to rule is claimed on the grounds of some special wisdom, insight, skill, or knowledge; as authority by convention, where the source of authority is assumed to have been voluntarily accepted by some commonly agreed upon procedure (highlighted in modern liberal political theories); or as authority by imposition, whereby the acceptance of authority is imposed by means of coercion, either overt or covert (accented by so-called realist political theory).[25]

Weber's typologies of domination ascribe authority over belief to both charismatic and traditional *Herrschaft*. Legal-bureaucratic domination is a form of authority by convention; yet in this type also, authority over belief must be accorded to the procedures and structures (and representatives of such) that have been formulated by common agreement. The notion of authority by imposition presumes that power is coercive control maintained by some in the community over others, to the benefit of the former, and against the will and interests of the latter. As we shall see, Karl Marx interprets political rule as a system of imposed authority that, thanks to mystifying ideology, is able to masquerade as legitimate authority over belief. The emphasis Weber places on legitimacy would seem to prevent his typologies of domination from including relations where obedience is simply imposed. To ascertain whether

---

[24]Mommsen, *The Age of Bureaucracy*, 19.
[25]Lukes, "Power and Authority," 640-44.

this is so, however, requires a closer examination of his theory of legitimation.[26]

"Legitimation," for Weber, refers to the different principles by which *Herrschaft* is justified from the point of view of ruler and ruled. The most stable political arrangements are those which elicit obedience not just on the grounds of expedience, coercion or habit, but are obeyed because they are viewed, for a variety of reasons, as having the right to be heeded.[27] Such persuasive warrants for obedience constitute the legitimacy of a given regime.

Weber asserts that identifying different forms of legitimation is the best way to distinguish what he calls "pure types" of domination. Three different principles of legitimation are isolated, which are linked in turn to three major types of *Herrschaft*. A first principle of legitimation is rational rules, whereby obedience is to norms rationally delineated. This principle is characteristic of legal, or bureaucratic domination. Second, legitimacy may derive from a principle of authority founded on tradition, whereby obedience is to authority figures who are themselves bound to traditional norms--hence, traditional domination. Finally, the principle of legitimation may be personal authority founded on charisma, whereby obedience is to the person of a gifted, inspirational leader; this Weber identifies as charismatic domination. Bureaucratic/ rational, traditional and charismatic domination each issue in distinct forms of organization and political relations. Major sections of *Economy and Society* are devoted to theoretical descriptions of these three types, accompanied by historical examples that illustrate concrete forms that each type has taken.[28]

---

[26]Max A. Myers grapples with the relations between Weber's "legitimation" and Marx's "ideology," and the significance of both terms for Christian social ethics in "'Ideology' and 'Legitimation' as Necessary Concepts for Christian Ethics," *Journal of the American Academy of Religion* 69 (Spring 1981): 187-210.

[27]Weber, *Economy and Society*, 2:946-48.

[28]Ibid., vol. 2, chs. 10-15.

Legitimacy, then, is a formal term attributed to social or political relationships wherein leaders and followers agree and act upon on compelling reasons--be they traditionally, charismatically, or rationally grounded--why commands ought to be obeyed. This formulation begs the question of whether those who judge a system of rule acceptable might be mistaken or deceived. By basing legitimacy on the beliefs of those who command and obey, Weber on the one hand ignores (and hence provides no critical purchase upon) power-over relations that might, despite such acceptance, be illegitimate on other grounds.[29]   On the other hand, this view of legitimacy accents the potential fragility of *herrschaftlich* relations: when the web of beliefs that supports rule deteriorates or breaks, social power-over is jeopardized and may vanish completely.[30]

These were not, however, the issues that caught Weber's attention as he considered social and political power. His own concern was combatting the threats to individual freedom posed by modern bureaucratic power-over. Significantly, Weber's theory of legitimate domination circumscribes the frame of reference within

---

[29]These "other grounds" might be normative (e.g., when a system of rule is accepted that nevertheless lacks the right to claim obedience) or descriptive (e.g., when a system of rule is accepted for reasons that are mistaken or incorrect), or, as in the case of ideology, a combination of both (as when a rule is accepted because its followers have been led to believe it is conducive to their flourishing to do so, but this is not in fact the case; therefore, they ought not to submit to it.)

[30]Why, then, in the case of bureaucratic domination especially, did Weber notice not the fragility but rather the fixed and intransigent nature of the power-over relation? One reason may be that, unlike charismatic and traditional authority, which clearly depend upon a community's shared *Wertrationalität* (agreement on non-rational values, such as the value of tradition, or the inspired message of a charismatic leader), Weber saw bureaucratic rationality as working according to supremely rational--and hence unquestionable--*zweckrational* principles, whose very effectiveness would assure bureaucracy's unremitting and ever-increasing sway over its subjects.

which his exploration of this problem remains confined. In his search for solutions to the problems of bureaucratic domination, he thinks mainly in terms of other forms of *Herrschaft*, especially charismatic domination, as avenues for retaining individual freedom. On this point, greater attention to power as transformative efficacy would have lent Weber's analysis more breadth and probity.

Wolfgang Mommsen persuasively argues that *Economy and Society* is in the end concerned with one central theme: the ceaseless struggle of charisma as a particularly powerful social force--which Weber more or less identified with individual creative activity--on the one hand, and the routinizing forces of bureaucratic rationalization on the other.[31] Rationalization tends to produce rigid and eventually ossified social structures dominated by institutionally oriented forms of social interaction, a trend Weber viewed as having dire anthropological ramifications. He feared a completely bureaucratized world that would be inhabited by fully adjusted, routinized "organization men;" such beings, drained of both freedom and power, would be but pathetic shadows of the creative, dynamic individuals Weber's own normative anthropology affirmed. Weber looked to new forms of charismatic leadership as offering the most promising, if only partial, defense against the incursion of bureaucratic routine on individual freedoms.[32] This line of thought is clearly incorporated into Weber's consideration of political power and the state.

*Political Domination as a
Dyadic, Asymmetric Relation*

Weber's analysis of political power recognizes that power is actuated in a two-way interchange of agents. There is no *Herrschaft*

---

[31]Mommsen, *The Age of Bureaucracy*, 20. Again, the conceptually awkward identification of charismatic domination with individual freedom illustrates a limitation of Weber's exclusive reliance on a power-over model.

[32]Ibid., 79-80.

unless subordinates cooperate by responding to commands, a cooperation that arises from their belief that an order of command is justified, for the different reasons which characterize each pure type. *Herrschaft* rests in the "power of command," but, "the power of command does not exist unless the authority which is claimed by someone is actually heeded to a socially relevant degree."[33] A form of *Herrschaft* possesses legitimacy when both commander and obeyer evidence a subjective belief in the validity of the order which governs the command.[34]

Despite this interactive description of *herrschaftlich* relations, each type of domination assumes a strictly hierarchical structure. In bureaucratic, traditional, and charismatic forms of domination alike, the power of command resides at the top, with the leader or ruling staff. As Mommsen puts it, Weber's theory of authority "is derived from the assumption that there is a fundamental dichotomy between qualified, i.e. charismatic leadership on the one hand, and the unreflected, submissive obedience of the governed on the other."[35] That Weber's analysis of dominative power is primarily concerned with leaders or managers reflects this assumption of an asymmetrical distribution of agency and significance between commanders and followers. The power-over cast of this formulation is heavy indeed.

---

[33]Weber, *Economy and Society*, 2:948.

[34]Ibid. Giddens criticizes Weber's notion of legitimate power, first, for reflecting a dualism between action and structure whereby action unconstrained by structure is considered the realm of freedom, and structure is presumed to be the realm of constraint; and second, for not taking account of the fact that human action logically implies an exercise of power understood as transformative efficacy--power-to. Giddens, *Central Problems in Social Theory*, 256-57.

[35]Mommsen, *The Age of Bureaucracy*, 19.

*Political Struggle, the State
and Violence*

Political domination, quintessentially embodied in the modern nation state, is defined by the possession of a monopoly on the use of legitimate force within a given territory.[36]   Other forms of *Herrschaft* involve the use of coercive influence; for instance, religious domination may entail psychic coercion, or economic *Herrschaft*, monetary coercion.   But the state as locus of political domination holds sole claim to the legitimate use of *physical* coercion--"power backed by violence"--to achieve its ends.   While "violent social action (resort by a group to force to protect the interests of its members) is obviously absolutely primordial," the monopoly on legitimate violence held by the associations we refer to as modern states is the product of a long historical evolution.[37]

Weber does not assume that force and violence are politics' constant or only means, but he does assume that these are the identifying means. He describes the state and politics in terms of their characteristic means because he believes that the political can not be identified by the pursuit of any particular ends. "There has been no purpose . . . which has not been pursued on occasion by some political association; and there has been no purpose . . . which *all* political associations have sought to achieve."[38]   This instrumental description of politics and the state reflects the same distinction between formal, rationally organized means and non-rational ends found in Weber's analysis of other modern institutional structures, particularly bureaucracy.

Weber's discussion of international relations demonstrates his tendency to assume that political power is not only violent, but

---

[36]Weber, *Economy and Society*, 1:54-55, 2:901-903.

[37]Ibid., 2:904-905.

[38]Weber, "Basic Categories of Social Action," in Runciman, ed., *Selections*, 40-41. See also Weber, *Economy and Society*, 1:55.

zero-sum in nature.[39]   He speaks of "power prestige" among
nations, that is, the belief in one's own national might, typically
expressed in efforts to expand territorial or other kinds of
dominion. There is, according to Weber, a dynamic of glorying in
power and prestige by nations, whereby "one claim to prestige calls
forth the competition of all other possible bearers of prestige,"[40]
competition that frequently escalates into violent conflict. Weber
does not preclude a complementary distribution of power among
separate spheres of societal action.   However, within a single
political territory or structure, *Herrschaft* as power of command is
generally zero-sum, since only one party at a time can hold the
monopoly on the use of force that identifies political domination.[41]

Political Power and Modern Democracies

Weber's   treatment   of   modern   plebiscitary   democracy   in
Economy and Society sheds further light on his attitudes toward
power in political processes.[42]   Rejecting the possibility that a
social arrangement can wholly eschew domination, and denying that
a "pure" democratic arrangement is feasible for anything beyond
face-to-face interpersonal settings, Weber portrays democracy as a
system wherein bureaucratic administration is mitigated by the vying

---

[39]A "zero-sum" relationship is one in which a gain by one party
necessarily entails a loss by the other. A zero-sum view of power assumes
that any increase in the power of one party must come at the expense of
someone else's power.

[40]Weber, *Economy and Society*, 2:911-12.

[41]In taking this position Weber appears to join the nay-saying side of the
modern debate over the question of whether political sovereignty is divisible.

[42]For a post-1989 critique and development of Weber's treatment of
democratic power and its cultural contexts, in light of the work of Michel
Foucault, Charles Taylor, and others, see Paul R. Harrison, "Power, Culture,
and the Interpretation of Democracy," *Praxis International* 11:3 (October
1991): 340-53.

of politicians for charismatic sway over the voting masses.[43] Genuine--that is, charismatic--leaders have the opportunity to emerge through this process. Weber perceived such leaders as the conduits through whom vitality and fresh direction might yet flow in an increasingly bureaucratized society.

Weber admitted that modern mass democracies engender "Caesarist" tendencies in their political leaders, since under conditions of universal suffrage politicians must exude the charismatic qualities needed to attract a mass following.[44] The inordinate tendencies of leaders can be checked by political institutions such as parliaments, which both serve as training grounds for competing political leaders, and incorporate procedures for withdrawing the mandate of leaders who overstep the bounds of their legal authority. Mommsen puts Weber's view this way: "There ought to be as powerful a rule as possible by responsible charismatic leaders, and at the same time effective control of their doings by rival leaders, in order to gain a maximum of mobility in politics and society, and hence maximum opportunity for individual creativity on the political level."[45]

Weber argues that "machine" or "leadership" democracy (*Führerdemokratie*) is the form best suited to modern technological societies. "In the contemporary state, there is only the choice between leadership democracy with a 'machine' and a leaderless democracy, namely the domination by professional politicians without a calling, without the inner charismatic qualities that make

---

[43]"Weber pointed out time and again that the strength . . . and stability of bureaucratic governments . . . depends on whether the system allows dynamic personalities with charismatic, that is to say, 'leadership' qualities to attain the top positions." Mommsen, *The Age of Bureaucracy*, 79.

[44]Giddens, *Central Problems in Social Theory*, 181. Weber, *Economy and Society*, 2:1126, 1415.

[45]Mommsen, *The Age of Bureaucracy*, 113. As Chapter II will demonstrate, this is very similar to Reinhold Niebuhr's advocacy of a "balance of power" as the means for mitigating the dangers of unchecked political domination.

a leader."[46] Weber regards leadership democracy as best able to
support modern forms of charismatic leadership. Modern
plebiscitarian democracy is described as a special, anti-authoritarian
version of charismatic domination, and the most important type of
leadership democracy.[47] This kind of democracy derives its
legitimacy formally from the vote or consent of the governed
(hence, its plebiscitarian character), and, in a more substantive way,
from the emotional devotion of the populace to the plebiscitary
leader (hence Weber's categorization of it as a form of charismatic
domination).[48]

Weber's appreciation for plebiscitary democracy is so influenced
by his focus on power-over that his description of it all but excludes
features, such as popular empowerment or self-governance, that
would be highlighted by a power-to paradigm. Analysts of his
political thought have pointed out the consequent underemphasis
and underappreciation for practical democracy in Weber's work.[49]
As Mommsen documents, Weber most certainly did not believe in
popular sovereignty, regarding the notion as a pipe-dream born of
the illusion that a world without domination might be possible.
Weber wrote in 1908, "All ideas aiming at abolishing the dominance
of men over men are 'Utopian.'"[50] He favored democracy not

---

[46]Giddens, *Central Problems in Social Theory*, 181. By a machine,
Weber means a highly bureaucratized party organization completely
subservient to the political leader. See Mommsen, *The Age of Bureaucracy*,
87-88; Weber, *Economy and Society*, 1:269.

[47]Weber, *Economy and Society*, 1:268.

[48]Ibid., 1:269; Mommsen, *The Age of Bureaucracy*, 113.

[49]See, e.g., Ira J. Cohen, "The Underemphasis on Democracy in Marx
and Weber," in Antonio and Glassman, eds., *Weber-Marx Dialogue*, 274-99.

[50]Mommsen, *The Age of Bureaucracy*, 87. In 1908 Weber wrote to
Robert Michels, who at the time was working to answer the question of how
to reconcile the ethical postulate of the sovereignty of the people with
evidence that political life gave birth to ever new oligarchies. Weber
commented drily, "Such concepts as 'will of the people,' [or] 'genuine will of
the people,' have long since ceased to exist for me; they are fictitious." Ibid.

because he espoused such democratic values as self-governance or equal rights, but because it offered maximum dynamism and the greatest room for creative leadership.[51]

Politics always involves the struggle for power-over, but when this is pursued as a "vocation" or "calling" within a leadership democracy, it engages participants in perpetuating a space of action which, while within bureaucratized society, itself escapes the confines of bureaucratic routine. In this way, the arena of political struggle can be a continual source of charismatic leadership. Here also, however, Weber is hobbled by his zero-sum, power-over stress. Lacking an accent upon power-to, Weber's analysis relegates the values of creativity and freedom to charismatic leaders who garner mass followings, and fails to identify such values in efficacious collaborative efforts among citizens themselves.

Politics, Power, and Ethics

Weber considers the moral dimensions of politics as the struggle for and exercise of power-over in a 1918 lecture, "Politics as a Vocation."[52] Here he distinguishes sharply between the ethics that characterize the political realm and those germane to interpersonal relations. Weber calls moral codes that require loyalty to values regardless of the consequences--such as the caritative neighbor love preached by Christianity--an "ethics of conviction," "inspiration", or "ultimate ends" (*Gesinnungsethik*). Such an ethics, Weber holds, reflects a form of rational behavior--*Wertrationalität*--that pursues the expression of values, but refuses to compromise moral means for the sake of practical consequences.

Wertrational action is the hallmark of saints and idealists. It is

---

[51]Ibid. Giddens offers a somewhat modified view of Weber on this point in *Central Problems in Social Theory*, 180.

[52]Max Weber, "Politics as a Vocation," in *From Max Weber: Essays in Sociology*, trans., ed., introduction by H. H. Gerth and C. Wright Mills (New York: Oxford University Press, 1946), 77-128.

not, however, appropriate for the effective negotiation of political life. Instead, politics demands the adoption of what Weber names an "ethics of responsibility" (*Verantwortungsethik*), whereby politicians put first the desired political consequences of action, recognizing that achieving political ends must often involve means that an ethic of conviction would deem morally reprehensible--in particular, politics' specific means: the use of power backed up by violence.[53] An ethic of responsibility reflects the adoption of means-ends rationality, *Zweckrationalität*, in the political arena.

There is a connection between Weber's discussion of *Zweckrationalität* and *Wertrationalität* in political life, and the differences he cites between bureaucratic and charismatic forms of political domination.[54] Whereas bureaucratic organization involves the ascendancy of means-ends rationality, the typical charismatic leader, marching to the drumbeat of unique ultimate values, upsets structure and routine with new insights and fresh goals to be embraced. Charisma does become routinized, but it then ceases to be charismatic domination and takes on some other form. This linkage of bureaucratic power-over with means-ends rational behavior, and charismatic power-over with value rationality is played out in Weber's picture of the political process as the interaction between routinized structures and charismatic leaders.[55]

---

[53]Ibid., 126-28.

[54]Löwith says of the ethic of responsibility, "If one opts for the ethic of responsibility one also decides in favor of rationality as means-ends rationality. . . . The real and primary reason for Weber's obvious preference for the purposive-rational schema is not the fact that it affords the greatest measure of constructive understandability of human conduct, but the specific responsibility of purposive-rational action itself. Inasmuch as rationality thus has its roots in the ethos of responsibility, it refers back to Weber's concept of 'man'." Löwith, *Max Weber and Karl Marx*, 47.

[55]The political leader's "ethic of responsibility" involves *means-ends* rationality, which seemingly contradicts Weber's association of charismatic leadership with *Wertrationalität*. Here is revealed an inconsistency found in all of Weber's formulations of value-rationality. Since values themselves are

Contributions and Limitations of
Weber's Power-over Theory

Weber's description of socio-political power as inhering in structures of legitimate domination on the one hand, and in the struggle for ascendancy among competing political forces on the other, has remained enormously influential in subsequent social scientific work. Though they may disagree with particular aspects or ramifications of his constructs, a host of scholars accepts his general understanding of socio-political power's meaning and functions. Weber's legacy includes his insights on the independence of political from economic power (this contra Marx), his use of the historically saturated ideal type for studying socio-political processes and structures, his actionist understanding that keeps social power firmly bound to the intentions of agents, his attention to the impact of unintended consequences of rationally initiated social action, and his elaboration of rationalization--expressed in both the means-ends rationality of political action, and the bureaucratic organization of political structures--as the modern context within which power must be understood.[56]

---

relegated to the sphere of the non-rational, *Wertrationalität* entails the use of rational means for the achievement of valued ends, chosen non-rationally. A charismatic leader is motivated by value-rationality, but to successfully pursue new ends or values appears to require the introduction of a consequentialist ethical mode. This shift contributes to the eventual supersedence of charisma by some other form of rule, and frequently some other orienting form of rationality. Also confusing is Weber's failure to distinguish adequately between charismatic *leaders*, and charismatic *Herrschaft* as a structure of domination. By definition, charisma defies strict routine, so that any "charismatic *Herrschaft*" would appear to be either a short-lived or a self-defeating phenomenon. Mommsen, *The Age of Bureaucracy*, 93.

[56]Marx regards the economic sphere of production and ownership as the primary locus of the struggle for human dignity and fulfillment. Weber acknowledges the importance of material and economic relations at every point, but he focuses more decisively on leadership in both economic and political relations.

Weber's normative contribution on the issue of power, while not as frequently acknowledged, has also left its mark on later theorists, including Christian ethicists. To the extent that Weber's description of power is based on undemonstrated but normative anthropological and sociological assumptions, those who adopt Weber's position on power also import related views of society and the relation of the individual to it. As Löwith, Mommsen, and others show, these underlying tenets include Weber's conception of society as a collection of individual agents, his emphasis on struggle and conflict among societal members, and his assumption that endemic social conflict is resolved only by establishing varied forms of hierarchical command. Weber's vantagepoint on human nature and on society prompted him both to notice and to value freedom and individuality over communal solidarity. In this he reflects the predilections of much modern western political theory, while differing profoundly from Karl Marx, for whom human being *is* social being.

Affecting all this is Weber's overriding concern: the fate of individual freedom and creativity amidst the constrictions of a bureaucratic world. He viewed the great danger of our age not as the detachment of individuals from their communities--Durkheim's *anomie*, not the squelching of genuine community by the alienation of workers from their labor and its products, as Marx would have it, but instead, the eclipse of individual genius within the specialized roles and routines required by the nearly complete ascendancy of bureaucratic organization. Weber does not deny that developing other forms of power and influence may allow some to temporarily escape the iron cage of bureaucratic domination, but power as *Herrschaft* remains the sociologically significant, enduring, and characteristic feature of socio-political relations. As such, it is within the parameters of power-over that the battle for human dignity and fulfillment is fought, a struggle in which Weber anticipated only limited and sporadic victories. Systems of political domination acquire institutional stability by establishing legitimacy. Politicians grasp for control over the governed, and genuine leaders are an individualistic, personalizing, creative minority who sway their followers in the directions those leaders choose. Both political leadership and structures of political rule always involve the dyadic relations of command and obedience typical of the power-over model.

As we close the discussion of Weber's theory of socio-political power, two problems of particular relevance for ethics should be noted. First, Weber's famous typology of legitimate domination is of little use for distinguishing "moral" from "immoral" versions of domination. Indeed, though Weber's types cover the terrain of legitimate domination, there is no mention of morally illegitimate domination, either by leaders or through structures.[57] So long as the governed accept a leader or government, that instance of domination qualifies as legitimate. Mommsen attributes the types' inability to distinguish good from bad regimes (except on the basis of success in legitimating themselves) to Weber's deliberately functional approach to his definitions of domination.[58] Weber means to exclude normative preferences from the discussion of the pure types of domination. If, however, success in dominating--on whatever grounds--is the *de facto* criterion for legitimacy in Weber's theory, and "legitimacy" is accorded its more usual, normative connotation, the upshot of Weber's theory is to connect efficient domination with moral validity. Recent efforts such as that by David Beetham to retrieve and clarify Weber's understanding of the legitimation of power do not succeed in overcoming this inherent normative difficulty.[59]

A second, related problem is that a Weberian interpretation elucidates how power-over operates to maintain social stability far

---

[57]Weber briefly discusses tyranny as a form of illegitimate domination in *Economy and Society*, 2:1315-18. He also treats the notion of the "city" under the category, "non-legitimate domination." Ibid., ch. 16. But in neither case is any content given to the notion of legitimacy beyond the explicit acceptance by the people of some form of the power to command.

[58]Mommsen, *The Age of Bureaucracy*, 90.

[59]See David Beetham, *The Legitimation of Power*. (Atlantic Highlands: Humanities Press, 1991).

better than it captures power's place in enabling social transformation. In this regard, Giddens's comments are on target.

> Weber associated 'meaning' with *legitimacy.* Consequently, his account of bureaucracy is very much written 'from the top'; the ideal type of bureaucratic organization is heavily weighted towards how the 'legitimate order of a rational-legal form' is sustained.[60]

This imbalance is another consequence of Weber's strong stress on power-over, and inattention to power-to.

The conceptual cargo that Weber's approach to socio-political power carries inevitably influences the shape of a social ethics that employs Weberian categories. Ethicists who rely on Weberian understandings of power tend to redirect the broader notion of power into the channels of *Herrschaft*, its forms, and its pursuit. What is possible and desirable in socio-political interactions involving power becomes focused, and in the end limited, by theframework Weber constructs. We will uncover similar problems in some Christian ethical assessments of power in the chapters to come.

---

[60]Giddens, *Profiles and Critiques in Social Theory*, 205. Giddens argues that Weber also ignores the fact of "the dialectic of control": the fact that, as organization increases, so does interdependence of the upper echelons of power upon the cooperation of the lower. While not claiming that power is wholly redistributed or dissipated in a complex bureaucratic organization, Giddens, along with Levine and others, does contend that "there is no simple movement of power" upward or downward with increasing bureaucratization; normally there are various kinds of possible tradeoffs in the resources which can be actualized by various levels of organization." Ibid., 204. See also Levine, "Rationality and Freedom," 21-23.

Karl Marx

As is well known, one of Max Weber's principal interlocutors as he developed his sociology of domination was the figure of Karl Marx.[61] Marx's description of socio-political power in the modern epoch is interest-oriented, structurist and asymmetrical. Though his portrayal of the communist society of the future incorporates a second vision of power as mutual and oriented toward the common good, much of his analysis concentrates on the power dynamics characterizing the existing capitalist system. Neither in his allusions to other, less alienated forms of society, nor in his talk of the coming communist one does Marx provide a complete description of a socio-political community in which power-to is wholly to the fore.[62] It is as the supreme analyst of dominative power-over that Marx makes some of his greatest contributions to social theory; it is this analysis, particularly its political implications, that will now be examined.

---

[61]A concise overview of contemporary interpretations of the relationship between the theories of Marx and Weber is found in Val Burris, "A Neo-Marxist Synthesis of Marx and Weber on Class," in Norbert Wiley, ed., *The Marx-Weber Debate* (Newbury Park: Sage Publications, 1987), 67-90. See also, ibid., editor's introduction, 1-31.

[62]Whether Marx believed that power-over in the form of chains of command would disappear entirely from communist society is a point of contention. Engels argued that, even though political power-over in the form of the state would "wither away," the activity of industry even in the communist society would continue to require power-over in the form of authority and discipline for the purposes of efficient production. See Friedreich Engels, "On Authority" (1874), in *Marx & Engels: Basic Writings on Politics and Philosophy*, Lewis S. Feuer, ed. (Garden City, New York: Doubleday Anchor Books, 1959), 481-484. On the deficiencies of Marx's treatment of "substantive democracy," see Cohen, "Under- emphasis," esp. 281-284.

Marx's Economic-Materialist Perspective

Marx's work, like Weber's, is animated by a concern with the characteristics and consequences of modern industrial capitalism. The work of both men is informed by normative notions of the human and of human community. Unlike Weber, however, Marx views the material, specifically the economic, sphere as the bedrock that determines every other dynamic and structure of social life. Marx's theory of capitalist society rests on the connection he draws between the development of the division of labor and the emergence of a polarized class structure.[63] The arena of political rule and process, with which we are particularly concerned, is construed from Marx's economic starting point as a significant, but not the central, dimension of bourgeois society.[64] Marx's central concepts of alienation and ideology contribute to a description of power in the political sphere as structurist, dominative, and derivative of the deformed economic relations characterizing capitalism.

---

[63]Anthony Giddens, *Studies in Social and Political Theory* (London: Hutchison Press, 1979), 239. In Marx's view, Western European capitalism originated with the expropriation of producers from their means of production, and the emergence of a propertyless working class at dialectical odds with the bourgeoisie in whose hands productive control came to rest.

[64] Whether Marx has a genuine political theory has been a matter of dispute. Bernard Quelquejeu's extensive study of Marx's notion of political power concludes, "As acute as is [Marx's] critique of the modern bourgeois state, as rich in heuristic fruit as is his democratic perspective, neither [of them] constitute a positive theoretical proposal. Between critique and utopia, the place for a [Marxist] political theory remains empty." "K. Marx a-t-il constitué une théorie du pouvoir d'état?" I. Le débat avec Hegel (1841-43). *Revue des sciences philosophiques et théologiques* 63 (1979): 60.

Individual and Society

Marx's interpretation of power in capitalist political economy is founded on a set of anthropological and sociological suppositions at variance with those held by Weber. In brief, Marx's materialist perspective leads him to describe the human person as a being with needs that must be fulfilled through engagement in, and reliance upon, the environment. This primal fact means that "Each man is condemned to dependence upon . . . nature, and upon other men, to help supply his needs."[65] Humans' essential neediness is, however, not merely a debit to be minimized, as some modern political theorists imply. In Marx's normative anthropology, human interdependence is indicative of an intrinsic sociality. Humans are first and always, not isolated individuals, but "species-beings" whose identity is achieved in community. Establishing social structures and patterns that acknowledge and facilitate this social identity is the key to human flourishing.

Society at every stage in history is the product of human interaction, and the direct reflection of the contemporary stage of the forces of economic production.[66] In Marx's terse formula, "The

---

[65]Joseph Cropsey, "Karl Marx," *History of Political Philosophy*, Leo Strauss & Joseph Cropsey, eds. (Chicago: Rand McNally, 1969), 703.

[66]Marx wrote in 1846: "What is society, whatever its form may be? The product of men's reciprocal action. Are men free to choose this or that form of society for themselves? By no means. Assume a particular state of development in the productive forces of man and you will get a particular form of commerce and consumption. Assume particular stages of development in production, commerce and consumption and you will have a corresponding social structure, a corresponding organization of the family, of orders or of classes, in a word, a corresponding civil society. Presuppose a particular civil society and you will get particular political conditions which are only the official expression of civil society." Letter to P. V. Annekov, December 28, 1846; quoted in Cropsey, "Marx," 699. Cf. Tucker, ed., *Marx-Engels*, 136-37. A provocative elaboration of Marx's thinking on this matter is offered by Philip Kain, *Marx and Modern Political Theory* (Lanham, MD: Rowman & Littlefield, 1993), esp. 279-90, 314-18.

hand-mill gives you society with the feudal lord; the steam-mill, society with the industrial capitalist."[67] Genuine human well-being requires a socio-economic setting of a sort yet to be achieved, a communist system wherein completely socialized relations of production will allow "an association in which the free development of each will be the condition for the free development of all."[68]

Marx's social perspective is in plain contrast to the more individualistic anthropological and sociological premises which guide Weber's analysis of modern capitalism.[69] What are the ramifications of this difference for the two thinkers' notions of power, especially socio-political power? Marx delivers a searing critique of the dominative and oppressive power-over relations endemic to all non-communistic, especially capitalist, systems. Fueling his diatribe is a normative notion of society--and of power-- sharply distinct from their historical expressions in modern capitalism.[70] Implied by Marx's vision of the future communistic

---

[67]Karl Marx, *The Poverty of Philosophy*, ii. 1. 2nd observation. (New York: International Publishers, 1967). Quoted in Cropsey, "Marx," 699. Cf. Tucker, ed., *Marx-Engels*, 136-42.

[68]Karl Marx, "Manifesto of the Communist Party" (1848). Tucker ed., *Marx-Engels*, 491.

[69]Löwith points out that because for Marx, "man himself *is* his social world," his study of society is always a study of anthropology, and vice versa. "Marx was convinced . . . that man is by nature 'man in society,' that is, a social being; it is the *conditio sine qua non* of his anthropology." Löwith, *Karl Marx and Max Weber*, 96, n. 11. Hence, Marx's "critique of man in bourgeois society culminates in a critique of society and the economy, without thereby losing its basic anthropological meaning." Ibid., 75.

[70]Nancy Hartsock similarly observes, "The Marxian account of the process of production . . . implicitly contains two accounts of power--the one a description of relations of domination in the present form of society, the other an indication of the possibilities inherent in human activity." Implied in the different accounts of power are two different understandings of community and human activity within community. Nancy C. M. Hartsock, *Money, Sex, and Power: Toward a Feminist Historical Materialism* (Boston: Northeastern University Press, 1985), 137.

society is a judgment that dominative power-over is something that ought not to be, something destined to fall away and be replaced by a power of the people which fits our type of power-to. Weber, while also critical of the human toll taken by industrial capitalism, neither condemns political power-over as immoral, nor envisages a world in which such domination would be overcome.

Alienation and Ideology:
Source and Supporter of Domination

The notions of "alienation" and "ideology" capture two crucial features of Marx's interpretation of the structures and processes of dominative power in capitalist political economies.[71]   Both concepts are multifaceted and each has provided a rich legacy to subsequent social and political theory.   Let us consider these notions in turn, beginning with alienation.

In what does alienation consist? From what does Marx believe persons in capitalist society are alienated?   The theme of estrangement or alienation (*Entfremdung, Entaüsserung*) works in a number of ways for Marx.[72]   In its primary usage, *Entaüsserung*

---

[71]Marx discusses alienation most extensively in his "Economic and Philosophical Manuscripts of 1844," Tucker ed., *Marx-Engels*, 66-125. In later works, the idea of alienation or estrangement of labor continues to play an important, but less explicit role. See Gayo Petrovic, "Alienation," in *Encyclopedia of Philosophy*, Paul Edwards, ed. (New York: MacMillan and The Free Press, 1967), 1:76-81; Quelquejeu, "Marx et l'étât", 224-30. The most concentrated source of Marx's thought on ideology is his "German Ideology," written with Engels in 1845-46, though never published in their lifetimes. See Tucker, ed., *Marx-Engels*, 146-202); David Braybrooke, "Ideology," *Encyclopedia of Philosophy*, 4:126.

[72]On differences among English translations of these Marxist terms, and their Hegelian links, see Tucker, ed., *Marx-Engels*, xl-xli. For an illuminating analysis of Marx and Marxism on alienation, see Alvin W. Gouldner, *The Two Marxisms* (New York: Oxford University Press, 1980), 177-88.

refers to the separation of producers from the means and results of their production, a process which is intrinsically related to the severing of persons from their power of action.[73] This separation takes place first as a morally neutral process of objectification, insofar as through action, I produce something other than myself. It becomes alienation when the object I have produced is lost, obscured or forgotten as *mine* and becomes seen as alien, a power over me rather than an expression of my own power.

In capitalist economies, a vicious cycle assures that the more workers spend themselves, the more powerful becomes the alien objective world which they create over-against themselves. This original, material alienation is elaborated into a whole institutional set in which knowledge, culture, decision-making capacity, truth--in short, all that contributes to people's sense of being effective agents in the world--become attributed to forces, groups, structures or ideas understood as external to, beyond the control of, and over-against those affected by them. In the terminology of this study, alienation is a historical process whereby people's communally generated transformative efficacy, or power-to, is wrested from them and re-introduced as an alien force, which is then experienced as dominative power-over the community.

Marx develops his notion of alienation from the thought of Hegel and Feuerbach, amending these writers' definitions in more materialistic (vs. Hegel) and more inclusive (vs. Feuerbach) directions. Humans not only alienate themselves by projecting their best aspirations onto the idea of God, as Feuerbach saw; we also alienate other products of our spiritual activity in forms such as philosophy, common sense, morals, and art. We alienate products of our economic activity in the form of commodities, money, capital, and so forth; we alienate products of our social activity in the form of the state, law, and social institutions.[74] In numerous ways, we

---

[73]See Petrovic, "Alienation," 76-81.

[74]See, e.g., Marx, "On the Jewish Question" (1843), Tucker, ed., *Marx-Engels*, 26-52. "Objectification is the practice of alienation. Just as man, so long as he is engrossed in religion, can only objectify his essence by an *alien*

make the products of our own action into a separate, independent, and powerful world of objects and structures toward which we are related subserviently and dependently.[75] Over time, alienated labor estranges people from the activity through which these products are generated, from the natural world, and from one other.[76] In its various manifestations, alienation represents a root estrangement of humankind from its own "essence."[77]

Marx's economic-materialist philosophy leads him to attribute the causes of alienation to historical developments in the forces and relations of production. In a class-differentiated society, social power, that is, the multiplied productive force that arises through the cooperation of individuals by the division of labor, appears to these individuals as an alien force existing outside their understanding and control.[78] In bourgeois capitalist society,

---

and fantastic being; so under the sway of egoistic need, he can only affirm himself and produce objects in practice by subordinating his products and his own activity to the domination of an alien entity, and by attributing to them the significance of an alien entity, namely, money." Ibid., 52. Alienation is at the heart of money-based capitalist political economies.

[75]See Petrovic, "Alienation," 77. Marx states, "the object which labor produces--labor's product--confronts it as *something alien*, as a *power independent* of the producer." "The Jewish Question," Tucker, ed., *Marx-Engels*, 52.

[76] Marx, "Economic and Philosophical Manuscripts of 1844," Tucker, ed., *Marx-Engels*, 75, 77.

[77]Petrovic says that for Marx, "the self-alienated man is . . . really not a man, a man who does not realize his historically created human possibilities. A non-alienated man would be a man who really is a man . . . . who fulfills himself as a free, creative being of praxis." Petrovic, "Alienation," 77.

[78]Marx, "German Ideology," Tucker, ed., *Marx-Engels*, 161. Clearly, for Marx, alienation and oppression are intimately intertwined. Some recent feminist analysis suggests, however, that non-waged work performed in the home may be a case of socially oppressive conditions wherein the work performed, such as that of child care, nevertheless retains a genuinely non-alienated character. See Philip J. Kain, *Marx, Housework, and Alienation* (*Hypatia* 8 (Winter 1993): 121-43.

money, with its insidious capacity to reduce human values to units of exchange, thereby mutating human powers into alien, commodified forces, is the quintessential symbol of the degradation of humanity wrought by alienation.[79]

Alienation, then, is the deformative process by which people are estranged from their effective capacities and fall under the sway of alien forces, as socially generated power-to is transformed into power-over wielded by the few. Distortions spawned by capitalist modes and relations of production are the source of alienation; renovating economic forces and relations is key to overcoming it. Avenues toward change at this basic level are opened by another crucial aspect of Marx's project, the critique of ideology.

Ideology is used in two related ways by Marx. On the one hand, ideology refers to intellectual discourse that mistakes for science the "illusions of the age", thereby causing people to see the world upside down, as in a *camera obscura*. On the other hand, and most prominently for Marx, ideology means the ideational web by which, in a given historical setting, economic, social and political relations of alienation and domination are legitimated and perpetuated. Ideology includes the prevailing political, religious, cultural, and even scientific belief patterns whereby the dominant class maintains its privileged position.[80]

---

[79]See "Economic and Philosophic Manuscripts of 1844," Tucker, ed., *Marx-Engels*, 101-105. "The overturning and confounding of all human and natural qualities . . . the *divine* power of money--lies in its *character* as men's estranged, alienating, and self-disposing *species-nature*. Money is the alienated *ability of mankind*." Ibid., 104. "Since money, as the existing and active concept of value, confounds and exchanges all things, it is the general *confounding* and *compounding* of all things--the world upside-down--the confounding and compounding of all human and natural qualities." Ibid., 105. Cf. Quelquejeu, "Marx et l'état," 227-30.

[80]Giddens's essay, "Ideology and Consciousness," delineates and critiques this twofold understanding of ideology in Marx. Giddens, *Central Problems*, 165-97, esp. 165-68 and 185-88. A more detailed treatment is Walter Carlsnaes, "Marx and the Concept of Ideology," in Carlsnaes, *The Concept of*

"False consciousness," a term introduced by Engels, refers to the fact that ideology is most successful when it works unbeknownst to those affected by it, whether negatively or positively. A thriving ideology lends an aura of facticity and legitimacy to social and economic arrangements and structures, encouraging participants to view as natural, permanent, and justified that which is in reality artificial, transitory, and oppressive.[81] Beliefs purveyed by various institutional spheres conspire to reinforce the collective illusion of normative actuality to which false consciousness refers.

At its zenith, bourgeois ideology perpetuates a communal mindset that corresponds perfectly with the needs of the capitalist system. "This ideology conceives of the laws of the competitive market as natural and impersonal; it accepts the institution of private property . . . as natural and permanent; it professes that workers are paid all in the market they can be paid; and it sanctions without question the expropriation of surplus value by claims founded on private property."[82] Ideology accomplishes this as much

---

Ideology and Political Analysis (Westport, CT: Greenwood Press, 1981), 23-100. On Weber's treatment of ideology versus that of Marx, see Gerth & Mills, *From Max Weber*, 47, 269-70; Runciman, *Selections*, 135-37.

[81]See Giddens, *Central Problems*, 168. Unlike some of his predecessors and successors, Marx gives ideology a consistently negative connotation. Braybrooke, "Ideology," 126.

[82]Ibid.

by the questions it deters people from asking as by the false answers it affirms.[83]

Bourgeois ideology, like alienation, is rooted in capitalist relations of production. The materialistic "base" of society consists of its productive forces (including resources, capital, equipment, technological expertise), and its relations of production (the relations among capitalists and workers, and among members of society that control the productive forces and determine how the productive output of a society is to be disposed). Ideology is the ideational "superstructure" erected upon, and in service to, the material "base." It consists of all the institutionally embodied beliefs that motivate societal members to heed the essential requirements of the relations of production in the course of mobilizing the productive forces.[84]

Historically, Marx argues, bourgeois ideology arose because, as intellectual and material laborers became increasingly differentiated, the former developed products such as religion and philosophy, which were put to work shoring up the position of the dominant economic class. Marx contends, however, that, "as mystification is a social phenomenon with institutional causes, it requires an institutional remedy as much beyond the powers of its critics as its

---

[83]Ibid. See also the oft-cited Peter Bachrach and Gordon Baratz, "Two Faces of Power," *American Political Science Review* 56 (1962): 947-52. Bachrach and Baratz highlight a second face of power-over which controls by setting the context in which decision making takes place. A significant feature of the power held by those who control that context is the ability to prevent certain questions from ever being raised for debate. Bachrach and Baratz's position has been augmented, modified, and challenged. See, e.g., Steven Lukes, *Power: A Radical View* (New York: MacMillan, 1974) and scholarly responses to Lukes; or more recently, the intriguing work on counter-ideological "offstage discourse" in James C. Scott, *Domination and the Arts of Resistance* (New Haven, CT: Yale University Press, 1990).

[84]Braybrooke, "Ideology," 125. Different groups in capitalist society, however, experience the hold of ideology in distinctive ways. On this see John A. Maguire, "Marx on Ideology, Power, and Force," *Theory and Decision* 7 (1976): 315-29, esp. 318-21.

dupes to bring about by argument alone."[85]   Only a fundamental shift in economic relations, abetted by the revolutionary action of the proletariat, will enable escape from the morass of alienation and mystification on which capitalist society depends.

Marx, then, employs the concepts of alienation, ideology, and false consciousness to portray the pernicious consolidation and perpetuation of the power-over of the capitalist ruling class, and the powerlessness of the underclasses.   His censure of capitalism is fueled by commitment to a socio-economic arrangement in which ruling class hegemony and its ideological props will be abolished and replaced by communistic relations of equality and effective action.   With the elimination of capitalist modes and relations of production, we infer, power will take on a dramatically different, non-dominative, and morally desirable face.[86]

---

[85]Braybrooke, "Ideology," 125. Cf. Giddens, *Central Problems*, 167-168, 187.   Marx is convinced that bourgeois ideology arose because, as intellectual and material laborers became increasingly differentiated, the former developed products such as religion and philosophy, which were put to work shoring up the position of the dominant economic class. "German Ideology," Tucker, ed., *Marx-Engels*, 164-65.

[86]"Equality" in the sense of treating each person strictly identically regardless of circumstances is not the goal of communist society. The real goal--which only advanced communist society will be able to approximate--is to garner "from each according to his ability," and to distribute "to each according to his needs." See the discussion of false bourgeois notions of equality (which in fact protect only the rights of the privileged) versus the communist understanding in Marx, "Critique of the Gotha Program," Tucker, ed., *Marx-Engels*, 530-31.

Hartsock explains that the community Marx envisages "is one in which persons relate to each other directly, their products operating as an expression rather than denial of their individuality, and as a means of connecting rather than separating them both from each other and from the world of nature." Here his theory "points beyond relations of domination and allows for a reformulation of power (both in theory and in fact) as not simply power over others but as competence and effective action in dealing with both the natural and the social worlds." *Money, Sex, and Power*, 137.

Political Power and the State

Because economic relations are the linchpin of his social theory, Marx's theory of politics has been criticized for being underdeveloped, or even non-existent.[87] There is cause to agree with analysts who, like Quelquejeu, look in vain for a full theory of politics between Marx's trenchant critique of the capitalist state and his description of "authentic democracy" in the not-yet-existent communist society. Yet, as recent treatments by Richard Miller and others highlight, Marx certainly intended his analysis to be an interpretation of politics as it was manifested within western capitalism.[88] He not only discoursed extensively about the workings of the capitalist state, but articulated strong claims about the dissolution of state apparatus under communism.

In Marx's historical-materialist theory, political relations are unmasked as epiphenomenal and in ideological service to the relations of production under capitalism. For Marx and Engels, power is class power, and political power merely the organized power of one class for oppressing another. "All struggles within the state . . . are merely the illusory forms in which the real struggles of the different classes are fought out among one another."[89] Class power, by nature asymmetrical, is exercised by superordinate over subordinate classes in ways that range from ideological

---

[87]See, e.g., Quelquejeu, "Marx et l'état;" Isaac D. Balbus, *Marxism and Domination: A Neo-Hegelian, Feminist, Psychoanalytic Theory of Sexual, Political, and Technological Liberation* (Princeton, NJ: Princeton University Press, 1982), chap. 3, esp. 109-122.

[88]See Richard W. Miller, "Social and Political Theory: Class, State, Revolution." in Terrell Carver, ed., *The Cambridge Companion to Marx* (Cambridge: Cambridge University Press, 1991), 55-105, esp. 72-79 on ideology and links between class and racism.

[89]Marx, "German Ideology," Tucker, ed., *Marx-Engels*, 160. Cf. Lukes, "Power and Authority," 657. Gouldner points out tensions and anomalies in Marx's treatment of the state as epiphenomenal to class interests in *The Two Marxisms*, 302-307, 341-52.

mystification, inducement, persuasion, influence and control, to outright force. This last is typically exercised by the state.[90]

A striking feature of politics in capitalist systems is its subsumption under a sharply drawn division between a "public" civic or political sphere, and a "private" sector of economic life and the intimate relations of family and friendship. Marx identifies in the privatization of the bourgeois citizen the specifically political dimension of human alienation under capitalism.[91] Political alienation consists in the fact that the bourgeois person exists in a contradiction: she or he is predominantly a private yet partly a public being, but in neither case a completed person. "What is distinctive about bourgeois man, what separates and removes him from the universality of public life, is that his human existence is primarily that of a private individual, and in this sense, 'bourgeois.'"[92] The political ideology consonant with capitalism celebrates a self-contradictory notion: the *citizen* as *private* individual. Political rights, freedoms, and duties center around the enhancement of the individual and private interests of citizens. The conditions of modern society thus presuppose a separation and abstraction of "real" life, that is, the actual day-to-day experience of societal members--which is relegated to the "private" sphere--and

---

[90]Lukes, "Power and Authority," 657; cf. Weber, *Economy and Society*, 2:904-905.

[91]The ideological functions of the separation of politics from a so-called "private realm" are developed by many Marxian thinkers. See, e.g., Giddens, *Central Problems*, 194-95; Jürgen Habermas, "Further Reflections on the Public Sphere," in Craig Calhoun, ed., *Habermas and the Public Sphere* (Cambridge: MIT Press, 1993), esp. 430-32.

[92]Löwith, *Weber and Marx*, 84. See Marx's "Critique of Hegel's Philosophy of Right," and "On the Jewish Question," Tucker, ed., *Marx-Engels*, 16-25; 26-52. The German *bürgerliche* can be translated as either "bourgeois" or "civil" (as in "*bürgerliche Gesellschaft*"); this highlights the paradox of a privatized civil/bourgeois sphere. Cf. Hannah Arendt's discussion of the subsumption of the political realm into the modern category of the "social" in *The Human Condition*, 68-73.

"public," or political, life.[93]   The upshot is that political life becomes one more instance in which people's transformative efficacy, or power-to, is wrested away, only to return in the form of estranged power-over.

Within this false division of private and public life, the state is estranged from the control of the populace and becomes a tool by which the ascendant class secures its own sectional interests.[94] For Weber, the bureaucratic state represented the rational coalescence of general interests; for Marx, state bureaucracy is the administrative organ through which the domination of the ascendant class is institutionalized.   The formal hierarchy of bureaucratic authority, far from forming a link between citizens and the state, acts to concentrate political power and to shield it from popular control: the bureaucratic state is "an organ superimposed on society."[95]

In short, the privatization of bourgeois citizens under capitalism strips persons of their social identity, and disempowers them by promoting a state which, abstracted from the citizenry, imposes on them the interests of the ruling class.   Within such regimes, declarations of human rights are naively believed to be universal, but in reality apply only to the "bourgeois citizen"--in itself a delusory notion.[96] None of these so-called rights go beyond the

---

[93]Löwith, *Weber and Marx*, 83-86.

[94]See, e.g, Marx, "German Ideology," Tucker, ed., *Marx-Engels*, 187.

[95]Karl Marx and Friedreich Engels, *Selected Works*, vol. 2 (New York: International Publishers, 1968), 32; cf. "Contribution to the Critique of Hegel's Philosophy of Right," Tucker, ed., *Marx-Engels*, 23-25. See also Giddens, *Studies in Social and Political Theory*, 236-37; and the comparison with Weber on bureaucracy in Gerth and Mills, *From Max Weber*, 49.

[96]Löwith, *Max Weber and Karl Marx*, 88. Marx argued that in France and America, the so-called rights of man were not human rights but bourgeois privileges, and the historically situated "man" these rights referred to, alienated bourgeois man. Given this, "Man is far from being considered, in the rights of man, as a species-being; on the contrary, species-life itself--society--appears as a system which is external to the individual and as a

egoistic man, an individual separated from the community, withdrawn into himself and wholly preoccupied with his private interest and private caprice. On this view, "[t]he only bond between men is natural necessity, need and private interest, the preservation of their property and their egoistic persons."[97] Bourgeois politics is thus the issue of the unholy marriage of perverted anthropology and sociology that forms the ideological superstructure for capitalist relations of production.

In the communist future Marx describes, the contradictions between private and public life will be overcome and people will participate together, fully and personally, in the public arena. "The privatized humanity of the bourgeois individual is to be transcended in a form of communal life which encompasses the whole being of man, including his 'theoretical' existence, and transforms him into a universal, communist being . . . ."[98] Marx dismissed as superficial or inadequate programs of political emancipation advanced within the confines of capitalism, insisting that

[h]uman emancipation will only be complete when the real, individual man has absorbed into himself the abstract citizen; when as an individual man, in his everyday life, in his work, and in his relationships, he has become a *species-being*, and when he has recognized and organized his own

---

limitation of his original independence." Marx, "On the Jewish Question," Tucker ed., *Marx-Engels Reader*, 43. For recent critiques of the bourgeois public sphere influenced by the work of Habermas, see Calhoun, ed., *Habermas and the Public Sphere*, esp. Nancy Fraser, "Rethinking the Public Sphere," 109-142.

[97]Ibid. See also, Löwith, *Max Weber and Karl Marx*, 88-89.

[98]Löwith, *Max Weber and Karl Marx*, 86. Note the affinity between Marx's point and later feminist claims that self-understandings and social structures must be realigned in reconfigured public and private realms. On the relation of Marxism to contemporary feminism, and for a creative contribution toward their integration, see Balbus, *Marxism and Domination*, esp. chs. 2 and 9.

powers (*forces propres*) as *social* powers so that he no longer separates this social power from himself as *political* power.[99]

These words suggest the difference Marx envisages between the conception and exercise of power in capitalist and in communist societies. Also implied are the grounds on which Marx can speak of the dissolution of political power and the withering away of the state, once the communist society has been finally established.[100] Though the future of political power and the state is discussed in many places by Marx, his views are summarized well in Friedreich Engels's essay, "Socialism, Utopian and Scientific"(1880).

Here Engels stresses that in order for the current capitalist system to be abolished, the proletariat must reclaim social productive forces by which they are now dominated. As with the forces of nature, so long as productive forces are allowed to work in spite of and in opposition to the oppressed, so long do those forces master them. "But when once their nature is understood, they [productive forces] can, in the hands of the producers working together, be transformed from master demons into willing servants."[101] Under capitalism, what passes for social order is

---

[99]Marx, "On the Jewish Question," Tucker, ed., *Marx-Engels*, 46.

[100]"The working class, in the course of its development, will substitute for the old civil society an association which will exclude classes and their antagonism, and there will be no more political power properly so-called, since political power is precisely the expression of antagonism in civil society." Karl Marx, *The Poverty of Philosophy*, 174. "When in the course of development, class distinctions have disappeared, and all production has been concentrated in the hands of a vast association of the whole nation, the public power will lose its political character. Political power, properly so-called, is merely the organized power of one class for oppressing another." Marx quoted in Balbus, *Marxism and Domination*, 110.

[101]Friedreich Engels, "Socialism, Utopian and Scientific," Feuer, ed., *Basic Writings on Politics*, 105. He continues: "Then the capitalist mode of appropriation, in which the product enslaves first the producer and then the

actually social anarchy; in the renovated communist regime, authentically *social* regulation of production consistent with the needs of the community and of each individual will hold sway.

A society based on class antagonisms requires a state. Engels provides a definition:

> [The state is] an organization of the particular class which was *pro tempore* the exploiting class, an organization for the purpose of preventing any interference from without with the existing conditions of production, and . . . especially for the purpose of keeping the exploited classes in the condition of oppression corresponding with the given mode of production (slavery, serfdom, wage labor).[102]

Purported to officially represent the whole citizenry, in reality it the state belongs to the historically ascendant class. Marx and Engels predict that at the critical revolutionary moment, the proletariat will seize political power and turn the means of production into state property. In so doing they will assure the eventual dissolution of themselves as a proletarian class, and indeed of all class distinctions and antagonisms.

When, through the revolutionary action of the proletariat, the state at last becomes truly the representative of the whole society, it will simultaneously render itself unnecessary:

> The first act by virtue of which the state really constitutes itself the representative of the whole of society--the taking possession of the means of production in the name of society--this is, at the same time, its last independent act as

---

appropriator, is replaced by . . . direct social appropriation as means to the maintenance and extension of production . . . [and] direct individual appropriation as means of subsistence and enjoyment." Ibid.

[102]Engels, "Socialism, Utopian and Scientific," Feuer, ed., *Basic Writings on Politics*, 106.

a state.[103]

In one sector after another, state interference in social relations will become superfluous, till, with the completion of a process whereby "the government of persons is replaced by the administration of things," the state finally withers away. "The state is not 'abolished.' *It dies out.*"[104]

The Marxist tradition shares with anarchism a commitment to the proposition that power as domination, and authority insofar as it conflicts with equality, freedom, and reason, are to be eliminated. At times, this vision of the dissolution of power-over seems to entail the expectation that coercive authority structures in the economic sphere would also disappear. Marx suggests, for instance, that the necessary coordination and unification of labor in the workshops of the future will be accomplished by leadership he likens to "an orchestra conductor."[105] On this point Engels demurs, arguing that it is impossible to have economic organization without "the imposition of the will of another upon ours." Economic organization, he holds, "presupposes subordination." "[A] certain authority, and . . . a certain subordination are things which, independent of all social organization, are imposed upon us, together with the material conditions under which we produce and make products circulate."[106] Concerning the fate of state power under communism, however, Engels and Marx were in accord. Both anticipated that a genuinely rational social order whose relations of production reflected and assured the de-alienation of social power would be accompanied by the evaporation of political power-over

---

[103]Ibid.

[104]Ibid.

[105]Marx, *Capital*, vol. 3 (Moscow: Foreign Language Publishing House, 1962), 376, 800, 859. Quoted in Lukes, "Power and Authority," 659.

[106]Engels, "On Authority," in Karl Marx and Friedreich Engels, *Selected Works*, 2 vols. (Moscow: Foreign Language Publishing House, 1962), 1:639. Quoted in Lukes, "Power and Authority," 659-60. Cf. Tucker, ed., *Marx-Engels*, 732.

(understood as the apparatus of class oppression). For Marx and Engels, as for Weber, consideration of political power is circumscribed within the limits of a power-over model. This explains why the communistic ideal, which so centrally features social empowerment or power-to, is described as a situation in which political power will have disappeared.

Marx and Weber on Power: Comparative Notes

As they examined socio-political power and its setting in the Western industrial capitalism of their day, Marx and Weber considered many of the same pathologies. They diverged, however, in their diagnoses, prescribed remedies, and long-range prognoses for bourgeois capitalism and its political structures.

Both thinkers concern themselves with the forms of disempowerment bred by capitalist society. Weber's chief worry is the way that individual freedom and creativity are being crushed in the gears of bureaucratic-rational routine. Marx, apprehending the situation in light of his social and economic understanding of the human, centers on the alienation of persons from their products, their environment, and each other--in short, from their power of action and interaction--within class society.

What role do structures of rule and political practices play in this situation of general disempowerment identified by both thinkers? How do these two draw the relationship between political power and social power more broadly construed? On the one hand both authors are acutely aware of the lack of power, whether power-over or power-to, experienced by the vast majority of modern people. On the other hand, when they consider the socio-political arena, both nearly exclusively attend to the analysis of dominative power--power-over.

By selecting a focus on types of legitimate authority, Weber puts political structures defined by sorts of leadership at the center of his sociology of domination. In any authority structure, the state is the organ of public administration which holds the right to command backed by the legitimate use of force over a given geographic territory. In Weber's scheme, legitimate use of force backed by violence distinguishes political power from all other forms of social and economic power, whether construed more broadly as *Macht*, or more narrowly as *Herrschaft*. The form of legitimate authority that characterizes modern capitalistic society, Weber found, is bureaucratic, legal, or rational domination. In it, personal leadership and personal loyalty to leaders are replaced by rational procedures and formal routines to which administrators and ruled alike are subject. While representing an advance in the rational organization of society, this shift has had disempowering effects on both leaders and followers.

Weber does not anticipate the dissolution of bureaucracy in any future social or governmental arrangement. He pins his hopes on charismatic political leadership and leader-democracy as offering the best chances for freedom and creativity within the irrevocable constraints of the bureaucratic system. In this Weber reveals his bias in favor of those few special people who, as charismatic leaders, can incarnate the individuality that will continue to elude most others. Modern political power works through structures to administer the life of the masses in generally uninspired and mundane ways, and through individual politicians to preserve a small space wherein an elite few can still aspire to personal fulfillment--and service to their devoted subjects--as dynamic, creative leaders.

Marx, we have seen, essentially denies the independent status of political power, viewing it as epiphenomenal to the economic relations of modern capitalism. This granted, Marx describes the state--in a manner not unlike Weber's--as the administrative organ which has resort to the use of force. But because it is a tool of the oppressor class, Marx presumes that the state is always repressive and negative, a conclusion not shared by Weber. Weber speaks of legitimacy based, in various ways, on the consent of the governed; Marx in effect denies the possibility of genuinely legitimate political authority. What passes for legitimate rule in modern society is an ideological mirage, a smoke screen for the tyranny of the privileged.

Through the communist revolution, alienated *political* power will recover its rightful meaning and function, as the *social* power of those groups presently most disenfranchised by the bourgeois capitalist system.

Plainly, a Marxist view levels considerable ideological suspicion at the Weberian account of political power. Yet Weber intended his own position to be a response and challenge to major tenets of Marx's analysis. Most prominently, Weber argued that political domination, while related to economic realities, was not merely a residue of the relations of production, but rather a social force in its own right which will operate in any communal arrangement. Scoffing at Marx's assertion that the domination of men over men ought to and could be overcome, Weber looked instead for ways to make the best of the inevitable continuance of bureaucratic forms of rule. Even under the most socialized relations of production, Weber was convinced, bureaucratic administration would eventually spring up, simply because it *is* the most efficient and rational way to organize common pursuits. And, since social life can not be completely subsumed under the aegis of the economic, political rule as such would also continue to be necessary.

In the end, both of these theories of political power, and the analyses of democracy they engender, must be found lacking. This is because, as Ira Cohen observes, the presuppositions of both Marx and Weber each contain an unnecessary exaggeration. Marx on one hand exaggerates the extent to which democracy divested of authoritarian structures is attainable; Weber, conversely, overstates the degree that the "iron law of oligarchy" limits the potential for democratization.[107]   This opposing difference, Cohen notes,

---

[107]Cohen affirms Alvin Gouldner's early critique of Weber's concept of democracy: "Weber's stress on the authoritarian implications of organizational constraints stacks the deck against democracy. Weber overlooks the fact that moving against the 'iron law of oligarchy' is the 'iron law of democracy': 'if oligarchical waves repeatedly wash away the bridges of democracy, this eternal recurrence can only happen because men [and women] doggedly rebuild them after each inundation.'" Cohen, "Underemphasis," 293-294,

reflects the theory of power each view harbors. "For Marx, the possibility exists that a society can be created in which the exercise of power [over] poses no problems; for Weber, the exercise of authoritarian powers of command by those who possess superior resources is inevitable."[108]   For those interested in a comprehensive notion of power for Christian social ethics, perhaps the most serious weakness of these treatments is their lack of attention to "the central problem of substantive democracy," that is, "the maintenance of vigorous public spheres in which democratic interest is formed and advanced."[109]   A robust Christian social ethics must redress this deficiency, even as it benefits from Marx's and Weber's insights into capitalist and bureaucratic threats to democratic empowerment.

Conclusion

These two classic treatments of socio-political power illustrate the prevalence of the power-over model in contemporary social theory. Marxian and Weberian theorists continue to challenge each other on the specifics of their formulations. Viewed from Marx's materialist and critical perspective, the legitimate authorities

---

quoting Alvin Gouldner, "Metaphysical Pathos and the Theory of Bureaucracy," *American Political Science Review* 49 (1955): 506.

[108]Cohen, "Underemphasis," 294. Cf. Alan Gilbert, "Political Philosophy: Marx and Radical Democracy," in T. Carver, ed., *Cambridge Companion*, esp. 188-95.

[109]Cohen, "Underemphasis," 295. North American ethicists focusing on practical empowerment will benefit from other strands of modern political theory, such as American pragmatism (e.g., John Dewey, *The Public and its Problems* (Chicago: Swallow Press, 1927), the work of feminist political theorists such as Nancy Hartsock, Jean Elshtain, and Nancy Fraser; and recent popular social movement studies such as Sara M. Evans & Harry Boyte, *Free Spaces: The Sources of Democratic Change in America* (Chicago: University of Chicago Press, 1992).

delineated by Weber appear as superstructures that mask the dynamics of domination rooted in relations of production. Weberians fault Marx's interpretation for its monocausal tendencies and failure to acknowledge the independent status of forces other than the strictly economic. But whether described as consciously accepted and existent in its own right, as for Weber, or operative in relations of production and often below the surface of actors' awareness, as for Marx, socio-political power in both theories is highlighted as command and obedience, superordination and subordination, domination and subjection. As power-over, these relations are asymmetrical and always include, at least potentially, coercion. The focal point for analysis and evaluation of power from this perspective tends to be dominative leaders, processes, or structures.

Important and varied streams of power analysis have proceeded from the work of these two seminal figures. Amidst great diversity, the emphases of these successor theories mirror the differences we have indicated between the theories of Marx and Weber themselves. Those more inspired by Marx underscore ideology, alienation, and the economic and class contradictions that underpin political structures and processes. Heirs to Weber accent types of domination, legitimation, and the role of leadership in political power. The impact of Marx can be detected in the literature of critical social theory, (including but not limited to the so-called Frankfurt School of Theodor Adorno, Max Horkheimer, and others), certain versions of stratification and (to a lesser extent, since it is more directly heir to the Italian Neo-Machiavellian sociologists) elite theory, the school of dependency theory, and, by way of Antonio Gramsci, class-state theory. Weber's influence is clear on those who approach socio-political processes by way of comparative historical studies, such as Richard Bendix and Edward Shils, stratification and conflict theory as represented by C. Wright Mills, and other studies of class and status that do not reduce social and political power to strictly economic determinants. Some of the most creative recent theoretical work on power is indebted to both Marx and Weber, yet attempts to redress perceived deficiencies in their predecessors' incorporation of power-to. Jürgen Habermas's analysis of civil society, Anthony Giddens's theory of structuration, and James C. Scott's examination of empowering, "backstage" discourses that parallel and foment the charismatic upheaval of "official transcripts" of domination, are examples.[110]

An adequate notion of power in Christian social ethics must integrate both models of power, power-over and power-to. This brief survey of Weber and Marx has illustrated the importance of power-over theories in the social scientific literature and political practices that shape the context for Christian ethical thinking. Analysts of power-over are, to be sure, not the only voices in recent social theoretical discussions, as Chapter Three will document. But such theories have predominated, and U.S. Christian ethicists have been most heavily indebted to power-over models as they have gone about their own thinking on socio-political power. Our task in Chapter Two will be to show how the power-over understanding is incorporated into the social ethics of two representative contemporary Christian thinkers.

---

[110]See, e.g., Jürgen Habermas, *The Structural Transformation of the Public Sphere*, trans. T. Burger and F. Lawrence (Cambridge, MA: MIT Press, 1989), *The Theory of Communicative Action* (Boston: MIT Press, 1987); Robbie Pfeufer Kahn, "The Problem of Power in Habermas," *Human Studies* 11 (1988): 361-87; Scott, *Domination and the Arts of Resistance*; and the works of Anthony Giddens cited in Chapter III.

CHAPTER II

POWER AS SUPERORDINATION
IN CHRISTIAN SOCIAL ETHICS:
CATHOLIC AND PROTESTANT INSTANCES

Social and political theorists of the past century have conceived of power primarily in terms of superordination, or power-over. The preceding analysis of two giants of modern western social thought illustrated this; it also illumined ways that social theorizing about power reflects assumptions regarding human nature and society. These assumptions, and the power theories they underwrite, significantly influence judgments about social flourishing and how to achieve it.

When Christian ethicists consider social or political matters, the social sciences guide them in establishing the descriptive lineaments of their subject. If the favored definition of power among social theorists has been superordination, it is no surprise that Christian social ethicists reveal a similar orientation. The power-over description predominates, in various forms, in the bulk of 20th century mainline Catholic and Protestant social thought, as well as in a good deal of revisionist and even radical religious reflection on social and political life.

This chapter examines the understandings of socio-political power in the work of two important 20th century figures, Roman Catholic political philosopher Jacques Maritain, and Protestant social ethicist Reinhold Niebuhr. Both thinkers work with a notion of power that emphasizes superordination. Each author provides a sophisticated illustration of the interaction between Christian perspective and sociological and political theory. Comparing Maritain's Catholic approach to that of the Protestant Niebuhr will also highlight some prominent divergences within mainstream Christian social thought, both in the doctrinal convictions out of which Christian theories regarding power emerge, and in those descriptive and prescriptive understandings of social life in which thinking about power is implicated.

Power-over is given a distinctive formulation by each thinker. Differences between their interpretations of socio-political power are rooted in their respective ways of conceiving human persons, the relationship between individual and community, and political society. Maritain, we will show, espouses a personalist anthropology and an organic social theory which envisages the person both as irreducible whole, and as participant in the common good of society. Power is seen within this scheme essentially as power-over, but, couched within Maritain's normative theory of authority and society, this power-over shows a mild and beneficent face. In the thought of Niebuhr, by contrast, a dynamic, paradoxical anthropology and a conflictual notion of society converge in a portrayal of power-over as more thoroughly ubiquitous, and more maleficent than that of Maritain.

The peculiar emphases of these treatments of power are related to distinctive interpretations of the Christian doctrines of creation, fall, redemption, and human destiny. Maritain places central emphasis on the doctrine of creation when he discusses social and political life. Niebuhr, by contrast, focuses on the doctrines of sin and the fall. Other major doctrines are configured in relation to the teaching that is the linchpin of each author's interpretation of social and political life.

After briefly describing the religious horizons that inform Maritain's and Niebuhr's approaches, their understandings of human agency, social structures, and socio-political life will be considered as these impinge on their theories of socio-political power. The final part of the chapter will compare and critically evaluate the two positions on the basis of our criteria for a comprehensive treatment of power.

Jacques Maritain on Power[1]

Christian Doctrines and Socio-Political Life

Jacques Maritain interprets the doctrine of creation within a teleological, Aristotelian-Thomistic framework. Humans are described as beings, made in the image of their Creator, who incline toward both proximate-earthly and final-spiritual *teloi*. The earthly *telos* is pursued within the limits of the created order, and it is within these limits that social and political life have their significance. The purpose of the structures and communities of this world is to provide directly for the temporal good which is the "final, natural end" of the human creature.[2] The temporal order

---

[1]This analysis of Maritain's political philosophy draws from his major writings over a span of several decades. Etienne Borne details the historical context and chronological development of those writings in "La philosophie politique de Jacques Maritain," in Jean-Louis Allard, ed., *Jacques Maritain: philosophe dans la cité* (Ottawa, Canada: Editions de l'Université d'Ottawa, 1985), 247-62. On Maritain's complex relation to social scientific sources, see Ralph Nelson, "Maritain's Account of the Social Sciences," in Peter A. Redpath, ed., *From Twilight to Dawn: The Cultural Vision of Jacques Maritain* (Mishawaka, IN: American Maritain Association, 1990), 143-54.

[2]Maritain envisages a threefold natural *telos* to the world, consisting in 1) the conquest of human autonomy (progressive liberation from subjection to natural or human forces); 2) the development of the multiple spiritual activities of persons (especially of knowledge, of art, and of moral understanding); 3) the progressive manifestation of all the spiritual potentialities of human nature in accordance with the impulse, testified to by history, "to make manifest what is in man." Jacques Maritain, *The Peasant of the Garonne* (New York: Macmillan Company, 1968), 40-41. In social life, these freedom-oriented goals are pursued as features of the common good.

also promotes humans' approach toward their final, supernatural end--everlasting enjoyment of the beatific vision of the Divine; it does so, however, only in an indirect and intermediate way.[3]

Maritain situates socio-political life within this temporal/spiritual division by means of his theory of "the distinction of planes."[4] According to this theory, the concrete realities of self and world inhabit two simultaneously existing realms or orders, ordained to specific ends. The natural/temporal order is oriented toward the real but passing good of time, matter, and this-worldly history. The spiritual order is directed toward God as its final good. The human being as incarnate spirit participates simultaneously in both dimensions, and both *teloi*.[5] Socio-political communities operate on the natural plane, which is distinctly the sphere of creation.

Sin affects the communal realm when persons ignore the God-given norms of justice and civic amity that govern it, and pursue individual or sectional gain without regard for the common good. Because both sin and redemption primarily concern humans' spiritual destiny, they relate only indirectly to events in the socio-political sphere. When properly ordered and pursued, however, social life fosters conditions in which the growth of the final kingdom can, in Maritain's term, "fructify." Social and political activity can promote conditions favorable to persons' pursuit of

---

[3]Political society, as part of the larger sweep of human history, has a natural, but not a supernatural end. The absolutely final, spiritual end of the world and history is the supratemporal Kingdom of God. Maritain, *Peasant*, 36.

[4]See Jacques Maritain, *Integral Humanism*, J. Evans, trans. (Notre Dame, IN: University of Notre Dame Press, 1968), 291-308.

[5]Maritain describes the relationship between these two realms as interlocking, but never thoroughly interpenetrating. Though the spiritual is superior, both planes, with their respective goals, are part of the Divine ordering. Consistent with the Thomistic dictum that grace does not destroy but completes nature, Maritain affirms that pursuing their natural, proximate purpose serves to ready humans for their final, spiritual end. Ibid.

their supernatural purpose, or conditions in which that pursuit is more difficult; but such activity can neither finally frustrate nor fully accomplish that purpose.

Having made the doctrine of creation central to his discussion of socio-political life, Maritain is inclined to view the problems of the social realm, including those involving the exercise and distribution of power, as caused primarily by the finitude which is our creaturely lot, and to focus only secondly on the toll taken by human sinfulness. Here, we shall see, is a key difference between Maritain's appropriation of the Christian doctrines and that of Reinhold Niebuhr.

Human Agency and Sociality

Following Thomas Aquinas, Maritain sees intellect and reason as the pre-eminent mark of humanity. As creatures who are in God's image, but other than God, we simultaneously inhabit two dimensions of reality: the realm of the spiritual and immaterial, to which our interior life especially corresponds, and the realm of the material and history, the temporal, to which our practical and bodily life directly relates.

Maritain locates the dignity of humans in the fact that each is a unique, spiritual *person*.[6] The purpose of human life includes

---

[6]As person, "I am a whole, a universe unto myself; a microcosm in which the whole universe can be encompassed through knowledge." Jacques Maritain, *The Rights of Man and Natural Law* (New York: Charles Scribner's Sons, 1943), 3. According to Maritain, personhood is rooted in a spiritual soul whose final destiny of union with the Almighty renders it of endless worth. Human freedom and rationality (which ground our ability to love) are evidences of this spiritual personality. It is to this mystery of personhood that the Christian doctrine of *imago dei* refers.

working for the perfection of the created order,[7] but worldly social structures remain instrumental to the ultimate *telos* of each person. "The whole universe and every social institution" must ultimately serve, foster, and protect "the conversation of every soul with God."[8]

In Maritain's eyes, the human person, albeit a whole unto itself, is an "open whole" which tends by nature to social life and communion.[9] As Aristotle affirmed, we are political animals, and society is something required by human nature. Born of a natural human craving, society then must be fashioned by the work of reason and will. A true society is "a whole made up of wholes," constituted by persons who, while organically related to the community, retain their own genuine independence.[10] The twofold destiny of humanity gives each member a dual relation to society:

> In short, the human person, so far as he is made for God
> and for participation in absolute good, transcends the
> earthly society of which he is a member; but, so far as he

---

[7]"Human creatures are ordained to the perfection of the created whole and are related to the order and perfection of the created universe, of which they are the most noble constitutive parts." Jacques Maritain, *The Person and the Common Good* (Notre Dame: University of Notre Dame Press, 1946, paperback ed., 1966), 17.

[8]Maritain, *Common Good*, 15-16.

[9]Maritain, *Natural Law*, 5. "The subjectivity of the person has nothing in common with the unity without doors or windows of the Leibnitizian Monad. It demands the communication of intelligence and love. . . . The person as such aspires naturally to the social life." Jacques Maritain, *Freedom in the Modern World* (New York: Charles Scribner's Sons, 1936), 49. This is so because we depend upon others for necessities of life, but also because of the "radical generosity inscribed within the very being of the person." A natural openness to communicating intelligence and love makes the person one who "wants to tell what it knows and what it is--to whom if not to other people?" Maritain, *Natural Law*, 5; cf. Jacques Maritain, *Scholasticism and Politics* (London: Geoffrey Bles, [1940] 1954), 59.

[10]Maritain, *Natural Law*, 7.

owes to society what he is, he is a *part* of society as of a whole that is greater and better than he is."

Maritain uses the terms *personhood* and *individuality* to distinguish between the human in respect to spiritual nature and destiny (as such, one is a person), and the human in respect to temporal nature and destiny (as such, one is an individual).[12] Individuality attains moral goodness only when it is properly related to personality.[13] Individuality uninspired by spiritual personality becomes oriented by "the detestable ego whose law is *to grasp* or absorb for itself," as, in an ultimately self-defeating trajectory, the

---

[11]"The Conquest of Freedom" (1944), in Jacques Maritain, *The Social and Political Philosophy of Jacques Maritain: Selected Readings*, ed. J. W. Evans & L. R. Ward (New York: Charles Scribner's Sons, 1955), 21.

[12]As corporeal beings, humans are individuals "by reason of their transcendental relation to matter understood as implying position in space. . . . Individuality is that which excludes from me all that others are." Maritain, *Common Good*, 37. As individual, one is "a fragment of a species, a unique point in the immense web of physical, cosmic, ethnic, and historical forces, . . . bound by their laws, [and] subject to the determinism of these aspects of the world." Ibid., 38; cf. *Freedom in the Modern World*, 46-47. Because it is incomplete and contingent, individuality is always threatened, and always tends to grasp for itself. Personhood, by contrast, is constituted by a principle of creativity and freedom--what Maritain calls the spiritual soul--that transcends the limits of individuality. As an "imprint or seal that enables one to possess one's existence, to perfect it, and to give oneself freely," personality is most clearly exemplified in the act of love. *Common Good*, 41, 38-39. Maritain cautions against construing the individual/person distinction dualistically. Our whole being, and every act, is individual by reason of that in us which derives from matter, and personal by reason of that which derives from spirit. Ibid., 43.

[13]Each free human act tends, says Maritain, in one of two directions: either toward "the supreme center toward which personality tends," or toward the dispersion into which material individuality, left to itself, is inclined to disintegrate. Ibid., 44.

personality becomes adulterated and dissolute.[14] On the other hand, activity consistent with one's spiritual personality shapes a character modeled after "the generous self of heros and saints."[15]

Maritain's articulation of human agency and sociality guides his normative thinking on social power in both its power-over and power-to forms. When power is understood and exercised from the limited perspective of material individuality, it is not only misconstrued but inevitably disordered. Precisely this distortion is reflected in the self-serving and oppressive uses of power so common in socio-political life. When actuated from a standpoint that correctly integrates individuality and personality, power is enlisted in the generous pursuit of mutual flourishing. These claims are borne out by a closer look at Maritain's theory of political society.

Society and its Purposes

Maritain's ethic of socio-political power is developed in relation to carefully delineated notions of society and of the body politic.[16] "Society" is defined as a collective union of people, a product of

---

[14]Ibid. Cf. Reinhold Niebuhr's similar description of the self-defeating effects of sin in *The Nature and Destiny of Man: A Christian Interpretation*, 2 vols. (New York: Charles Scribner's Sons, 1941, 1943), esp. vol 1, ch. 7, 8.

[15]Maritain, *Common Good*, 44. Education's vital task is to promote in each the organic development toward full personhood, by "pruning and trimming" personality and individuality in such a way that genuine personality and its generosity may flourish. Ibid., 45-46.

[16]John W. Cooper, *The Theology of Freedom: The Legacy of Jacques Maritain and Reinhold Niebuhr* (Atlanta, GA: Mercer, 1985) compares Maritain's view of political society with Niebuhr's. See esp. ch. 4, 90-100, 118-24.

reason and moral strength."[17]   For Maritain society is a fully human, hence rational and ethical reality.   Consonant with the Aristotelian-Thomistic tradition, politics is defined as the moral pursuit of the good society.   Political institutions exist for the good of the body politic, and structures and practices of political power must conform in both means and ends to norms of justice and civic amity.[18]

Because it is composed of persons, society is, for Maritain, "an organism composed of liberties." Yet the good that society pursues is not simply the sum of the individual goods of its members. Rather, the goal of society is the achievement of a *common good*, "the good of the social body, a good of human *persons*," consisting in "the good human life of the multitude."[19]   Participation in the

---

[17]This definition of society is in contrast to "community," which Maritain describes as an ethico-social reality whose origin and object "precede the determinations of human intelligence and will . . . and involve common unconscious psyche, common feelings and psychological structures, common mores." *Man and the State*, 2-3. Examples of communities can be regional, ethnic, and linguistic groups, social classes, and "nations" properly understood. Ibid., 2-4. Niebuhr makes a comparable distinction between the organic bonds that underlie a community, and a genuine political society. See, e.g., Reinhold Niebuhr, "The Illusion of World Government," *Foreign Affairs*, 27 (April 1949): 385-86.

[18]"The subordination of politics to ethics is absolute and even infinite, being based on the subordination of [natural and supratemporal] ends; for the good of the state is not God Himself, and remains far, far inferior to the supreme beatitude of man." Jacques Maritain, *The Things That Are Not Caesar's* (New York: Charles Scribner, 1930), 2-3.

[19]Maritain, *Natural Law*, 8. The common good is a good that persons receive and communicate; it "presupposes persons and flows back upon them, and is in this sense achieved in them." Ibid. Elsewhere, Maritain explains "the good life" as "a life conformable to the essential exigencies and essential dignity of human nature, a life--both morally straight and happy--of the social whole . . . such . . . that it is in some way spilled over and redistributed to each individual part." "The End of Machiavellianism," (1952), *Selected Readings*, 301-302.

commonweal neither abrogates personal rights nor supersedes membership in smaller communities within the social unit; the common good, in fact, implies and requires a vital pluralism in which the fundamental rights of persons, of the domestic family, and of smaller scale communities encompassed by the whole, are protected.[20] But in political society, these various subunits are caught up and encompassed by a shared good which both reflects and enhances them.

In picturing the common good Maritain explicitly focuses on the value of freedom. His notion of the common good contains, as well, rich implications for a normative theory of socio-political power, though Maritain's power-over focus limits his apprehension of these. He names as the chief value fostered by the common good "the highest possible attainment (compatible with the good of the whole) of persons to their lives as persons, and to their freedom of expansion or autonomy, and to the gifts of goodness which in turn flow from it."[21] In *The Rights of Man and Natural Law*, Maritain enumerates three essential characteristics of the common good. First, the common good implies a *redistribution* of social benefits among persons in a way conducive to their development. Second, it is an *intrinsically ethical reality*, consisting not merely of a set of advantages and conveniences, but essentially of the good and just life of the multitude--for this reason the common good requires a virtuous citizenry Finally, the common good founds a genuine *authority* that serves the good of the whole, and is exercised in a manner appropriate to free persons; this means that self-serving or oppressive authority betrays its political essence, and is thereby illegitimate.[22] In short, the common good implies and demands a

---

[20]Maritain, *Natural Law*, 8-9.

[21]Ibid.

[22]Ibid., 9. An insightful critical analysis of Maritain's articulation of the common good is M. Duquesne, "La philosophie politique de Jacques Maritain," *Centre d'archives Maurice Blondel, Journée d'études* 4: (November, 1974): 39-55; esp. 50-53.

society wherein power's structure and exercise is strictly oriented to the flourishing of each and all.

Political society, then, the public form under which persons, animated by justice and civic friendship, join in pursuit of their this-worldly, natural purposes.[23] Those purposes are most fully realized in a common good that orchestrates persons' flourishing within a thriving social body.   Of course, attaining the socio-political common good does not make human destiny complete.[24] Christianity reveals the supreme, transcendent and all-embracing "common good" to be God, and the ultimate goal of human life as union with the divine. This places socio-political life in its proper context as a good in itself, a *bonum honestum*, but one that remains bound to the temporal plane.[25]

---

[23]"Political society," or the "body politic," is essentially a rational/spiritual order, but, because it presumes and encompasses communities, Maritain conceives it as having "flesh and blood, instincts, passions, reflexes, unconscious psychological structures and dynamisms," all subject, by legal coercion when necessary, to the guidance of reason toward the common good. Maritain, *Man and the State*, 9-10. Justice and civic amity are prime ethical characteristics of a genuine body politic, and Maritain frequently describes them as the cement of the common good. See, e.g., "The End of Machiavellianism," *Selected Readings*, 302. The shared interests and passions Maritain identifies with community can also serve, albeit in a more ambiguous fashion, as social "glue." Ibid., 321-22; *Integral Humanism*, 204.

[24]"Here Maritain goes--with St. Thomas--beyond Aristotle. . . . Revelation liberates political philosophy--as all philosophy--from the limitations which are the consequences of the factual weakness of human reason."   Waldemar Gurian, "On Maritain's Political Philosophy," *The Thomist* 5 (1943): 19.

[25]Gurian, "On Maritain," 10-11. For a recent retrieval of Maritain's concept of the common good with reference to ecclesiology as well as socio-political theory, see Kibujjo M. Kalumba, "Maritain on 'The Common Good': Reflections on the Concept," *Laval théologique et philosophique* 49 (février 1993): 93-104.

Socio-Political Power

Maritain speaks of socio-political power in two different contexts. Though they involve distinctive ethical evaluations, both discussions highlight power as superordination.

Power in service to the common good. Power is first discussed as contributive to the common good of political society. In this treatment, power is joined to authority, from which it derives legitimacy and moral value. Maritain defines "power" as an ascendant party's ability to successfully elicit the obedience, compliance, or aid of others in pursuing ends set by the ascendant. Power is "the *force*, which one can use and with the aid of which one can oblige others to listen or to obey."[26] Superordination, power-over, is the heart of this description. In collective life, power-over's purpose is to serve the common good. For this reason, the decisive ethical determinant for power is whether or not it is exercised under the auspices of genuine authority.

While power for Maritain is the force by which one obliges others to listen or obey, authority refers to "the *right* to direct and command, to be listened to or obeyed by others."[27] Maritain draws his two definitions from the medieval distinction between *auctoritas* and *potestas*. He cautions, however, against regarding the notions in isolation from one another, for the two ought to be, and most frequently are, linked:

> All authority, insofar as it concerns social life, demands to be completed (under some mode or other, which need not be juridical) by power, without which it threatens to become useless and inefficacious among men. All power which is not the expression of authority is iniquitous.

---

[26]Maritain, *Scholasticism and Politics*, 73.
[27]Ibid.

Practically, it is normal that the word authority should imply power . . . [and vice versa].[28]

Maritain sees power as the material, physical capability which the moral, legal right of authority needs in order to be practically effective.[29]   Conversely, power requires authority in order to achieve positive moral status. "To separate power and authority is to separate force and justice."[30]   To gain power is important for anyone who wants to act on the community, but, "to acquire authority--the right to be followed by the minds and by the wills of other[s] . . . (and consequently the right to exercise power)--is more important still."[31]   The primacy he gives to authority flows from Maritain's conviction that politics is an intrinsically ethical enterprise.   Indeed, power is genuinely political in Maritain's normative sense only when it is exercised under the auspices of authority.

How is political authority acquired? Maritain explains that all government, whatever its form, is grounded in the right of people to govern themselves. This right of governance originates in God, the Maker and Governor of human life, and is known to us by advertence to the natural law. We possess the right of self-government by participation in God's absolute right to govern us. For

---

[28]Maritain, *Scholasticism*, 74. See also, Maritain, "Problems Concerning Authority," *Selected Readings*, 89. "Authority and power are two different things. Power is the force by means of which you can oblige others to obey you. Authority is the right to direct and command, to be listened to or obeyed by others. Authority requests power. Power without authority is tyranny." Ident. Maritain, *Man and the State*, 126. Cf. Reinhold Niebuhr's near-equation of authority and power in the introduction to *The Structure of Nations and Empires* (New York: Charles Scribner's Sons, 1959), 8-10.

[29]"Insofar as it has power, authority descends into the physical order; insofar as it has authority, power is raised to the moral and legal order." Maritain, *Scholasticism*, 92-93.

[30]Ibid., 74.

[31]Ibid.

every member of a society to exercise directly this right to self-government, however, is counter-productive; this arrangement only works successfully in very small groups or in the occasional case of popular referendums. Inevitably, certain citizens need to be placed in public service and invested with authority by the people.[32]

Maritain argues that the facts of human creaturehood, not the effects of sin, make government and command-obedience relations natural necessities in social life. Since the common good and common action must be sought amidst the contingency and singularity that marks historical existence, the agreement of minds possible in mathematics and other speculative fields cannot be expected in politics. Political life thus requires practical direction by people with the requisite skills, knowledge, and judgment. Political community entails a hierarchic distribution of its organs. It is necessary that some parts "should have as their work those functions which concern the unity of the whole and the direction of the common work and the common life, and that these should consequently possess an authority over the others."[33] The upshot is that superordination and subordination are endemic to human social living. "Even if all individuals possessed perfect reason and perfect rectitude of will, the unified conduct of social affairs would still require a political authority and a hierarchy."[34]

Maritain acknowledges that modernity's appreciation of human rights and freedoms has contributed to the development of democratic political structures. His own work weds Thomistic political theory with an appreciation of democracy and the impulses that animate it. An affirmation of the rights of persons as rooted

---

[32]Maritain, *Man and the State*, 135; *Selected Readings*, 97.

[33]Maritain, *Scholasticism*, 78. Max Weber and Reinhold Niebuhr also view political authority as encompassing the coordination and regulation of the various forces and smaller units that compose a society.

[34]Ibid.

in God's natural and eternal law is decisive for the "personalist" or "organic" form of democracy Maritain advocates.[35]

Personalist democracy is a form of political society that, as it pursues the common good, integrally embraces the dignity of each human person. Its goal is the free expansion of persons in a milieu of civic friendship. Such freedom and friendship are not givens, but rather goals that are arduously pursued and attained only at cost.[36] Pursuant to these goals, personalist democracy entails specific understandings of power and authority.

First, personalist democracy suppresses neither authority nor power, but seeks to assure that both emerge from the people, and that both are exercised in their name. With freedom of persons one of its primary goals, this organic democracy affirms the fact that to obey those rightfully holding civic authority is neither irrational, nor an abdication of freedom. "[To] obey the one who really fulfills the duty to direct the common work toward the common good (as in a game of football or hockey a player obeys his captain) is to act as a free man . . . ."[37]

Second, personalist democracy understands that the power of constraint (and Maritain regards the ability to constrain as a constitutive feature of power) is not the substance of authority. Rather, power (the ability to compel) is only one attribute of authority, which authority needs to complete itself and to be

---

[35]The term "organic" alludes to the grounding of this form of political life in the natural design of the Creator. "Active participation of all human persons in political life; control of the state by the people, and fraternal cooperation in common work under a leadership based not on inherited privileges and hereditary selection but on the necessity of having an authority to determine unity of action, are characteristic of this democracy, which is inspired by Christianity, even though its members may not be Christians." Gurian, "On Maritain," 17.

[36]See Maritain, *Scholasticism*, 78-93.

[37]Ibid., 80. Maritain's use of the sports metaphor is interesting but problematic; such a metaphor may imply a purely voluntarist understanding of relations of power inconsistent with our author's wider political vision.

efficient, "especially as regards children, or the vicious and obstinate."[38] A truly organic democracy seeks to eradicate all traces of power without authority. To do this, merely declaring principles or ratifying legal formulae will not suffice. "The only efficacious means is the enlargement of the rights and of the power of action of persons, and spontaneous groups of persons, and the state of tension thus developed."[39] Here Maritain apparently has in mind something similar to Niebuhr's principle of the balance of power. Both Niebuhr's balance of power and Maritain's stress on enlarging persons' power of action imply the idea of power-to; yet, in both cases, the power-over emphasis in their operative socio-political theories prevents our authors from making this explicit.

In Maritain's democratic theory, the obligation to obey depends on the justice immanent in the authority who commands. Here the classic objectivist meta-ethic that grounds Maritain's system shines through clearly. Free persons submit to law and authority not because they are coerced, but because it is just to do so. "At the origin of the democratic sense, then, there is not the desire to 'obey only oneself,' but rather the desire to obey *whatever is just to obey*."[40]

Organic democratic theory recognizes the right of all holding authority (in whatever societal arrangement) to obedience, yet sees this right as originating in God, and passing through the people to the rulers. By reason of the consensus which lies at the origin of political community, "the authority which derives from the principle of being, as its transcendent source, also derives from the people as passing through it in order to reside in its legitimate holders . . . ."[41]

---

[38]Ibid., 81. What apparently joins children, the vicious, and the obstinate here is their need for externally imposed limits, and beyond that, perhaps, the administration--one presumes, despite their resistance--of contributive or retributive measures deemed "for their own good," and for the good of society.

[39]Ibid., 81.

[40]Ibid., 82.

[41]Ibid., 84.

Civil authorities govern as representatives for the multitude. To explain, Maritain appeals to Aquinas' notion of the prince as vicar of the people, re-interpreting this principle for a democratic context.[42]

[Vicariousness is] the typical law of . . . authoritative structure, in such a way that authority passing through the people rises, degree by degree, from the base to the summit of the hierarchic structure of the community; and so that the exercise of power by men in whom authority is brought periodically to reside through the designation of the people, attests the constancy of the *passage* of sovereignty through the multitude.[43]

It is on the notion of representation or vicariousness that all the theory of power in democratic society rests.[44]

Vicariousness is constituted, first, by the fact that when they invest rulers with authority, the people turn over the *exercise* of governance to the ruler, but they do not thereby relinquish *possession* of their basic right to self-government. Second, the representatives of the people are not for that reason mere instruments or puppets of the people, but are invested with the real right to command essential to authority.

Though it is not altogether clear that they are the same, Maritain links the notion of vicariousness to what he calls a "homogenetic" view of authority, in which the leader is seen not as

---

[42]Ibid., 86. Organic democracy recognizes that the prince governs as representing in his person the entire people, *ut vices gerens multitudinus*, (*Summa Theologiae*, I-II, 90, 3.) Cited by Maritain, Ibid. See also, Maritain, *Selected Readings*, 95.

[43]Ibid., 84. In support of this claim, Maritain appeals to Leo XIII, Pius X, Suarez, Bellarmine, and Thomas Aquinas's *Summa Theologiae* I-II; 90, 3. Ibid., 84 ns. 1, 2.

[44]Maritain, *Selected Readings*, 92.

a separated majestic being but rather as first among equals: here, "the holder is as a companion who has the right to command his fellows."[45] All types of paternalist domination are excluded in a homogenetic authority relation. Furthermore, he avers, the means of exercising authority, "rather than promoting a military-like discipline," ought to be appropriate to the ends of freedom and civic friendship being sought.[46]

Thus detailed by Maritain, social rulership possesses the two components of political authority that Reinhold Niebuhr also identifies: majesty and force. Force, or the ability to coerce consent, is accorded the rulers by the people as the necessary back-up to the right to command. Majesty, says Maritain, is borne by the civil power not because it represents either God or itself, but because it represents the people, the whole multitude and its common will to live together.[47] Political majesty arises not because the ruler is sovereign, since, "in the political domain there is no such thing as sovereignty," but because the ruler is the image of the people, their topmost deputy. And, behind this majesty as its first foundation, is the eternal law of "the primary cause of being," God, Source of the authority which is in the people and in which the vicar of the people participates.[48]

Finally, from the base up through the whole hierarchy, the rights of the human person must be recognized and guaranteed so thoroughly that an organic democracy will be essentially "the city of

----

[45]Maritain, *Scholasticism*, 106.

[46]Ibid., 109.

[47]Maritain, *Selected Readings*, 93; Niebuhr, *Nations and Empires*, 8-9. The legacy of French social theory is evident in similarities between Maritain's treatment of majesty and select features of Rousseau's General Will, or again, Emile Durkheim's later claims about the reverence that "society" evokes from its members. Maritain, of course, explicitly distances himself from what he regards as the errors of a Rousseauian view. See Maritain, *Man and the State*, 28-53.

[48]Maritain, *Selected Readings*, 94.

the rights of the person."[49] To this end, a "just pluralism" ought to be fostered. Such pluralism also provides the best remedy for what Maritain calls the difficulties inherent in all democracies, difficulties that arise from the evil and foolishness--the sin and finitude--of the persons who inhabit them.[50]

Distortions of power and authority. Maritain asserts that in theory and practice modern democracies have often succumbed to false ideologies flowing from erroneous, anthropocentric political theories.[51] He also criticized distorted thinking that underlay the national and international "power politics" of his day. In these cases a second, more negative treatment of power occurs.

In a first error that plagues modern democracies, what Maritain calls Rousseauist democratic theory elaborates a "democracy of the individual" which "suppresses authority and preserves power." The root of this view of democracy is the assertion that "since every individual is 'born free,' his dignity demands that he should *obey only himself.*"[52] Elaborating this premise, it is declared that authority resides in the whole multitude, and is expressed in a mythical "General Will." But, charges Maritain, this general will eludes identification, and hence the escapes control of the people whose will it supposedly expresses. In the authority-less vacuum that results, those able to marshal the most coercive power easily step. Proclaiming themselves the bearers and interpreters of the general will, these power holders also claim absolute authority for their organ of rule, the state. Ironically, this approach to

---

[49]Maritain, *Scholasticism*, 88.

[50]Ibid., 89.

[51]The conceptions of democracy that Maritain rejects embody the same destructive extremes which Reinhold Niebuhr speaks of as the "Scylla of anarchy"--the Proudhonian pitfall, and the "Charbydis of tyranny"--the tendency of the Rousseauist. See Niebuhr, *Nature and Destiny*, 2:258.

[52]Maritain, *Scholasticism*, 74-75. "Rousseauistic Democratism is opposed because its sentimental equality makes all social order impossible." Gurian, "On Maritain," 13. Note Gurian's assumption, shared with Maritain, that social order requires hierarchy.

democracy, while aiming to preserve all individual rights and freedoms, ends in either "communist sociolatry or totalitarian stateolatry."[53]

Maritain identifies a contrasting error: an approach to democracy that suppresses both authority and power. In championing an open, anarchic society without hierarchy or centralized government, this utopian, "Proudhonian" theory seeks "to substitute the administration of things for the government of men." (Here Engels and Proudhon were in accord.) The root of this thinking is "the idea of a non-hierarchic totality," whose intra-historical possibility Maritain firmly rejects. "A totality without hierarchy--a whole without subordination of the parts to the whole--such a supernatural marvel can only be found in the Divine Trinity, in Uncreated Society, where the persons are precisely not parts."[54]

Besides criticizing misconstruals of power and authority in certain democratic theories, Maritain decried two other lines of thought about power that had gained ascendance in modern-day politics: the ideology of state sovereignty, and Machiavellian or *Realpolitik* theories of political relations.

The evil issue of Rousseauian democratic theory was sovereignty--the notion of an indivisible, transcendent and supreme power-over that originates, resides in, and is wielded by a state, a nation, or a people. As we have seen, on Maritain's interpretation, Rousseau's General Will, the locus of sovereignty, arises from the people but then rules separately, from above. But a figment of the imagination cannot hold the reins of government, so in practice sovereignty is inevitably transferred to the state. Since, moreover, sovereignty cannot be shared, the state will eventually usurp the

---

[53]Ibid., 76.

[54]Ibid., 78. Recently, feminist theologians, some also appealing to Trinitarian theology, have questioned the judgments about social hierarchy represented by Maritain here. See, e.g., Elizabeth A. Johnson, *She Who Is: The Mystery of God in Feminist Theological Discourse* (New York: Crossroad, 1993).

supreme power-over claimed for the people.   The resulting understandings and practices of political power tend to be zero-sum and oppressive. Ultimately, the theory of sovereignty is an ideology which ascribes to human structures an absolute power proper to God alone. This makes it not only erroneous, but blasphemous. Politics carried out under the principle of sovereignty is bound to issue in abuse, injustice, and eventual failure.[55]

On another front, Maritain castigates the approach to power taken by Machiavelli and adopted by his "realist" heirs on three fundamental counts. First, it is based on a radically and inaccurately pessimistic interpretation of human nature. Second, the ethical character of politics is denied, and hypocritically so, since Machiavelli claims morality is irrelevant for leaders but that the prince must rely on morality's perdurance among those he seeks to manipulate. Maritain's third charge against Machiavellianism is directly related: it treats the people as passive objects to be shaped and directed, thus denying them their dignity.[56]

Maritain's disputes with various manifestations of modern political thought center, finally, around their anthropocentrism. The differences between a politics inspired by secular, anthropocentric ideals and one motivated by a Christian conception of the world are best elaborated in his 1936 work, *Integral Humanism*.   In the theocentric humanism to which modern Christians should aspire, the profane realm is of independent but subordinate importance (it is *un fin intermediare*), whereas in secularized humanistic views, individuals or particular temporal orders are absolutized and perceived as ultimate rather than

---

[55]Maritain, *Man and the State*, 129-32, *Selected Readings*, 92-94. Maritain acknowledges that while oppressive power practices wreak great destruction, they can also, at times, attain convincing short-term success. Yet, he argues, insofar as unjust power practices contravene God's natural and eternal law, they are, in the long run, doomed. *Selected Readings*, 305-316.

[56]Ibid., 292-304. For more on Maritain's reflections concerning the problem of "dirty hands" in political action, see Duquesne, "Philosophie politique de Maritain," 42-45.

proximate ends.[57] His criticisms of aberrant interpretations politics reflect Maritain's conviction that socio-political power must be understood and pursued within the bounds of a theocentric and ethical vision of the human world.

Conclusion

The thought of Jacques Maritain provides an entrypoint into Roman Catholic Thomistic thought about socio-political power through one of its most influential 20th-century representatives. Maritain's understanding of power as superordination is a sophisticated one, set as it is within a normative picture of social flourishing that power-over is supposed to serve. Maritain's typically Catholic emphases on creation and natural law afford him a relatively positive descriptive and prescriptive vantagepoint from which to discuss power-over. Power-to, or transformative efficacy, is not given an explicit place in this theory. Yet when political or social superordination functions properly, the shared human flourishing it promotes, especially as articulated in Maritain's important notion of the common good, implies the presence of shared empowerment for effective action, or power-to. Maritain subsumes some qualities attaching to what we here call power-to within his notion of freedom. However, a political theory that more explicitly attended to power-to would have permitted Maritain to more effectively articulate notions of both freedom and power.

While it is strikingly different from Maritain's in many ways, we shall find a similarly deficient treatment of power-to in the thought of Reinhold Niebuhr.

---

[57]Gurian, "On Maritain," 15-16. Some have thought to find in Maritain a critic of liberation theologies, which purportedly uncritically commingle the spiritual and temporal destinies of the human person. For an analysis of issues surrounding this debate see J. Dean Brackley, *Salvation and Social Transformation in the Theologies of Jacques Maritain and Gustavo Gutierrez* (Unpublished Ph.D. dissertation, The University of Chicago, 1981).

Reinhold Niebuhr

In contrast to Jacques Maritain's accent on humans' natural sociability and the organic character of society, Reinhold Niebuhr's descriptive and ethical assessment of power emerges from an analysis of social life as so many individuals in dynamic tension.[58] Niebuhr argues that the anxiety accompanying existence as finite beings with infinite aspirations prompts human beings to transmute the wholesome drive to self-transcendence into egoistic graspings after security and domination that express "the will to power." Interpreted from the perspective of biblical faith, this will-to-power is the premier expression of sin in both individual and communal life. The special impact of human sinfulness on collective life dictates that social norms and structures be geared toward checking and balancing the adverse effects of group egotism and its expression in the will to dominative power-over.

Christian Doctrines, Theological Method, and Socio-Political Life

Niebuhr's interpretation of the doctrine of creation carries a normative understanding of power as the dynamic interrelation of self-actualizing wills without conflict or coercion--a sort of idealized version of our power-to. His understanding of sin stresses the corruption of the will that arises from egoistic pride, and that issues in a will-to-power which radically skews and distorts relations with self, God, and others. By introducing hostility, conflict, and disorder into relationships, sin precipitates a change in the historical

---

[58]Niebuhr and Maritain were contemporaries and acquaintances who expressed appreciation for each others' work. Unfortunately, aside from several reviews of Maritain's early books published by Niebuhr, they never dialogued in print on matters of common concern. See Cooper, *The Theology of Freedom*, 12-18.

appearance of power: now coercion becomes one of its permanent ingredients. Sin-tainted power-over is a primary tool for the accomplishment of "social sin," yet, ironically, Niebuhr also views it as the primary weapon for checking that sin. The use of power-over is thus at once temptation and necessity.

Finally, Niebuhr's interpretation of the doctrine of redemption focuses on God's power "above" history as forgiveness, and portrays God's work "within" history principally in terms of the freely chosen weakness of Jesus, the Suffering Servant.[59] The cross reveals the significance yet impotence of pure goodness in history, particularly collective history.[60] Jesus' teachings on agapaic love are thus directly relevant to individual life, but only indirectly to social interaction.[61] Redemption as the inbreaking of God's power-- through the *exousia* and *dunaimos* of Jesus' words and works, and the outpouring of the Holy Spirit--will have a minimal impact on group life.[62] The consequences of this theological framework, which maximizes the effects of sin and severely constricts the effects of grace on collective life, are played out in Niebuhr's interpretation of the nature and functions of social and political power. Niebuhr

---

[59]See, e.g., Niebuhr, *Nature and Destiny*, 2:71-72, 2:98-99.

[60]Dennis McCann explains that for Niebuhr, the cross represents both the perennial relevance and the historical unattainability of the ideal of sacrificial love, especially in political and social life. In social situations, sacrificial love serves to symbolize undefined higher possibilities that should prevent self-satisfaction with any partial realization of justice. Dennis McCann, *Christian Realism and Liberation Theology: Practical Theologies in Creative Conflict* (Maryknoll, NY: Orbis Books, 1981), 90-91.

[61]See, e.g., Reinhold Niebuhr, "The Power and Weakness of God," in *Discerning the Signs of the Times: Sermons for Today and Tomorrow* (New York: Scribner's, 1946), esp. 141-43; Reinhold Niebuhr, "Christian Faith and Social Action," in J. A. Hutcheson, ed., *Christian Faith and Social Action* (New York: Charles Scribner's Sons, 1953), 241-42; Niebuhr, *Nature and Destiny*, 2:72.

[62]On this see Paul Lehmann, "The Christology of Reinhold Niebuhr," in *Reinhold Niebuhr: His Religious Social and Political Thought*, ed. Charles W. Kegley and Robert W. Bretall (New York: MacMillan Co., 1956), 251-79.

interprets the historical workings of power primarily in terms of power-over, and as irremediably marred by human egotism.

The theologies of history and the eschatologies developed by Niebuhr and Maritain exhibit similarities and differences consonant with their overall treatments of core Christian doctrines. Niebuhr interprets the relation between intra-historical possibilities and the Kingdom of God in a dialectical fashion, imaging the Kingdom and its ethical features as an "impossible possibility" standing over every concrete realization of justice as both possibility and judgment.

> Love is both the fulfillment and the negation of all achievements of justice in history. . . . There are therefore obligations to realize justice in indeterminate degrees, but none of the realizations can assure the serenity of perfect fulfillment. . . . Sanctification in the realm of social relations demands recognition of the impossibility of perfect sanctification.[63]

Maritain's understanding of history in relation to God's kingdom also contains dialectical elements, but more prominently features a conception of history progressing toward its own natural end, concomitant with a deeper, at times undetectable, "supra-historical" movement of persons in history toward their final, supernatural end. Maritain also speaks of the law of "two-fold, contrasting progress" in history, according to which good and evil both can increase in indeterminate degrees, as the wheat grows with the tares, to be finally separated only by God's action at the end of time. We proceed, but from "fall to fall."[64]

Niebuhr and Maritain's different appropriations of the Christian message are accompanied by divergences in theological method. Maritain's theological framework places all existence in organic

---

[63]Niebuhr, *Nature and Destiny*, 2:246-47.

[64]Jacques Maritain, *The Philosophy of History* (New York: Charles Scribner's Sons, 1957).

relationship owing to its transcendent source and end. The schema is the traditional Dionysian-Thomistic one of *exitus-reditus*, all things coming from and returning to God. The human person and human community are described using participative and organic imagery. Ethics relies heavily on notions of natural and divine law as elaborated by Thomas Aquinas, laws which contribute in different spheres to the realization of the respectively ordained ends of different forms of life.

Niebuhr employs a dialectical-paradoxical theological method which highlights the inseparable link between human beings' noble destiny and potential, and the dismal depths of failure and evil to which they can sink. Ethics, especially social ethics, involves discovering ways of dealing with the tension between possibility and finitude, and with the distortions of sin that mark all phases of human experience. Whereas Maritain conceives of dynamic yet persistent orders and harmonies in social life, Niebuhr's approach retains a keener sense of the precariousness and conflict endemic to human structures, and of their susceptibility to perversion and disintegration.

Power and the Human Situation

The human being as seen from Niebuhr's Christian perspective is a multidimensional unity, a dialectical synthesis of nature and spirit, finitude and self-transcendence, necessity and freedom.[65]

---

[65]While recognizing the importance of reason and rationality, Niebuhr, in the tradition of St. Augustine, views the will as the center of human selfhood. The Christian doctrine of *imago dei* in his eyes pertains primarily to the capacity for choice, grounded in self-conscious freedom. The will is the center wherein human capabilities coalesce, and from which freedom and creativity radiate. Niebuhr's belief, which he attributes to both Augustine and Thomas Hobbes, is that "in all historical encounters the mind is the servant and not the master of the self." Reinhold Niebuhr, *Christian Realism and Political Problems* (New York: Charles Scribner's Sons, 1953), 146.

While he gives his most sustained attention to power as it is displayed in socio-political contexts, Niebuhr also discusses power as an attribute of the freedom that defines human personhood. Humans are distinguished from other creatures primarily by their freedom which allows them both to transcend the forms and vitalities of life as they find it, and to create new forms and dynamic configurations.[66] In this context, human power is at times described on the model of effective capacity, or power-to. Niebuhr tells us, for example, that most cosmically, "Life is power." Broadly applied to humans, power refers to "all the vitalities by which men pursue their goals."[68] Power on this definition exudes from different dimensions of the personality and coalesces in the will, which acts as a sort of "center of power" within each individual. Rooted in freedom, power as effective capacity may reside in persons' ability to transcend, direct, or channel natural forms and vitalities, as well as in the ability to create new realms of coherence and order.[69] Speaking in this general way, Niebuhr focuses on power as the capacity of agents to effect goals, especially by eliciting responses from other agents. "The spiritual and physical faculties of man are able, in their unity and interrelation, to create an endless variety of types and combinations of power, ranging from that of pure reason to pure physical force."[70]

The dynamic and static aspects of spirit and nature which the will harnesses and directs as "power" may be tools for either creation or destruction, good or evil. Power as a human capacity to

---

[66]Niebuhr, *Nature and Destiny*, 1:26-27. "Form" refers to the fixed, determined, uniform aspects of reality; "vitality" designates its dynamic, unpredictable, indeterminate aspects. Human life is marked by form and vitality, both in its status as nature and its status as spirit.

[68]Comment on a Quaker Publication, "Speak Truth to Power." *The Progressive*, October, 1955. In Reinhold Niebuhr, *Love and Justice: Selections from the Shorter Writings of Reinhold Niebuhr*, ed. D. B. Robertson (Philadelphia: Westminster Press, 1957), 299.

[69]Niebuhr, *Nature and Destiny*, 1:26-27.

[70]Ibid., 2:260.

effect ends is of neutral ethical status; indeed, Niebuhr speaks at points of the moral irrelevance of power.[71] The purposes for which power is enlisted determine its moral status.

In Niebuhr's estimation, however, human sinfulness has had a decisive impact on power's historical appearance. This is especially true for collective life, where power connotes almost exclusively power-over, and where, due to its inextricable relation with conflict and coercion, every concrete exercise of power is at best morally ambiguous.

The theocentric vision articulated by biblical faith discerns the basic law of human existence as "love, the harmonious relation of life to life in obedience to the divine center and source of life."[72] Niebuhr employs the concept of original righteousness as a symbol for "essential man," the self as God created it to be. In our concrete historical situation, original righteousness stands as a perduring norm and "law." "It is the sense in which there ought not to be a sense of ought."[73] *Justitia originalis* reveals humans' essential or original nature to be in perfectly harmonious relations between the self and God, the self and all its desires and impulses, and the self and other selves. Original righteousness' social term is love of neighbor, the perfect accord of life with life and will with will. This normative harmony implies a dynamic coordination of the various facets of social life without recourse to coercion. Social relations appear as unity-in-difference, plurality without conflict.[74] This description of original righteousness suggests that, to be consistent, Niebuhr ought to posit power relations as the harmonious actualization of capacities and intentions--power-to--as the essential ideal for both personal and communal life.

But within actual historical experience, this situation of perfect harmony is nowhere to be found. The Christian doctrine of sin and

---

[71]Reinhold Niebuhr, *Faith and History: A Comparison of Christian and Modern Views of History* (New York: Charles Scribner's Sons, 1949), 129.

[72]Niebuhr, *Nature and Destiny*, 1:16.

[73]Niebuhr, *Nature and Destiny* 1:293.

[74]Ibid.

the fall illumines "a tragic reality about human life."[75] The book
of Genesis portrays in mythic language the disintegrating
consequences wrought when humans respond to their existential
anxiety by misusing freedom in an attempt to arrogate to themselves
the infinite value and power belonging to God alone.[76] The
misuse of human freedom combines with finitude to spawn sin's
pernicious results. Sin produces estrangement--alienation from
appropriate relations with self, God and others. As sinners we
actively perpetuate this alienation as the "will to live" is transmuted
into the "will to power."[77]

Niebuhr views the will-to-power as a primary expression of the
basic sin of human pride. What he calls the pride of power may be
expressed by separation and isolation from relationships, as when
"the human ego assumes its self-sufficiency and self-mastery, and
imagines itself secure against all vicissitudes,"[78] or by the pursuit
of ever-greater dominative control, as when, disregarding the costs
to others, one seeks to amass more and more power-over in an
effort to guarantee one's own security.[79] As for means, the will-to-

---

[75]Reinhold Niebuhr, *An Interpretation of Christian Ethics* (New York:
Harper and Brothers, 1935), 88.

[76]"Evil cannot be equated purely with ignorance of the mind or passions
of the body. Human evil, primarily expressed in undue self-concern, is a
corruption of the essential freedom of human selfhood and grows with that
freedom." Ironically, the freedom that is the source of human dignity also
initiates our downfall. Niebuhr, *Nature and Destiny*, 2:viii (preface to the
1963 edition).

[77]Niebuhr's "will to live" is the natural impulse of all life for survival,
which in humans is normatively a "will to live truly," orienting us toward
loving self-transcendence. The notion is similar to Maritain's description of
the human creature as naturally inclined to the good and the true. But
whereas Maritain accents the perdurance of the will to live truly despite sin,
Niebuhr underscores the ways that sin undermines this positive orientation
of the will.

[78]Niebuhr, *Nature and Destiny*, 1:188.

[79]Ibid., 1:190.

power is unprincipled "in principle," using any expedient measure in its quest for control and dominance. For the person or group under its sway, the will-to-power generates a vicious cycle of insatiable grasping, which, over time, delivers less and less satisfaction or security. This is so because, whether it seeks to dominate matter, individuals, or nations, "The will-to-power . . . involves the ego in injustice. It seeks a security beyond the limits of human finiteness, and this inordinate ambition arouses fears and enmities which the world of pure nature, with its competing impulses of survival, does not know."[80]   Individual abuses of freedom feed the sinful will-to-power, and are magnified and compounded on the level of collective relations.

Gordon Harland is correct to claim that Niebuhr's work is dominated by one persistent concern: "to clarify the resources and insights of the faith in such a way that they may be savingly related to the structures, dynamics, and decisions of large social groups."[81] Niebuhr recognizes that human beings need, naturally tend to, are deeply formed by community.[82]   But humans' indeterminate potential for both creativity and destructiveness make social relationships inherently ambiguous. Political and social forms are necessary to foster creativity and to protect individual dignity; at the same time their participants must be defended against the opposing

---

[80]Ibid., 1:192.

[81]Gordon Harland, *The Thought of Reinhold Niebuhr* (New York: Oxford Press, 1960), vii.

[82]See Reinhold Niebuhr, *The Children of Light and the Children of Darkness: A Vindication of Democracy and a Critique of its Traditional Defense* (New York: Charles Scribner's Sons, 1944), 48-49. "The individual is related to community (in its various levels and extensions) in such a way that the highest reaches of his individuality are dependent upon the social substance out of which they arise and they must find their end and fulfillment in the community. No simple limit can be placed upon the degree of intimacy to the community, the breadth and extent of community which the individual requires for his life." Ibid., 48. Niebuhr describes community as "primordial" in human life. Ibid., 53.

evils of chaos and oppression which always threaten to overcome them.

Niebuhr's contention that the doctrine of sin has particular relevance for social life rests on a contrast he draws between the moral capacities of individuals and groups, a contrast having direct ramifications for his descriptive and prescriptive approach to socio-political power. The thesis of his early work *Moral Man and Immoral Society* (1932), remained a hallmark of Niebuhr's political realism: "[A] sharp distinction must be drawn between the moral and social behavior of individuals and of social groups," and "this distinction justifies and necessitates political policies which a purely individualistic ethic must always find embarrassing."[83] Group egotism, expressed as a collective will-to-power, represents human pride's ultimate attempt to deny the finitude and contingency of its existence. A much more potent source of injustice than individual pride, "the very essence of human sin is in it."[84]

The self-transcendence that marks human persons in the image of God enables each individual to critically judge and--to an extent-- rise beyond the vicissitudes and constraints of self and community. Human groups lack this self-transcendent, critical faculty. Through the state, groups do possess a sort of organ of will, through which they may pursue domination and security. Yet the state remains incapable of either genuine self-criticism, or real self-sacrifice. To make matters worse, group egotism compounds the individual egotism of its members exponentially rather than arithmetically. This is because, by a tragic twist, the group (family, tribe, nation, etc.) can attract and employ even the individual's altruistic impulses in the service of collective selfishness. Patriotism frequently exhibits this perversion. Further, since a group has no real capacity for reflective or moral self-transcendence, leaders never have warrant

---

[83]Reinhold Niebuhr, *Moral Man and Immoral Society* (New York: Charles Scribner's Sons, 1932, Scribner Library Edition, 1960), xi.

[84]Niebuhr, *Nature and Destiny*, 1:213.

to "agapaically" sacrifice the multiple interests of their constituencies.[85]

The upshot is that possibilities for moral heroism are severely constricted, if not eliminated, when one moves from the individual to the group level, while the possibilities for injustice are indeterminately increased. The political realm thus remains, distinctly, a realm of sin.[86]

For Niebuhr, the first and greatest evil that the sinful will-to-power perpetrates against the would-be harmonies of social and political life is the evil of disorder and anarchy.[87] He notes that for a social unit, chaos is the equivalent of non-being; hence, his oft-repeated assertion that order is the first aim of social structures.[88] Yet a social structure concerned only with order lapses into the opposite perfidy of tyranny, which lays waste the freedom that grounds human dignity. Social and political arrangements must, therefore, guard against two extremes: tyranny, oppressive power-over prompted by an inordinate response to the need for order and form; and anarchy, the dissipation of order and cohesion resulting from an over-emphasis on vitality and freedom.

---

[85]Since "inevitably they [politics] involve the interests of others for whom the agent bears some responsibility," for political leaders, "the sacrifice of those interests ceases to be 'self-sacrifice.' It may be the unjust betrayal of those interests." Ibid., 2:88, quoted in McCann, *Christian Realism*, 91. Niebuhr's thinking here is influenced by the assumption, shared with Weber and Marx, that political power involves initiating decisions and goals for the sake of, or over against, subjects. Maritain's alternative interpretation of the leader's vicarious relation to the people allows for another possibility: agapaic action by leaders that genuinely represents the people's decision to be agapaic.

[86]Reinhold Niebuhr, *Reflections on the End of an Era* (New York: Charles Scribner, 1934), 247.

[87]"There is no level of human life or moral enterprise in which sin does not threaten life with anarchy." Niebuhr, *Love and Justice*, 97.

[88]Niebuhr, *Nations and Empires*, 8.

Niebuhr's awareness of groups' proclivity for injustice, yet also of the danger of destructive anarchy when individuals interact outside of a social order, is accompanied by pessimism regarding any substantive "common good" to which societies might aspire. While there are relatively general interests toward which social groups can devote themselves, through Niebuhr's eyes society appears less an organism with shared goals and goods than a dynamic, tension-filled field of interacting individuals. He describes communal life as "a vast series of encounters between human selves and their interests."[89] Whatever sort of shared good is possible within this sea of interaction must be continually renegotiated and skillfully managed:

> It is the business of politics so to organize the vitalities of human existence that a "commonwealth" will be created out of the conflicting forces and interests of human life, a task which has never been achieved in history without setting force, as the instrument of order, against force as the instrument of anarchy.[90]

---

[89]Niebuhr, "Christian Faith and Social Action," 241. Niebuhr does criticize liberal bourgeois "social contract" theories for assuming that "communities, and not merely governments, are created by a fiat of the human will," and for perpetuating "the illusion that communities remain primarily the instruments of atomic individuals, who are forced to create some kind of minimal order to their common life, presumably because the presence of many other such individuals in some limited area, makes 'traffic rules' necessary." *Children of Light*, 53-54. Yet when he turns from "primordial communities" such as families or ethnic groups to the political arena, Niebuhr's descriptions are more atomistic than either those of social theorists like Marx and Durkheim, or of Catholic thinkers like Maritain.

[90]Reinhold Niebuhr, "Force and Reason in Politics," *Nation* 150 (Feb. 10, 1940): 216.

The basic problem of politics then, is "how to prevent the force which is an instrument of order on one level of social organization from becoming the instrument of either anarchy or tyranny on the next level of social integration."[91] These comments point us to the heart of Niebuhr's theory of socio-political power.

Socio-Political Power: Descriptions and Prescriptions

Niebuhr's analysis of the actual workings of power in social and political life places overriding emphasis on dominance or control, power-over. There are many forms of social power; in fact, "every skill, or every organization of skill, in industry or trade, is a form of social power."[92] All holders of social power seek to enhance and stabilize their positions through the acquisition of property and other forms of economic power. Up to this point, much social power could be fairly described as merely or mainly power-to. But Niebuhr puts it as a general rule that "whenever a power, which is generated in specific functions, becomes strong enough to make the step possible or plausible, it seeks to participate in organizing the community. Thus the societies of the past have been organized by various types of oligarchies who had the most significant or most dominant social power of their epoch."[93]

Political power, then, is "the ability to use and manipulate other forms of social power [economic, religious, military, etc.] for the particular purpose of organizing and dominating the community."[94] Such power has two sources and components. The first is force or coercion, the ability to elicit consent against others' wills by compelling physical or spiritual means. The second source of

---

[91]Ibid.

[92]Niebuhr, *Children of Light*, 62-63.

[93]Ibid., 63.

[94]Niebuhr, *Nature and Destiny*, 2:263.

political power, "prestige" or "majesty," is the capacity to win the uncoerced support of followers by evoking respect and reverence. When exercised through government, political power serves a dual purpose. Negatively, it checks anarchy. Positively, it promotes social cohesion by providing a center of unity. In both cases, force proves a necessary but not a sufficient element of political domination. Without prestige and majesty, no government long survives.[95] Yet the limitations of force do not obviate its necessity for the exercise of political power under the conditions of history.

Historical experience attests to the moral ambiguity--if not perversity--that inevitably accompanies the wielding of political power. As we have seen, Niebuhr attributes this to the permeation of human life by sin. With sin's insinuation of the will-to-power into history, coercion and conflict arise. To check the lawless use of force, lawful uses of force become necessary.[96] Curbing anarchic contests for domination requires political arrangements which introduce central organizing control through government. The state manufactures relative degrees of harmony through a combination of force and prestige.[97] This is the pole of "order" found in all political structures. Since order requires that society have an organizing center, there is in any community a concentration of ruling power in the hands of some minority.[98]

This concentrated governmental power can protect individuals from the will-to-power of their neighbors. But with it comes the danger that leaders will misuse their dominant position to wreak new and greater injustice. Needed, therefore, are countervailing loci of social power that can deter this. The conviction that centralized authority must be offset by decentralized positions of strength, thereby making possible minimal levels of social justice, animates Niebuhr's well-known theory of the balance of power. Based on the

---

[95]Niebuhr, *Nations and Empires*, 8-12; Niebuhr, *Faith and Politics*, ed. R. H. Stone (New York: George Braziller, 1968), 185.

[96]See, e.g., Niebuhr, *Moral Man*, xv.

[97]Niebuhr, *Nations and Empires*, 8.

[98]Cf. Paul Tillich's very similar analysis, analyzed in Chapter IV below.

premise that "the domination of one life by another is avoided most successfully by an equilibrium of powers and vitalities, so that weakness does not invite enslavement by the strong,"[99] the principle of the balance of power is meant to interact with the principle of government to produce a tolerably just social arrangement. A dynamic balance of power checks the central government's tendency to become oppressive; conversely, effective government prevents the tension among competing centers of vitality from degenerating into chaos.[100]

The organization of power and the balance of power (which appear to express Niebuhr's fundamental categories of "form" and "vitality") both serve and imperil social life. As responses to the finitude and sinfulness that mark the public sphere, these two strategies deflect, but do not reduce collective egoism.[101] For Niebuhr, the danger and the dynamism of socio-political relations spring from this paradox: we can never eliminate the potential contradiction to brotherhood implicit in the two political instruments of brotherhood (the balance of power and the center of power), but no moral or social advance can redeem society from its dependence upon them.[102]

Maritain and Niebuhr on Socio-Political Power: Comparison and Evaluation

This study contends that an adequate Christian social ethics incorporates and relates both models of power, power-to and

---

[99]Niebuhr, *Nature and Destiny*, 2:265-66.

[100]Ibid., 2:267.

[101]"A balance of power implies a conflict of wills and contest of interests in which injustice is prevented because contending forces are fairly evenly matched. Such a procedure does not remove the root of conflict which is to be found in the corporate egotism of contending groups." Niebuhr, *Reflections on the End of an Era*, 243.

[102]Niebuhr, *Nature and Destiny*, 2:257-58.

power-over, and does so in a manner coherent with the anthropological, sociological, and theological allegiances governing that particular Christian account. We have shown that both Jacques Maritain and Reinhold Niebuhr highlight the superordination model of power. Are these, therefore, inadequate treatments? The answer to this question turns in part on whether, and how adequately, power-to is recognized and accounted for in each author's thought.

Niebuhr posits the harmonious, non-coercive actualization of human capacities in common with others as a societal norm in his description of original righteousness. But this norm remains eschatological, an impossible-possibility that stands in judgment upon every historical social arrangement. In concrete history, power-to unsullied by asymmetrical, coercive interaction cannot be found.

What of the countervailing loci of power included in Niebuhr's theory of the balance of power? Are these understood primarily as concentrations of power-to, or power-over? Even these secondary reservoirs of strength take on, in Niebuhr's formulation, the face of power-over, insofar as their role consists in warding off the tendency of other holders of power-over to overrun them. As Niebuhr depicts it, the balance of political power resembles a dynamic state of mutual deterrence or stand-off, whereby parties refrain from encroaching on each others' turf in order to ward off damaging retaliation.[103] Ultimately, Niebuhr's overriding and compelling

---

[103]Not all balance of power theories give such overriding weight to power-over. Other theorists emphasize the importance of lower echelon groups' expressing power-to, and view the offsetting of tyranny as a side-effect, rather than the purpose of such expression. Examples include Evans and Boyte, *Free Spaces*, and Roman Catholic thinkers who emphasize the principle of subsidiarity articulated by Pope Pius XI in the 1931 encyclical, "Quadragesimo Anno." See *Seven Great Encyclicals*, ed. and introduction by William J. Gibbons, S.J. (Paramus, NJ: Paulist Press, 1939, 1963), chap 2. Allegiances to different sociologies--conflictual vs. integrative--also influence authors' leanings on this question.

focus on power-over in the political arena prevents him from considering power-to in its own right.

To the extent that power-to is incorporated into Jacques Maritain's socio-political thought, its role remains mostly implicit. "Freedom" is Maritain's watchword, and he appears to regard the effective capacity we have termed power-to as a feature of freedom. The focus generally remains on individual persons, though in Maritain's espousal of subsidiarity and the common good, and in his comments on other centers of strength, there are hints of a recognition of communal power-to. Most of his writings on political matters, however, consider ways to justly order power-over so that the freedom of societal members is protected and promoted.

We can detect a similar absorption of the notion of power-to into the notion of freedom in other recent Christian thought, for instance, in some strands of Latin American liberation theology.[104] Though this claim requires further substantiation, if it is correct, at least three undesirable consequences result. First, the concepts of power-to and power-over are most authentically understood in explicit and vital relationship to one another. To subsume power-to under freedom severs that relationship, thereby impoverishing the understanding of power in social life. Second, asking the concept of freedom to bear more than it ought by conflating it with power-to blurs the actual lineaments--positive and negative--of the former

---

[104]Gustavo Gutierrez's early work criticizes Maritain's theory of the distinction of the temporal and supernatural planes for discouraging liberative political action by the poor. Yet (like Maritain himself) Gutierrez fails to apprehend the resources for understanding transformative empowerment resident in Maritain's own concepts of subsidiarity, the common good, and of the "concrete historical ideal." See Gustavo Gutierrez, *A Theology of Liberation: History, Politics, and Salvation*, Sister Caridad Inda & John Eagleson, trans. and ed. (Maryknoll, NY: Orbis Books, 1973); cf. Brackley, *Salvation and Social Transformation.*

term. Given this, ethical analysis involving questions of freedom and power is bound to be negatively affected.[105]

What of the coherence between these authors' understandings of power and their sociological, anthropological, and theological background assumptions, as well as with actual social experience? Undoubtedly, the enduring appeal of Niebuhr's presentation is largely due to such coherence. Niebuhr's convincing analysis of sin's social expression as group pride and the will-to-power provides a focal point around which his religious and secular sources and arguments converge. Nonetheless, there are points at which the adequacy of his account may be questioned. One point concerns the sharp distinction Niebuhr draws between individual and group morality, and hence, between the appearance and ethics of power in the private and the public realms. The main warrants for this distinction seem to be a combination of anthropological and sociological presuppositions, and analysis of historical experience. But one must ask if this distinction, and the anthropological assumptions that undergird it, most adequately accounts for the full range and complexity of social experiences of power. Further, is such a distinction, which leaves the workings of socio-political power nearly bereft of the influence of redemptive grace, warranted by the Christian horizon Niebuhr upholds, even a Christian horizon that puts sin to the fore? In the face of these and other critical questions, closer attention to power-to, by providing a way to more fully grasp the phenomenon of power, may facilitate a more adequate and coherent stance.

Maritain, conversely, may be challenged on the limited extent to which his theory admits the impact of human sin on socio-political life. His critiques of Machiavellianism and sovereignty notwithstanding, there is considerable incongruence between the

---

[105]Religious ethicists are not the only ones who tend to blur distinctions between freedom and power. See the critique of similar confusions in the social theories of Steven Lukes and William Connolly in K. Kristjansson, "'Constraining Freedom' and 'Exercising Power Over'," *International Journal of Moral and Social Studies* 7:2 (Summer, 1992): 127-38.

creation-focused picture of political life Maritain's Thomistic Catholic vision upholds, and the negative impact that a serious treatment of sin must acknowledge. By relegating the socio-political sphere to the temporal plane, Maritain's analysis may tend to underplay the dynamics of either sin or redemption in relations and structures of power.

It is also instructive to compare Niebuhr's and Maritain's respective ways of describing the impact of redemption upon the possibilities of socio-political life. For Niebuhr, the effects of redemption remain principally in God's power over, rather than in, history.[106] Maritain appears to leave a bit more room for social activity and even institutions that bear redemptive effects, as Christians who undertake to fulfill their political obligations voluntarily submit to "the sufferings due to solidarity."[107] Yet for Maritain, redemption most directly concerns the person and the church. The social and political order have, in the end, only passing relevance. The constricted role they accord to redemption in the socio-political realm helps explain why, in distinctive ways, both Niebuhr and Maritain confine power-to to a normative feature of creation or final destiny. Very little place is found for social power unmitigated by hierarchy and coercion under the conditions of fallen history.

---

[106]On this point, Harvey Cox comments, "Secular thinkers could make sense of Niebuhr's reinterpretation of original sin. I have always regretted that Niebuhr never succeeded in redefining an equally central theological term--grace--with comparable persuasiveness. The result was that his 'Christian realism' was not sufficiently tempered by such elements as surprise and hope, which have therefore rightly come to the fore in more recent theologies." H. Cox, "Reply," *New York Review of Books* (Feb. 9, 1986): 40.

[107]Maritain, *Man and the State*, 207. Maritain's compelling remarks on the interdependence of the modern world and the relation of suffering to solidarity would evoke the hearty agreement of many, such as political and liberation theologians, who are highly critical of the French philosopher on other counts. Ibid., 207-208.

A final criterion for an adequate theory of power is the degree to which a specific formulation illumines actual political and social practice. Both Maritain and Niebuhr tend to articulate social problems and prescribe social practice using the idiom of power-over. Yet the particulars of their positions reflect the different ways each configures the impact of sin, creation, and redemption in interpreting the facts and possibilities of socio-political life. Their responses to post-World War II debates concerning world federalism are illustrative. Niebuhr feared chaos but distrusted the egoistic tendencies of a global meta-government even more, and came out soundly against movements for world government. Maritain's stress on the possibilities inhering in the created order made him somewhat more optimistic about the positive functions that an international governing body, properly constructed, might serve.[108]

Conclusion

The theories of Niebuhr and Maritain are related neither by simple opposition nor total agreement. Their formulations of socio-political power exhibit both points of complementarity, and of challenge. Both are astute interpreters of the Christian message and of human experience, whose nuanced approaches are not easily dismissed.

Maritain's Neo-Thomist analysis yields an illuminating, teleological interpretation of human nature and society. As he guides his reader through considerations of the many facets and functions of individual and communal life, integrating parts into ordered wholes, Maritain's work breathes a certain sweet reasonableness. Maritain's God has brought forth a creation that is, to be sure, finite and marred by sin, but which exhibits still a

---

[108]Compare Niebuhr, "The Illusion of World Government," 379-88, and Maritain, "The Problem of World Government," *Man and the State*, 188-216.

wondrous design and purpose that we humans may discern and serve.

Human beings are both limited and sinful, yet Maritain's faith in the natural capacities of a humanity endowed with the divine image, and a less enunciated faith in the effects of redemption, ground his more positive assessment of power's uses in political society. Nuanced distinctions between forms of social life in which organic, irrational bonds predominate (e.g. communities, nations) and those characterized by rational and ethical organization (society and the body politic), allow Maritain to highlight the role of reason in the polis. Niebuhr, who perceives a more acute and incorrigible conflict between the forces of reason and will in social interaction, professes less faith in reason's potential for guiding and shaping the direction of power in socio-political life.

Maritain's theory of the unity-yet-difference of the spiritual and temporal purposes of human life, and hence of the natural and supernatural planes of human action, is fraught with its own difficulties. Yet it has merits not found in Niebuhr's approach. Maritain's according of a finite but relatively final purpose to social historical existence allows a positive and constructive role for politics and for social institutions. Without being ingenuous, Maritain's appreciation for the good borne in these areas of activity --a good at least as real as the sin and finitude he also identifies-- highlights aspects of social experience that Niebuhr underplays. Maritain contends that social groups are not simply breeding grounds of collective egotism, but can also embody and express people's better aspirations. He thereby challenges the Niebuhrian view, in an appraisal that mitigates the bleakness of a purely "immoral society."[109]

---

[109]Maritain argues that wholesome social structures can at times promote the common good more effectively than individual acts of volition. "Social structures . . . are human things, they are not men; insofar precisely as they are things and not men, they can be purified of certain miseries of human life. . . . They issue from men and [can be] better than men, in their own order and under a certain relationship. They can be measured by justice and

This said, Maritain's system may still be criticized for lacks and weaknesses that comparison with Niebuhr has brought to light. Sin, finitude, and their tragic consequences do at times get short shrift in Maritain's political ethics. In his concern with the philosophical interpretation of human experience, Maritain sometimes gives fine analyses of *de jure* implications, but leaves the reader unadvised as to how to begin, within the messy, concrete *de facto*, to approximate the normative picture he outlines.

In emphasizing harmony and integration as societal norms, Maritain at times disregards the extent to which conflict and duplicity persist in collective interactions. The insights about ideology and false consciousness that Niebuhr gained from his early exposure to Marxism, and then ruthlessly applied to even the best-intentioned human endeavors, largely escape Maritain's attention. This leaves Maritain susceptible to criticisms of naiveté, and threatens the credibility of his arguments regarding the intrahistorical potentials of social and political relations.

Above all, what Niebuhr offers that Maritain does not is a fruitful suspicion, a critical viewpoint against which social attitudes, structures, and actions are constantly questioned. Niebuhr's stress on dialectic and paradox accommodates the conflict he views as part of the fabric of historical existence. This method seeks to protect the transcendent ideal for human life from vitiating compromise within the limited and corrupt realities of political interaction.

Maritain and Niebuhr have proven excellent representatives of the power-over emphasis in contemporary Christian social thought. In Chapter Four, we shall consider recent Christian thinkers who focus more clearly on the role of power-to. But first, we will survey contemporary social theory for what it may teach us concerning a more comprehensive approach to socio-political power.

---

fraternal love, whereas acts of men on the whole are rarely measured by that measure; they can be more just than the men who apply them. But they remain *things* . . . realities of a degree essentially inferior to that of persons whose communications and life they serve to regulate." Maritain, *Integral Humanism*, 111.

CHAPTER III

ALTERNATIVES TO POWER AS DOMINATION: RESOURCES IN SOCIAL THEORY

Introduction

We have analyzed representatives of the emphasis on power as domination in modern social theory and mainstream Christian social thought. The second part of this book is devoted to exploring alternatives to that majority view. In the literature of contemporary social theory, a countervailing stress on power as transformative capacity, rather than as superordination, is found in three different loci. First, this other way of looking at power is a significant element in some theories that focus on dominative power. This is the case in the work of a number of contemporary Marxian and post-Marxist European scholars.[1] These analyses of power uncover the oft-concealed scope, intensity, and pervasiveness of domination in social relations, yet may simultaneously highlight collaborative and mutually beneficial potentials of power that exclusively power-over treatments tend to overlook. Second, a small group of

---

[1] I denote as Marxian theories that embrace some ideas of Marx without professing strict allegiance to Marxism as a philosophical, political, or economic system. Theorists designated as post-Marxist are influenced by Marx's theories but in explicit disagreement with, and attempting to advance beyond, substantial features of Marx's theory.

thinkers have spurned the consensus about power-over's primacy, placing instead overriding weight upon a notion of power as effective capacity.[2] Finally, some few contemporary social theorists explicitly attempt to integrate what we have called the power-over and the power-to approaches in their analyses of society and politics.[3]

This chapter will map the treatment of power-to in recent social theory by examining examples of each of the three positions just cited. The concept of effective capacity will be concisely traced in the power-over theory of post-structuralist philosopher Michel Foucault, in the exclusively power-to theory of political philosopher Hannah Arendt, and in the integrations of power-to and power-over being developed by sociologist Anthony Giddens, and by selected North American feminist social theorists.

These writers have been chosen both for the lucidity of their treatments, and for the originality and significance of their contributions to the debates about power in different scholarly sectors. Both in their formulations of power-to, and in the ways agency, intentions, and structures figure into their overall theories, they represent a spectrum of positions.[4] Yet, in varying manners

---

[2]A key proponent of this position is Hannah Arendt, whose work will be examined here. Talcott Parsons, employing a Durkheimian, functionalist social theory, also puts power-to squarely to the fore. See, e.g., Talcott Parsons, "On the Concept of Political Power," *Sociological Theory in Modern Society* (New York: The Free Press, 1967).

[3]Besides being featured in social theories to be considered later in this chapter, this integrative approach is identifiable among practically-oriented thinkers concerned with community action and empowerment. See, e.g., Saul Alinsky, *Rules for Radicals* (New York: Harper Vintage Books, 1970); Gene Sharp, *The Politics of Non-Violent Action*, Part 1: Power and Struggle (Boston: Porter-Sargent, 1973).

[4]Arendt's theory of power centers wholly upon action; Foucault's is a decidedly structurist approach; Giddens, and to a certain extent, the feminists we shall consider, attempt to give equal weight to action and structure in their conceptualizations of social power.

and degrees, all these authors acknowledge the importance of the notion of transformative efficacy for an adequate description of socio-political power. They concur in regarding power as a desirable phenomenon, as a relation rather than a quantity, and as pertaining to collectivities as a whole rather than simply to individuals or authorities who "have" it. On these and other counts their conceptualizations correspond to our type of power-to.

After situating each power theory in the context of the writer's anthropological and sociological assumptions and concomitant analysis of the individual-society relation, we will briefly consider how that theory addresses one particular issue, the problem of collective oppression (be it racially, sexually, or economically based). These theorists' treatments of social oppression provide clues about the impact of particular notions of power upon the way situations of injustice are described, and their remedies prescribed. This examination of power-to notions will also contribute in a preliminary way to the final chapter's argument, that a Christian social ethic taking both models of power into account, and showing good reasons for the relationship espoused between the two, can offer the most satisfactory critique of social injustice, and the most adequate substantive proposals for just power relations.

Michel Foucault

French philosopher Michel Foucault has contributed an important, original, and provocative voice in contemporary debates about social and political power. Foucault's thinking on power resists easy categorization; indeed, throughout his career, he worked strenuously to avoid being theoretically pigeon-holed.[5] Foucault is

---

[5]My account highlights Foucault's middle and later writings. On the evolution of Foucault's thought concerning power and for an illuminating analysis of the Foucauldian view, see Kyle A. Pasewark, *A Theology of Power: Being Beyond Domination* (Minneapolis: Fortress Press, 1993), ch. 1; also Stephen Frederick Schneck, "Michel Foucault on Power/Discourse, Theory

critical of approaches to power that spring from western liberal political roots. He rejects, as well, analyses that describe power as a possessable "substance," exclusively located in, or owned by, specific persons, processes or institutions. This prompts him to distance himself from some prominent mainstream and leftist treatments of power. Finally, Foucault dismisses as mistaken those thinkers who take a purely negative view of power, seeing it solely in terms of oppression or restriction. In his formulation, power relations are simultaneously rife with antagonism, coercion, and struggles for control, *and* productive of the effective capacity we have been calling power-to.

General Theory of Socio-Political Power

Power, in Foucault's political thought, signals an ubiquitous kind of interaction which he most often calls "relations of force." Relations of force exist and seek to advance themselves not just in the political or economic realms, but in every corner of individual and social life. Foucault's theory of power emerges from analyses of discourses and practices in various historical arenas of human knowledge and interaction. These analyses elucidate ways in which relations of force develop, intersect, reinforce or clash with one another. Foucault spurns the search for a grand theory that would completely encompass power relations in a given society, and rejects

---

and Practice," *Human Studies* 10 (1987): 15-33. For reflections by Foucault on the development of his thought, see "The Ethic of Care for the Self as a Practice of Freedom: An Interview with Michel Foucault on January 20, 1984," conducted by R. Fornet-Betancourt, H. Becker, A. Gomez-Müller; trans. by J. D. Gauthier, S.J., *Philosophy and Social Criticism* 12 (Summer, 1987): 112-31. Cf. Pasewark, *A Theology of Power*, 39 n. 142.

the claim that all social power emanates from some single point.[6] Instead, he attends to local strategies of power, dissecting the ways in which relations of force and domination intertwine within very particular historical, geographic, and ideological settings.[7] Foucault conceives these relations as the fundamental discourse by which a society expresses itself, is itself. His various works are attempts to provide a microphysics of the "grammar" of power-and-knowledge in modern society, especially as that has developed around practices concerning mental health and illness, sexuality, and crime and punishment.

Foucault's theory of power is relational rather than substantial. But this is a structurist, rather than a subjectivist or actionist, interpretation. Foucault dislodges power from the will and subjective reflection, situating it instead in the structured features of social interaction. Power is a quality of collective interactions, not a possession of one or some. A further point is, for our purposes, the most significant. As Foucault sees it, power includes within its purview dimensions of positive enablement along with

---

[6]For an astute analysis of Foucault's "de-centering" social theory and for comparison with Marx's grand system approach, see Paul Wapner, "What's Left: Marx, Foucault and Contemporary Problems of Social Change," *Praxis International* 9:1/2 (April & July 1989): 88-111.

[7]"Power relations are rooted in the system of social networks. This is not to say, however, that there is a primary and fundamental principle of power which dominates society down to the smallest detail; but, taking as point of departure the possibility of action upon the action of others (which is coextensive with every social relationship), multiple forms of individual disparity, of objectives, of the given application of power over ourselves or others, of, in varying degrees, partial or universal institutionalization, of more or less deliberate organization, one can define different forms of power. The forms and the specific situations of government of men by one another are multiple; they are superimposed, they cross, impose their own limits, sometimes cancel one another out, sometimes reinforce each other . . . ." Michel Foucault, "The Subject and Power," in Hubert L. Dreyfus & Paul Rabinow, *Michel Foucault: Beyond Structuralism and Hermeneutics* (Chicago: The University of Chicago Press, 1982), 224.

negative constraint. Power is productive, insists Foucault, not merely obstructive. In short, transformative capacity, power-to, as well as power-over is entailed in the actuation of power.[8]

Foucault divides modern theories of socio-political power into two major types: contract/juridical, and war/repression. The first group of theories springs from classical liberal assumptions about the person and society. Power is understood as an original right residing in each individual or group that is then given over to the sovereign.[9] The contract is the image for understanding the proper operation of socio-political power; laws are the means whereby power is limited and channeled toward communal and individual flourishing. Problems with power arise when the contract between people and sovereign is overstepped and the laws, or rules of fairness, are transgressed. When this happens, oppression occurs. In the main, this liberal approach to power (traced by Foucault to the 18th century *philosophes*)[10] reflects a notion of society as an artifice created by individuals for their mutual protection and convenience. It sees power as originating in those individuals, and legitimates domination only insofar as it is organized in fair contract fashion between rulers and ruled.

More than war/repression versions, contract/juridical theories appear to highlight transformative efficacy or power-to. Yet Foucault criticizes this contract/juridical approach, which he discerns in both classical liberal and Marxist political thought. Such a position, he argues, makes the mistake of imagining power in

---

[8]On this last point Foucault understands himself as opposing the Frankfurt School theorists, whom he regards as putting singular emphasis on the negative and constraining features of power as *Herrschaft*. See Foucault, "The Subject and Power," 210.

[9]Michel Foucault, *Power/Knowledge: Selected Interviews and other Writings 1972-1977*, ed. Colin Gordon, trans. Colin Gordon, Leo Marshall, John Mepham, Kate Soper (New York: Pantheon Books, 1980), 91.

[10]Ibid., 91.

economistic ways." Power is construed as a *commodity* that may be quantified, owned, exchanged, given, bought, or stolen. For Foucault, by contrast, power is the multitudinous *relations* of force by which the actions of people and groups are produced, affected, and governed by other people or groups in crisscrossing ways throughout the social body.[12] The contract approach is blind to both the ubiquity and complexity of these endless relations, and to the fact that power is not an exchangeable "thing." Power only exists in actions and practices that influence, direct, and frequently subjugate, the actions and practices of others.[13]

Foucault also faults the contract/juridical approach for being subjectivist, in that it links power's exercise to the intentions and wills of agents, either individual or collective. Foucault does not deny to power a certain purposefulness, but that purposefulness is located in relations rather than in wills, in structures rather than in subjects. Arguing that "power is at the same time intentional and

---

[11]Ibid., 88-89. On one hand, Marx's "economic functionality" considers power primarily if not solely in terms of relations of production and class domination. For Marx, the historical *raison d'être* of political power is the economy; political power is always in a subordinate position relative to economic relations. Liberal contractarians do not so reduce or subordinate political power, but they err by assuming that power is analogous to an economic commodity--something that can be possessed, exchanged, or stolen.

[12]"Power is everywhere; not because it embraces everything, but because it comes from everywhere." Michel Foucault, *The History of Sexuality* vol. 1, Robert Hurley, trans. (New York: Vintage, 1980), 94. "Power's condition of possibility . . . is the moving substrate of force relations which, by virtue of inequality, constantly engender states of power, but the latter are always local and unstable." Ibid., 93. Cited by Mark Philp, "Foucault on Power: A Problem in Radical Translation?" *Political Theory* 11 (Feb., 1983): 29-52.

[13]As we shall see, by insisting that power exists only in relations, Foucault is in agreement with Hannah Arendt. But Arendt rejects Foucault's further claim that power always directs and subjugates the actions of others.

non-subjective,"[14] he urges the need to "cut the king's head off" in our ways of imagining it.[15]

A second kind of approach to power takes a perspective that Foucault calls war/repression. Here power relations are regarded as zero-sum, negative, and having mainly to do with struggles for ascendancy and domination. War and conflict are the orienting images for understanding the workings of socio-political power. For war/repression thinkers, von Clauswitz's aphorism--that war is simply politics carried on by other means--is equally truthful when inverted.

In the war/repression model, power's sole basis for legitimacy is the powerholder's possession of coercive advantage (due to wealth, brute force, or other reasons). Hence, while on the first model oppression is judged as the breakdown of power's normative function, in the latter model, repression--oppression that moves beyond external constraint to invade the psyche--is considered not a corruption but a logical extension of power. Repression, in which ideology and violence combine to squelch either the recognition of oppression or expressions of resistance, is, from this standpoint,

---

[14]Foucault, *Sexuality*, 94. Agents may act with clear intentions in mind, but they neither comprehend nor fully control the directions in which their particular exercises of power lead. "It is [thus] often the case that no one is there to have invented them [power strategies and their results] and few who can be said to have formulated them. . . . People know what they do; frequently they know why they do what they do; but what they don't know is what what they do does." Ibid, 95. See Henry Krips, "Power and Resistance," *Philosophy of the Social Sciences* 20/2 (June 1990): 173-74.

[15]Foucault's notion of "subjectless, yet intentional power" has occasioned much critical discussion. See, e.g., Michael Walzer, "The Politics of Michel Foucault," in David Couzens Hoy, ed., *Foucault: A Critical Reader* (Oxford: Basil Blackwell, 1986), esp. 63; Charles Taylor, "Foucault on Freedom and Truth," Ibid., esp. 85-88; Krips; "Power and Resistance," 173-77. Some of the criticisms Jacques Maritain levels at Rousseau's notion of the General Will might be raised against Foucault's claim that power has its purposes, but purposes that escape human intentionality or responsibility. See above, 81-83.

"not an abuse, but . . . the mere effect and continuation of a relation of domination. On this view, repression is none other than the realization, within the continual warfare of this pseudo-peace, of a perpetual relationship of force."[16]

In many ways, Foucault's own rendering of power favors this latter approach. Consonant with the war/repression conceptualization is Foucault's emphasis upon power as relationships of force and resistance that produce endemically unstable, and hence everchanging, patterns. The "agonal" picture of social life that emerges from his insight that power depends both upon differentiation (expressed as inequality) and upon the persistence of freedom, is also congenial with the war/repression model.[17] Yet other features of his treatment, especially his focus on freedom, reveal affinities with the contract/juridical approach.

Foucault envisages societal members as thoroughly enmeshed in external forces, yet as genuinely individuated agents nonetheless.[18] Power relationships spring up due to--and in turn produce--differences, variations, and inequalities among us. Freedom is likewise crucial to power relations. A wholly determined relation, or one in which there was no possibility for resistance on the part of the recipient of force, is no longer genuine power, but rather "a physical relationship of constraint."[19]

---

[16]Foucault, *Power/Knowledge*, 92.

[17]"*The system of differentiations* . . . permits one to act upon the actions of others: differentiations determined by the law or by traditions of status and privilege; economic differences in the appropriation of riches and goods, shifts in the processes of production, linguistic or cultural differences, differences in know-how and competence, and so forth. *Every relationship of power puts into operation differentiations which are at the same time its conditions and its results.*" Foucault, "The Subject and Power," 223.

[18]Foucault's later work gives the most attention to individual agency and responsibility, as Gauthier, "An Ethic of Care for the Self," illustrates.

[19]"Power is exercised only over free subjects, and only insofar as they are free. By this we mean individual or collective subjects who are faced with a field of possibilities in which several ways of behaving . . . may be realized.

Power is inextricably tied to the phenomenon of freedom, with each constituting for the other a kind of permanent limit, a point of possible reversal. This means there can be no zero-sum confrontation of freedom and power such that freedom disappears wherever power is exercised. Instead Foucault discerns a much more complicated interplay, wherein "freedom may well appear as the condition for the exercise of power (at the same time its *precondition*, since freedom must exist for power to be exerted, and also its *permanent support*, since without the possibility of recalcitrance, power would be equivalent to a physical determination.)"[20]

Despite these important similarities, Foucault distinguishes his perspective from typical versions of the war/repression approach. What he regards as inadequacies in that model are addressed in three dimensions of his analysis. First, the multifarious and intersecting relations of struggle in society are exposed and analyzed. Second, the modern emergence of a new kind of power, disciplinary power, is charted.[21] Finally, in a development of

---

Where the determining factors saturate the whole there is no relationship of power; slavery is not a power relationship when man is in chains. (In this case it is a question of a physical relationship of constraint.)" Foucault, "The Subject and Power," 221.

[20]Ibid.

[21]Disciplinary power refers to a set of modern dominative technologies developed gradually in disparate locales, which make the human being an object of manipulation. This manipulation may center on the body, as in the case of sexual codes or incarceration, or on the mind, as with psychiatry. The basic goal of disciplinary power is to produce a human being who is a docile and productive body. "The technology of discipline developed and was perfected in workshops, barracks, prisons, and hospitals; in each of these settings the general aim was a 'parallel increase in usefulness and docility' of individuals and populations. The techniques for disciplining bodies were applied mainly to the working classes and the subproletariat, although . . . they also operated in universities and schools." Dreyfus and Rabinow, *Beyond Structuralism and Hermeneutics*, 134-35, referring to Foucault, *Discipline and Punish* (London: Allen Lane, 1977), ch. 7.

Marx's insight concerning the ideological functions of political rights in bourgeois political economy, attention is given to the mutually reinforcing relationship between liberal systems of right (laws and the complex of means by which they are applied)[22] and the networks of domination that simultaneously enmesh and constitute social life.[23]

Truth, The Discourse of Domination, and Power-To

We see that for Foucault, power and freedom are linked insofar as the two both uphold and constantly threaten one another. This yields a picture of social relations as in a state of permanent antagonism. Any power relationship is in perpetual risk of breaking into a struggle because of the persistence--among all parties--of the twin urges toward freedom and toward control. For our purposes we must ask, is the urge to control that marks power exclusively oriented toward domination? What place, if any, does this theory have for power as transformative capacity?

---

[22]Foucault, *Power/Knowledge*, 95.

[23]"The theory of [popular] sovereignty, and the organization of a legal code centered upon it, have allowed a system of right to be superimposed upon the mechanisms of discipline in such a way as to conceal its actual procedures, the element of domination inherent in its techniques, and to guarantee to everyone, by virtue of the sovereignty of the State, the exercise of his proper sovereign rights. The juridical systems . . . have enabled sovereignty to be democratized through the constitution of a public right articulated upon collective sovereignty, while at the same time this democratization of sovereignty was fundamentally determined by and grounded in mechanisms of disciplinary coercion. . . . Modern society, from the 19th century up to our own day, has been characterized on the one hand, by a legislation, a discourse, an organization based on public right . . . and, on the other hand, by a closely linked grid of disciplinary coercions whose purpose is in fact to assure the cohesion of [the] social body." Ibid., 105, 106.

The complex relationship Foucault sees between power as superordination and power as effective capacity is moored in the deep interconnections between power, discourse, knowledge, and subjectivity his analysis uncovers.   The individual, or subject, emerges from within the network of discourses and practices generated by the dynamics of knowledge and power in modern society. Foucault tells us that the thread of continuity among his various studies is his concern to create "a history of the different modes by which, in our culture, human beings are made subjects."[24] It was his recognition that the human subject exists in and through complicated power relationships for which adequate tools of analysis were lacking that moved Foucault to consider the theme of power more directly.

In any society, knowledge, discourse, and the subject who knows and speaks are all products and expressions of power relations. In Foucault's relativist view, truth is itself a social product, born of the configurations of force that hold sway in any particular time and place. "Truth," he insists, "isn't outside power, or deprived of power . . . . Truth is of the world; it is produced by virtue of multiple constraints . . . ."[25]   At the same time, power relations depend upon accepted notions of the true which are incarnated in a functioning system of meaning, a discourse.

> [I]n any society, there are manifold relations of power which permeate, characterize and constitute the social body, and these relations of power cannot themselves be established, consolidated nor implemented without the

---

[24]Foucault, "The Subject and Power," 208. Foucault describes his work as dealing with three modes of objectification which transform human beings into subjects: modes of inquiry which objectify the person in the name of science; the objectivizing of the subject through dividing practices; and the ways persons turn themselves into subjects, such as through one's sexual self-identification. Ibid.

[25]Foucault, *Power/Knowledge*, 131. Cited in Philp, "Foucault on Power," 36.

accumulation and functioning of a discourse. There can be no possible exercise of power without a certain economy of discourses of truth which operate through and on the basis of this association. We are subjected to the production of truth through power and we cannot exercise power except through the production of truth. . . . In the end we are judged, condemned, classified, determined in our undertakings, destined to a certain mode of living or dying, as a function of the true discourses which are the bearers of the specific effects of power.[26]

For Foucault, then, truth exists in a circular relation of mutual production, sustenance, and influence with systems of power.

Foucault perceives a similar connection between knowledge and power. Against positions (including liberal humanism) which tend to separate the two, Foucault views his work as bringing to light the constant articulation of knowledge upon power and of power upon knowledge. This knowledge/power interplay, he argues, is not centralized, say, in universities, but is dangerously diffused in and through all the interactions of society.[27]

Modern humanism is therefore mistaken in drawing [a] line between knowledge and power. Knowledge and power are integrated with one another, and there is no point in dreaming of a time when knowledge will cease to depend on power; this is just a way of reviving humanism in a utopian guise. It is not possible for power to be exercised without knowledge; it is impossible for knowledge not to engender power. "Liberate scientific research from the demands of monopoly capitalism": maybe it's a good slogan, but it will never be more than a slogan.[28]

---

[26]Foucault, *Power/Knowledge*, 93. Cited in Philp, Ibid.
[27]See, e.g., Foucault, *Power/Knowledge*, 51-52.
[28]Ibid., 52.

If one reads these claims with only the meaning of power as counter-interest domination in mind, a bleak picture of collective life emerges. Foucault by his own admission lays greater weight on dominative, oppressive features of the web of forces and resistances by which language, knowledge, and the subject are carried and produced. Stress on the negative and constraining features of power is particularly strong in those of Foucault's writings that recount the ascendance of disciplinary power in modern society. Yet, for Foucault, power-over is not the whole story.

When Foucault speaks of power as the relations of force that emanate from every sort and level of social interaction, he does mean to describe relations of domination. But his analysis is complicated by the fact that he does not view relations of force as productive solely of constraint. In fact, transformative efficacy is a key feature of the networks of power that Foucault describes. Colin Gordon notes that, "for Foucault power is omnipresent in the social body because it is coterminous with the conditions of social relations in general."[29] These conditions entail power-to as well as power-over.

Ubiquitous relations of force have a positive function inasmuch as such relations genuinely (not only apparently) produce, and make accessible, that which we count and value as true, as selves, and as known. Relations of force are, then, the matrix in which capacity is put into action to become efficacy. Discourse, knowledge, and socially constructed subjectivity bind and limit, yet these things also enable. Society, then, is a dynamic realm, not simply of power-over, but also of power-to.

> If power were never anything but repressive, if it never did anything but to say no, do you really think one would be brought to obey it? What makes power hold good, what makes it accepted, is simply that it doesn't only weigh on us as a force that says no, but that it traverses and produces

---

[29]Colin Gordon, "Afterword," in Foucault, *Power/Knowledge*, 246.

things, it induces pleasure, forms knowledge, produces discourse. It needs to be considered as a productive network which runs through the whole social body, much more than as a negative instance whose function is repression.[30]

Power, then, must be considered not simply a constraining, limiting reality but far more as "the means whereby all things happen."[31] A crucial function of the dynamic and ever-shifting patterns of power-over in social interaction, it turns out, is to generate and carry power-to.

Social Oppression and the Economy of Power

Despite similarities of agenda, Foucault parts with Marxian critical theorists who essay a global investigation of Enlightenment rationality in relation to modern forms of *Herrschaft*. Instead he analyzes how power insinuates itself into the particular rationalities that characterize discourse and practices around different sectors of modern experience: madness, illness, death, crime, sexuality, and so

---

[30]Foucault, *Power/Knowledge*, 119. See also Foucault, *Sexuality*, 86-87. Giddens recognizes the significance of Foucault's position in this regard. "Power, for Foucault, is declaredly the opposite of that which it appears as in Marxist theory--a noxious expression of class domination, capable of being transcended by the progressive movement of history. Power, says Foucault, is not inherently repressive . . . . Power has its hold because it does not simply act like an oppressive weight, a burden to be resisted. Power is actually the means whereby all things happen, the production of things, of knowledge and forms of discourse, and pleasure." *Profiles and Critiques in Social Theory* (Berkeley: University of California Press), 219; cf. Anthony Giddens, *A Contemporary Critique of Historical Materialism*, vol. 1, *Power, Property, and the State* (Berkeley: University of California Press, 1981), 50-51.

[31]Giddens, *Profiles and Critiques*, 219.

forth.[32]   Foucault claims that if an investigation of the links between knowledge and power is to be empirical, related to the present situation, and effectively join theory and practice, it must take specific forms of resistance to power as its starting point. This approach, which he believes offers a way toward a new economy of power relations, involves employing resistance "as a chemical catalyst so as to bring to light power relations, locate their position, find out their point of application and the methods used. Rather than analyzing power from the point of view of its internal rationality, it consists of analyzing power relations through the antagonism of strategies."[33]

To illustrate this method, Foucault takes the example of resistance to oppression. He notes the rise, in the past several years, of a number of loci of opposition: "opposition to the power of men over women, of parents over children, of psychiatry over the mentally ill, of medicine over the population, of administration over the ways people live."[34]   These struggles have three distinctive features. First, they call into question the status of the individual. "On the one hand, they assert the right to be different and they underline everything which makes individuals truly individual. On the other hand, they attack everything which separates the individual, breaks his links with others, splits up community life, forces the individual back on himself and ties him to his own identity in a constraining way." As it turns out, these contests are not about the individual *per se*; rather they are struggles against what Foucault calls "the government of individualization."[35]

Second, these contemporary struggles oppose the dominative and restricting effects that are produced when power is linked with knowledge, competence and qualification. In this regard, those seeking liberation struggle to overcome the secrecy, mystifications,

---

[32]Foucault, "The Subject and Power," 210.

[33]Ibid., 211.

[34]Ibid.

[35]Ibid., 211-12.

and deformations of truth which are routinely imposed on oppressed people. What is thrown into question is "the way in which knowledge circulates and functions, its relations to power. In short, the *regime du savoir*." Lastly, these struggles are distinctive because they revolve around the question, "Who are we?" Any group working to overcome domination must resist persons and forces that would either ignore that group's own particular identity, or seek to impose one from without.[36]

Foucault contends that the main objective of these different emancipatory struggles is to attack "not so much 'such and such' an institution of power, or group, or elite, or class, but rather a technique, a form of power."[37] The target is disciplinary power, power-over that in everyday life categorizes the individual, and imposes a regime of reality which one is forced to acknowledge and which others have to recognize. "It is a form of power which makes individuals subjects." Foucault points out two senses of the word "subject" that reflect the wedding of intrapsychic and institutional determinants in this understanding of power. Those who oppose sexism, racism, and other forms of hegemony seek liberation from being *subject to* oppressive powers, and from being *shaped and determined in their subjectivity* by those same powers.[38] One way of opposing oppressive disciplinary power-over, practiced by Foucault himself, is to uncover and release the oppositional power of discourses and knowledge which the ruling forces have submerged. Foucault calls this "the insurrection of subjugated knowledges."[39]

His treatment of resistance to oppression confirms that despite his claim that power-over relations are constitutive of social bonds,

---

[36]"The Subject and Power," 212. Cf. the features of liberation as delineated by Gustavo Gutierrez, discussed in Chapter IV below.

[37]Ibid.

[38]Ibid. "There are two meanings of the word *subject*: subject to someone else by control and dependence, and tied to his own identity by a conscience or self-knowledge. Both meanings suggest a form of power which subjugates and makes subject to." Ibid.

[39]Foucault, *Power/Knowledge*, 81.

Foucault is not fatalistic about the lot of those who are oppressed by such relations. "For to say that there cannot be a society without power relations is not to say either that those which are established are necessary, or, in any case, that power constitutes a fatality at the heart of societies, such that it cannot be undermined."[40] When subjugated knowledges are unearthed, they have the potential to effect change. As Kathy Ferguson observes, for Foucault, "Opposition voices are a vehicle for bringing power to light as well as for altering that power. They are able to reveal the politics embedded in the dominant discourse, but are not simply a passive reaction to it."[41]

Yet Foucault regards power-over, in shifting guises, as a permanent feature of social existence. Relations of force (the power-over which is the condition for power-to) will be implicated not only in oppressive patterns, but in every form of resistance to oppression. Grand schemes for domination's complete reversal, whether through revolution or evolution, are thus illusory. Avenues for emancipatory change must be sought on local, strategic fronts.

---

[40]Foucault, "The Subject and Power," 223. Power *is* a "fatality" in the sense that it will not be eliminated; but every specific form and instance of power relations is unstable, and therefore may be sabotaged or replaced. Despite Foucault's claims, influential commentators have criticized what they perceive as the nihilistic or even conservative implications of Foucauldian power analysis. See, e.g., Jürgen Habermas, *The Philosophical Discourse of Modernity: Twelve Lectures*, trans. Frederick Lawrence (Cambridge MA: MIT Press, 1987); Anthony Giddens, "From Marx to Nietzsche? Neo-Conservatism, Foucault, and Problems in Contemporary Political Theory," *Profiles and Critiques*, 215-30. Also on the question of whether Foucault's position ends in fatalism concerning liberating social change, see David R. Hiley, "Foucault and the Analysis of Power: Political Engagement Without Liberal Hope or Comfort," (*Praxis International* 4/2 (July 1984): 191-207; Stephen David Ross, "Foucault's Radical Politics," (*Praxis International* 5/2 (July 1985): 131-43.

[41]Kathy E. Ferguson, *The Feminist Case Against Bureaucracy* (Philadelphia: Temple University Press, 1984), 155.

Given this, Foucault's advice to those seeking to overcome social, political, or economic oppression would be to eschew universal campaigns, and to aim for strategic victories within specific networks of domination.[42] Foucault's own vision of such victories increasingly focused on the attainment of "a less governed mode of living, where individuals would use the spaces in the networks of power relations to devote themselves to an 'aesthetics of existence' in which one's own life becomes 'the principal work of art.'"[43] Yet the wider social and historical context for this pursuit, constantly shifting patterns of domination, remains. Foucault's later emphasis on personal responsibility is accompanied by this stark reminder:

> [H]umanity does not gradually progress from combat to combat until it arrives at universal reciprocity, where the rule of law finally replaces warfare; humanity installs each of its violences in a system of rules and thus proceeds from domination to domination.[44]

In the end, Foucault's insistent call for strategic, local, and particular thinking and acting does not prevent him from advancing, at least performatively, much more general claims regarding the nature of modern society and of the modern individual, and the

---

[42]The potentials and limits of a Foucauldian approach to social struggle are more thoroughly debated in Ross, "Foucault's Radical Politics"; and from a feminist perspective, in Nancy Fraser, *Unruly Practices: Power, Discourse and Gender in Contemporary Social Theory* (Minneapolis: University of Minnesota Press, 1989), chs. 1 & 2.

[43]Ian Burkitt, "Overcoming Metaphysics: Elias and Foucault on Power and Freedom," *Philosophy of the Social Sciences* 23/1 (March 1993): 67, quoting Taylor, "Foucault on Freedom and Truth," 99. Cf. Pasewark, *A Theology of Power*, 35-51.

[44]Michel Foucault, "Nietzsche/Genealogy/History," in *The Foucault Reader*, ed. Paul Rabinow (Hammondsworth: Penguin, 1986), 85. Quoted in Burkitt, "Overcoming Metaphysics," 64.

meaning and role of power for each. For our purposes, Foucault's most interesting contention about the world of power-over he portrays is that this all-encompassing web of dominative struggle brings forth and sustains power-to: effective capacities that are expressed in the cooperative ventures of individual and communal knowing, doing, and being.

Some critics of Foucault argue that by placing dominative struggle at the heart of social interaction, he consigns himself to a reductionist, and thereby flawed analysis. The result is a skewed picture of social-political relations, and a constricted sense of the possibilities for shaping or transforming structures or patterns of power. Though not his contemporary, the next theorist to be considered would certainly share these criticisms of Foucault's approach. She roundly rejects his power-over starting point. Indeed, the power-to perspective that informs Hannah Arendt's analysis of socio-political life is, in many ways, precisely the converse of the Foucauldian view.

Hannah Arendt

The writings of political philosopher Hannah Arendt reveal a voice and a theory of power strikingly different from those of Michel Foucault, and at least as original and significant. Arendt's work is animated by a concern to understand human action. Emerging from her analysis of action is a singularly unadulterated theory of power as effective capacity, or power-to.

A central concern of Arendt's is to elucidate the significance of public life for human flourishing in an era when interest in the civic realm and civic engagement is on the wane. Concern for public things in the late twentieth century has, she observes, been nearly eclipsed by a preoccupation with the private and the social.[45] If a lively sense of the meaning and importance of public life is to be retrieved, Arendt is convinced, a fresh consideration of the basic terms of human being and acting together is required. Accordingly, her work probes such concepts as private and public; the social as distinct from the political and economic; labor, work, and action; and violence, authority, and power.

Like Foucault's, Arendt's style of study is distinctive, and idiosyncratically radical in its attempt to illumine the settings of word and deed in which basic political notions arose and developed. Historical sources receive insightful and original interpretation as Arendt seeks to rejuvenate important western ideas by boring down into their philosophical, historical and experiential roots. Not surprisingly, these excavations frequently lead to ancient Greece and Rome.[46]

Human Action and the Public Realm

Arendt's notion of socio-political power is situated within her theory of human action in general, and of action in the public realm in particular. She locates the source of power in humans' capacity to act.[47] Action, "the political faculty *par excellence*," is the process by which the new and unexpected is generated through human

---

[45]On the ascendance of the private realm, see Hannah Arendt, *The Human Condition* (Chicago: University of Chicago Press, 1958), ch. 2. On the eclipse of the political by the social, see also Hannah Arendt, *On Revolution* (New York: Penguin Books, [1963] 1973), ch. 2; n. 56 below.

[46]On the characteristics of, and tensions within, Arendt's peculiar historical approach, see Canovan, *Hannah Arendt*, 4-7; Seyla Benhabib, "Hannah Arendt and the Redemptive Power of Narrative," *Social Research* 57/1 (Spring 1990) 188-96; Benhabib, "Models of Public Space: Hannah Arendt, the Liberal Tradition, and Jürgen Habermas," in Craig Calhoun, ed., *Habermas and the Public Sphere* (Cambridge, MA: MIT Press, 1993), 76-78.

[47]Arendt, *The Human Condition*, 238.

interaction.[48]   In contrast to work, which, "as making, always incorporates some degree of violence as 'man overcomes nature,'" action is the performance in which power, a capability distinct from violence, is brought about. Power is the "can" that appears in the in-between-space created when humans get together and share words and deeds.[49]

For humans to act in the sense that Arendt intends requires that they be among others: action always involves interaction. By their words and deeds people distinguish themselves from one another; but the unique identity of each must be shown forth, it must appear in the world. Such appearance is impossible without others to whom to appear, and without a "space of appearances" in which to do the appearing. While work and labor are also human doings, for Arendt it is speech and action that distinguish and constitute full humanity. "A life without speech and without action . . . is literally dead to the world; it has ceased to be a human life because it is no longer lived among men."[50]   When we speak and do before and with others, we simultaneously participate in creating ourselves, a public realm, and power.

Speech and action depend upon the fact that we are many, that is, upon the *plurality* of the human species. Plurality grounds both the public realm and political power. In Arendt's estimation, plurality has a twofold character. First, it implies equality; we are the same in ways that link us fundamentally, and this gives us a common footing on which to meet. Second, plurality means distinction; we are unique and different each from the other.

---

[48]Hannah Arendt, "Collective Responsibility," in James W. Bernauer, S.J., ed., *Amor Mundi: Explorations in the Faith and Thought of Hannah Arendt* (Boston: Martinus Nijhoff Publishers, 1987), 50.

[49]See Arendt, *Human Condition*, 200-201. Power is simply "the potentiality in being together." Ibid., 201.

[50]Ibid., 176.

If men were not equal, they could neither understand each other and those who came before them nor plan for the future and foresee the needs of those who will come after them. If men were not distinct, each human being distinguished from any other who is, was, or will ever be, they would need neither speech nor action to make themselves understood.[51]

Linked to human distinctness is the fact that only humans are capable of actually communicating themselves, rather than something about themselves, to others. When, by expressing ourselves, we freely enter the "human world" and take responsibility for ourselves, it is "like a second birth, in which we confirm and take upon ourselves the naked fact of our original physical appearance."[52] Action creates, sustains, and involves us in a web of relationships that, though intangible, is not a bit less real than the physical things we may speak of or work on.

Through action and speech, we embody and express the commonality-in-difference, the plurality, of our human condition. And the space where humans may speak and act with one another-- and thereby become themselves--is the public realm. Although she does not impugn the private realm, Arendt wants us to appreciate that without action in public, human beings are radically stunted.[53]

---

[51]Ibid., 175-76. Cf. Maritain on individuality and personhood, Chapter II; and Foucault's discussion of differentiation and freedom, above. Significantly, Arendt connects differentiation with equality in her notion of plurality; Foucault emphasizes the doubly divisive combination of difference (or inequality) and freedom in relations of force.

[52]Ibid., 177. "In acting and speaking, men show who they are, reveal actively their unique personal identities and thus make their appearance in the human world. . . . This disclosure of 'who' in contradistinction to 'what' somebody is . . . is implicit in everything somebody says and does." Ibid., 179.

[53]Arendt's pivotal distinction between the public and private realms, and her related separation of the political from the social spheres, have been the subject of much critical analysis. See, e.g., Patricia Springborg, "Hannah

For Arendt the public sphere designates not simply a geographical space, but a way of relating that incarnates the equality and distinction that attend human plurality.[54] Rather than the hereditary or spontaneous communion of similarity that is characteristic of private life, in public we find the creative and enduring association of the different.[55] The concerns that belong to the public differ, too, from the concerns about nurturing and reproducing biological life that mark the private realm.[56] The public realm "happens" when different people, in their distinctness, meet, speak, deliberate, and act on matters of common concern to them as members of a shared world.[57]

Arendt and the Classical Republican Tradition," in Gisela T. Kaplan & Clive S. Kessler, eds., *Hannah Arendt: Thinking, Judging, Freedom* (Sydney: Allen & Unwin, 1989), 9-17; Margaret Canovan, *Hannah Arendt: A Reinterpretation of Her Political Thought* (Oxford: Cambridge University Press, 1992), 115-20; Nancy Fraser, *Unruly Practices*, 160 n. 32, 169-70.

[54]Arendt, *Human Condition*, 50, 52.

[55]I draw the phrase "enduring association of the different" from Robert Bellah, Richard Madsen, William Sullivan, Ann Swidler, & Steven Tipton, *Habits of the Heart: Individualism and Commitment in American Life* (New York: Harper and Row, 1985), 238.

[56]For this reason, Arendt castigates moderns for confusing the political with the sphere of the social. The "social" conflates political concerns with matters (such as feeding, clothing, and sheltering people, and economics) proper to the private realm. One noxious consequence of this confusion is that what should be non-debatable givens (e.g., the right of all community members to decent nutrition, shelter, and medical care) are mistakenly treated as political negotiables. Another is the tendency to misconstrue political action as having mostly to do with *techne*, the how-to of executing predetermined goals. Goals, then, lose the benefit of genuine public deliberation, which is the real function of the political sphere. Arendt, *Human Condition*, 38-49; *On Revolution* (New York: Penguin, [1963] 1973), 59-114. See also Canovan, *Hannah Arendt*, 116-22; 231-33.

[57]Many find Arendt elusive on the question of the substantive content or object of political deliberation and action. George Kateb argues that for Arendt, political deliberation and action pertain to the creation or

Where the public realm happens, so does the possibility of the new and unexpected. For action, which needs a public home if it is to thrive, is the generative, "miracle-making" capacity of humankind. As such, it is also the locus of power.

Power in Political Life

Hannah Arendt virtually identifies the genuinely public with the genuinely political. Her paradigm for the public realm is, in fact, the *polis* of the ancient Athenian city-state.[58] We may say then that political action is the defining activity of the public realm. For

---

preservation of conditions that make political deliberation possible, that is, "either to the creation (or founding) of a constitution or form of government, or to the defense of a constitution or form against internal erosion or external attack." *Hannah Arendt: Politics, Conscience, Evil* (Totowa, NJ: Rowman & Allenheld Publishers, 1984), 17; 16-25.

An analogous interpretation is offered by Catholic political theologian John Courtney Murray, S.J.. Describing the essence of civil society as "men locked together in argument," he names three central themes of the ongoing public conversation: 1) public affairs, "those matters which are for the advantage of the public . . . and which call for public decision and action by government;" 2) the affairs of the commonwealth, a concept denoting affairs that fall beyond the scope of government and legal resolution, but that bear upon the quality of the common life, e.g., education; 3) and most crucially, "the constitutional consensus whereby the people acquires its identity as a people and the society is endowed with its vital form, its entelechy, its sense of purpose as a collectivity organized for action in history . . . ." *We Hold These Truths: Catholic Reflections on the American Proposition* (New York: Sheed and Ward, 1960), 8-9. Arendt lays the greatest weight upon Murray's third theme.

[58] Arendt's political thought is widely considered to be a contemporary retrieval of the "classsical republican tradition." For a vigorous, historically-attuned analysis and critique of Arendt's apprehension of republican political traditions, see Patricia Springborg, "Arendt, Republicanism and Patriarchalism," *History of Political Thought* 10/3 (Autumn 1989): 499-523.

the ancients as Arendt interprets them, the political realm was "a man-made space of appearances where human deeds and words were exposed to the public that testified to their reality and judged their worthiness."[59]   Debate, through which opinions are interactively formed, is the stuff of political life, and participation in public debate requires face to face interaction where all have the ability to speak freely and to be heard. Freedom, not the inner freedom of the Stoics, but a public freedom to express oneself, is created and maintained by the activity of authentic political life.[60] From this free association springs forth power.

Three aspects of Arendt's notion of power distinguish it from other influential definitions, including those of Weber and Marx. First, she insists that power's essence is not rule, the triumph of one will over another, but the collaboration of persons for mutually agreed upon purposes. Second, she carefully differentiates power from both violence and authority. Third, Arendt separates power from materiality, holding that power is never something possessed, but is only present in the process of political action. Each of these points bears elaboration.

Against the venerable western tradition (originating, she says, with Plato, and culminating more recently in Weber and Marx, Nietzsche and Sartre) that focuses on power as rule or superordination, Arendt locates power in the capacity of humans to act together. This capacity appears in, and also sustains, the public realm. Power is, further, an inherently collective phenomenon:

---

[59]Arendt, *On Revolution*, 103. Concerning the complex relationship between Arendt's political theory and Greek thought, see Canovan, *Hannah Arendt*, esp. 115-16, 135-38, 224-25.

[60]Hannah Arendt, *Between Past and Future: Eight Exercises in Political Thought* (New York: Penguin, 1961), 146, 152, 153. Cited and discussed in Gordon Tolle, *Human Nature Under Fire: The Political Philosophy of Hannah Arendt* (Washington, D.C.: University Press of America, 1982), 110-111.

Power corresponds to the human ability not just to act but to act in concert. Power is never the property of an individual; it remains in existence only so long as the group keeps together. When we say of somebody that he is "in power" we actually refer to his being empowered by a certain group of people to act in their name.[61]

The history of political philosophy marks a saga of forgetfulness and fear of the seemingly fragile and insecure *dunamis* that originates in human getting-together. Unlike force, violence, and hierarchy, it eludes easy definition or possession. Thus, Plato, extrapolating from his normative anthropology, identified the notion of rule as constitutive of politics. In so doing, contends Arendt, Plato mistook relations of asymmetry and force for the heart of public life, and obscured its actual wellsprings in the power of action shared by the people. The preponderance of later political philosophy rests on this same false assumption, which has bred a retreat from authentic politics altogether.

From Plato up to the present, western political theory and practice has been hobbled by the too-frequently successful attempt to flee politics. Says Arendt,

The hallmark of all such escapes [from genuine politics] is the concept of rule, . . . the notion that men can lawfully and politically live together only when some are entitled to command and others are forced to obey.[62]

---

[61]Hannah Arendt, "On Violence," in *Crises of the Republic* (New York and London: Harcourt Brace Jovanovich, 1969), 143. Arendt's resolutely collective interpretation of power sets hers off from other recent philosophical treatments of power as activity which produces effects, e.g., Peter Morriss, *Power: A Philosophical Analysis* (Manchester: Manchester University Press, 1987), esp. chs. 11, 12.

[62]Arendt, *Human Condition*, 222.

The common definition of political community as consisting of those who rule and those who are ruled is not the result of deliberate mis-statement, however. It rests on what Arendt calls a suspicion of action rather than a contempt for human capability, and arose more from a sincere desire to find a more sturdy substitute for action than from any irresponsible or tyrannical will to power.[63]

But why has action perennially aroused such suspicion and ambivalence? The reason lies, Arendt proposes, in the frustrations inherent in action. These frustrations result from the paradoxical condition of potency and limitation that characterizes actors, and from the uncontrollable conditions and consequences that frame action. First, because they are effected by finitely free subjects, human affairs are unpredictable: no individual or group can rely on the perdurance of power-bearing action over time because there is no way to guarantee the continuance of the agents and relationships that produce it. This is due to external unknowns as well as the irrevocability of freedom: agents can always change their minds. The problem of unforeseen and unintended consequences constitutes another of action's built-in frustrations. The irreversibility of action and of its effects also lends ambiguity to the creative power of human doing. These problems reveal action as a fragile and risky enterprise, and, Arendt claims, help explain its abandonment in favor of the seemingly more stable and clear grounding of politics in relations of rule.

With the rise of the modern nation state, a further development of the notion of rule has emerged in the concept of sovereignty. This Arendt judges to be but one more station on the wrong track. Her own work pleads the unpopular case for restoring power-bearing action to its proper place, at the center of the theory and practice of politics.

In the history of experiments in genuine politics, ways for warding off the unpredictability and irreversibility of action that do

---

[63]Ibid.

not require its replacement by rule have been found in the human capacities to make and keep promises, and to forgive.[64] Besides being "the only alternative to a mastery [of action's unpredictabilities] which relies on domination of one's self and rule over others," these abilities correspond to the existence of a freedom under conditions of non-sovereignty that characterizes a vital public realm.[65] And, though forgiveness and promise-keeping are not foolproof remedies, their decided political potential is obscured insofar as rule by force becomes the generally supposed foundation of political power.

When the governmental dimensions of politics are considered, Arendt acknowledges a strong temptation to identify power with command and obedience.[66] This is because for governments, violence (the capacity to coerce obedience via force) remains "a last resort to keep the power structure intact against individual challengers." It can thus appear that coercion is a prerequisite of power, and power its epiphenomenon or facade, "the velvet glove which either conceals the iron fist or will turn out to belong to a paper tiger."[67] Yet, she claims, on closer inspection this equation of violence with power loses its plausibility.

The efficacy of a government rests not on its possession of the means of violence, but on the "power structure" which upholds it.[68] This power structure, which enables a government to rule, rests either on the people's consent (whereby government is lent citizens' power such that citizens are politically impotent until they decide

---

[64]See below, 144, n. 78.

[65]Arendt, *Human Condition*, 224, 244.

[66]Arendt, "On Violence," 146.

[67]Ibid.

[68]Ibid., 147. The event of revolution illustrates the divergence between violence and power. "In a contest of violence against violence the superiority of government has always been absolute; but this superiority lasts only so long as the power structure of the government is intact," that is, only as long as the people are willing to obey commands and the army or police are prepared to use their weapons in service of that government. Ibid.

to recover it) or upon their mutual promise (which keeps more obvious the fact that power originates in the people themselves who join together for "mutual benefit and increase").[69] Whatever the means of violence owned by a state, for a regime to continue, "everything depends upon the power behind the violence. The sudden dramatic breakdown of power that ushers in revolutions reveals in a flash how civil obedience--to laws, to rulers, to institutions--is but the outward manifestation of support and consent."[70]

A further difference between power and violence is the properly instrumental nature of the latter. Violence is a tool which, unless restrained and channeled by the power of a body politic, can overstep its bounds to become an end in itself. In such cases, violence can succeed in destroying the public realm and its power, as occurs in an efficient totalitarian regime. Yet violence can never create either power or the public. Necessary to the very existence of a political community, "power is indeed of the essence of all government; violence is not." While governments pursue policies and employ their power to achieve prescribed goals, "the power structure itself precedes and outlasts all aims, so that power, far from being a means to an end, is actually the very condition enabling a group of people to think and act in terms of the means-

---

[69] Arendt, *On Revolution*, 171.

[70] Arendt, "On Violence," 148. This notion of support and consent is linked to Arendt's understanding of authority, treated below. The idea that rulers require the consent of the ruled is certainly not original to Arendt. What distinguishes her rendition of this point is that she grounds that consent in an explicit understanding of communal power as power-to. Cf. Pasewark's provocative treatment of Arendt's understanding of the legitimation of power in *A Theology of Power*, 211-25, 246-50.

ends category."[71] As such, power--like peace--remains an ongoing concern of the *polis*.[72]

To summarize, Arendt holds that power and violence, though they frequently appear together in public life, are finally opposites. Where one pertains fully, the other is absent.

> Violence appears where power is in jeopardy, but left to its own course it ends in power's disappearance. This implies that it is not correct to think of the opposite of violence as non-violence; to speak of non-violent power is actually redundant. Violence can destroy power; it is utterly incapable of creating it.[73]

Before turning to the distinctions Arendt draws between power and authority, we must elaborate the third main feature of Arendt's concept of power, its immateriality. Arendt tells us that power is what keeps the public realm, the potential space of appearance between acting and speaking persons, in existence. Since "power is the only human attribute which applies solely to the worldly in-between space by which men are mutually related," it retains a decidedly intangible quality. "Power is always, as we would say, a

---

[71]Arendt, "On Violence," 150.

[72]Ibid. Like the body's health the city's peace, power is a valued end in itself insofar as it is an essential condition for the action and flourishing of the members of the polis. Also like health and peace, the importance of power-to is frequently noticed and appreciated more in the breach, when it has been eroded or lost. On this Arendt's political thought bears some resemblances to the treatment of peace by St. Augustine of Hippo, in *The City of God*, Books XIX and XX. Augustine's philosophy of love was the subject of Arendt's doctoral dissertation. See Canovan, *Hannah Arendt*, 8, 153.

[73]Arendt, "On Violence," 155. Arendt recognizes that in practice power and violence are often intertwined. "Nothing is more common than the combination of violence and power, nothing less frequent than to find them in their pure and therefore extreme form. From this, it does not follow that authority, power, and violence are all the same." Ibid., 146.

power potential and not an unchangeable, measurable, reliable entity like force or strength." It is "the potentiality in being together" that springs up between people when they act together, and vanishes the moment they disperse. Arendt finds power to be surprisingly independent of material factors; "the only indispensable material factor in the generation of power is the living together of people."[74] Despite its intangibility, power's positive role in actuating and perpetuating the public realm makes it the lifeblood of the humanly constructed world. Thanks to the efficacy constituted by power, the humanly-made world is the scene of action and speech, of the web of human affairs and relationships and the stories engendered by them, which together constitute its *raison d'être*.[75]

Power, Authority, and Government

Arendt's insistence that power is present only while people are acting in concert raises questions about institutional structures.[76] Since power appears solely in the worldly in-between space that allows human relatedness, the preservation of such space is imperative for power's continuance. Action and speech, and the power they generate, have a boundlessness that is characteristic of the new. The power-bearing action that the public realm makes

---

[74] Arendt, *Human Condition*, 200-201.

[75] Ibid., 204.

[76] My reading of Arendt's theory of authority stresses her foundational concerns with housing and preserving power-to. A critic who focuses on Arendt's elitism and her sharp separation of "social" and "political" is Sheldon Wolin, "Hannah Arendt: Democracy and the Political," in Reuben Garner, ed., *The Realm of Humanitas: Responses to the Writings of Hannah Arendt* (New York: Peter Lang, 1990), 167-86. Wolin deems inadequate Arendt's treatments of justice and of power--especially in its material, "social" aspects. (173) Yet his constructive political proposal (180-83) sounds much like the one I detect in Arendt's writings.

possible always sparks relationships, but their perdurance depends upon finding ways to protect, without stifling, the dynamism of the *vita activa*.

Arendt believes that by binding and promising, combining and covenanting, people create structures that foster the continued generation of power over time. Promise-making, promise-keeping, and forgiveness are activities crucial to sustaining the existence of a power-bearing community.[77] Wherever people succeed in keeping intact the power which sprang up between them during the course of any particular deed, "they are already in the process of foundation, of constituting a stable worldly structure to house, as it were, their combined power of action."[78] In Arendt's eyes, the American revolutionary era gives profound historical witness to "the enormous power potential that arises when men 'mutually pledge to each other their lives, fortunes, and their sacred honour.'"[79]

As we have seen, Arendt identifies power as the creative potential, springing from action, that constitutes the public realm. Action generates a dynamic field, or power structure, that consists in a web of relationships that supports and is reinforced by the capacity that is unleashed when people act and speak in concert. We have also seen that power so understood is subject to the

---

[77]Arendt, *Human Condition*, 238-39. The two "inherent remedies of human action," forgiveness and promising, mitigate the inherently present-bound character of communal power so that the power-generating community can endure through time. Arendt attributes the discovery of the profound importance of forgiveness for human action to Jesus of Nazareth. "Only through [forgiveness,] this constant mutual release from what they have done unknowingly can men remain free agents, only by constant willingness . . . to start again can they be trusted with so great a power as that to begin something new." Ibid. This feature of Arendt's thought invites further theological and social ethical analysis. For one effort, see Bruno-Marie Duffé, "Hannah Arendt, le 'religieux' dans le politique," *Revue de théologie et philosophie* 120 (1988): 161-78, esp. 169-77.

[78]Arendt, *On Revolution*, 181.

[79]Ibid., 176.

frailties that prey on human action, especially fragility and unpredictability. If political life is to flourish, this fundamental, "ontological" power structure needs to be augmented by other, more tangible structurings, such as are usually found in systems of authority or government. It is precisely at this point that theorists like Weber identify effective social power with some form of hierarchy, or power-over. Arendt challenges this formulation. But how can government genuinely serve and foster power-to, rather than replacing it with rule or force?

Arendt views authority, properly construed, as a relationship that is different from power, but one that can protect and promote power and public life. For her, authority is an alternative to violence that can provide needed stability and structure to the power generated by political action. Arendt's concept of authority separates it both from persuasion, which presumes that the parties involved are on equal footing, and from coercion, which introduces violence into the relationship and thereby makes it no longer genuinely political.[80] Genuine authority in her view is neither simply imposed, nor merely democratically agreed-upon and conventional. It perhaps comes closest to the kind of relation Steven Lukes calls "authority over belief," whereby the right to be heeded is claimed and acknowledged on the grounds of some special wisdom, revelation, insight, skill or knowledge.[81]

In elaborating her meaning, Arendt relies heavily upon an interpretation of the ancient Romans' understanding of *auctoritas*.

---

[80]Arendt, who rejects a relativistic approach to language and meaning, does not advance her definitions simply as alternatives to conventional usage. Her aim is to uncover the meanings of ideas as these are embodied in their origins and carried in their histories. Thus, Arendt's notion of authority is meant to be *experience derived*, that is, "based on the authority of meanings, which cannot be made but will only disclose or reveal themselves, pressing for our consent." Tolle, *Human Nature Under Fire*, 113.

[81]Steven Lukes, "Power and Authority," 640-44. Arendt's definition rejects authority by imposition, focuses on belief, but does not preclude elements of convention. See Chapter I, 26-27.

Authority for the Romans was drawn, says Arendt, from relationship to the foundations of the community. That authority was thought to reside uniquely in the Roman Senate, whose influence was based neither on coercive capability nor on the senators' persuasive skills, but on that connection to foundations.

Besides the authority of the Roman senate, the authority accorded the judiciary in a republic, as detailed by Montesquieu and later incorporated into the United States' system of government, is also a key reference point for Arendt. Authority considered in this way is, in Wolfgang Mommsen's words, "more than advice and less than a command, an advice which one may not safely ignore."[82] Most often, this "advice" and the process by which it is produced are incorporated into a legal system.[83]

The order of authority described by Arendt is hierarchical and commands obedience. Yet it is not violent. What binds the commander and obeyer together in an authority relationship is neither agreement about reasons nor the agreement of the obeyer that the one who commands is superior in dominative power. "What they have in common is the hierarchy itself, whose rightness and legitimacy both recognize and where both have their pre-determined stable place."[84] In a manner also described in Weber's formulations, the authoritative order elicits the free consent of both commander and obeyer.

---

[82]Quoted in Arendt, *Between Past and Future*, 123.

[83]Once such authority is incorporated into law, of course, it becomes part of a body of commands to which some sort of coercive capability may be attached. Nonetheless, Arendt refuses to make coercion constitutive of either authority or power.

[84]Arendt, *Between Past and Future*, 93. Cf. her distinction between "leading" and "ruling" in *Human Condition*, 189. Arendt's intent here is to affirm a stable way of "housing" the power-bearing action inherent in human community that can offset its dynamic unpredictability. Two pertinent questions are first, whether such dynamism and stability can really co-exist; second, whether the authority structure she describes is indeed the best or only adequate habitation for power-to.

Authority, government, and law introduce hierarchy into human affairs. Arendt accepts this, and also accepts the need for them. Together they provide organization and structure that can protect the public realm, a "worldly house" within which power-bearing action may be promoted and continued. But there seems to be a problem. Doesn't Arendt's appreciation for public authority contradict her conviction about the fundamental equality among persons rooted in plurality?

The solution to this apparent dilemma lies, first, in keeping clear Arendt's way of distinguishing authority, violence, and power. Authority is not in itself power but, we might say, power's servant or guardian. This is true to the extent that authority's purpose is to promote the common weal, which includes the community's transformative capacity or power. By also separating authority from coercion and force, Arendt protects the equality and freedom of citizens even as she acknowledges the necessity of obedience in its proper place. A government's recourse to violence is deemed possibly acceptable only as a limit action when authority--and more importantly, the power housed by authority--are at grave risk of dissolution. To use force is to descend from power and authority to a crude stop-gap measure, one that threatens to destroy the very values it is used to protect.[85] In the end, authority, government, and their instruments are legitimate to the extent that they serve and protect public space and foster political action, and thereby, power-to.

Authority thus understood is indispensable to a flourishing public. Yet, Arendt finds, genuine authority is in profound crisis in the contemporary period, and nearly absent from contemporary public life. Modern citizens are hardly able to imagine a relationship that could be legitimately authoritative without being either coercive or conventional.

---

[85]Recall Reinhold Niebuhr's articulation of this same point. But Niebuhr differs profoundly from Arendt in his emphasis upon the intrinsically coercive dimensions of all historical manifestations of power.

Where authority survives at all today, it is found in the private world, in the authority of parents over children, or in the pre-public arena of education, where teachers are given authority over students.[86] But the authority practiced in the private arena differs from that appropriate to the public realm. In fact, Arendt argues, inestimable damage has been wrought by those (starting with the classical Greeks) who have uncritically taken the fundamentally unequal and temporary relations that characterize parental and pedagogical authority as models for political authority. In contrast to the private sphere, public authority needs both to honor the fundamental human equality between commander and obeyer, and to provide a structure of relative permanence. Most often, transposing private models upon public authorities has encouraged the misconstrual of authority in both realms as a permanent relation of inequality, backed, when necessary, by force.

A second reason why Arendt's understanding of the power-authority nexus resists devolution into *Herrschaft*-by-another-name concerns her understanding of citizenship. Governmental apparatus is only legitimate when it is strictly in service to the citizenry; and the citizenry exerts its proper influence only when there are preserved local contexts wherein every member can actively and effectively enact political agency. Maurizio d'Entreves points out this strong link in Arendt's thought between active citizenship and effective political agency, a link that for Arendt was exemplified in Jefferson's proposal for preserving local wards system of direct democracy within the growing nation.[87] Without vital channels for learning and participating in direct democracy, citizens are deprived

---

[86] Arendt does not consider in her essay the authority accorded to persons perceived as "experts" in modern technological society. Needed, it seems, are criteria for sorting out how different forms of noetic activity constitute or reflect power-to, and when knowledge becomes power-over in either authoritative or violent guise.

[87] See Maurizio Passerin D'Entreves, "Agency, Identity, and Culture: Hannah Arendt's Conception of Citizenship," *Praxis International* 9:1/2 (April & July 1989): 16-17; Arendt, *On Revolution*, 254.

of the flourishing that can only be attained through public action; structures of authority, cut off from their civic lifeblood, become vitiated and perverted. Indeed, only through re-invigorated spheres of popular political action can Arendt's theoretical claims about the proper relation between power and authority become practically effective.[88]

We have by now identified a number of key distinctions and relationships between power and authority in Hannah Arendt's thought. First, power generates the new when humans get together and act. Authority, on the other hand, preserves what has been generated over time. Action and power found and express the body politic; authority and government can house and preserve it. Power is equalizing and emerges as a shared feature of the group who acts in concert. Authority implies hierarchy and for this reason is asymmetrically distributed within a community, and associated with a requirement of obedience (though not one accompanied by violent sanctions).

Power is uniquely related to the present; it is the "can" that emerges like spontaneous combustion when people get together and share words and deeds. Authority, both in ancient Rome where the notion originated, and in much of its subsequent political usage, is

---

[88]"If the ultimate end of the Revolution was freedom and the constitution of a public space where freedom could appear, . . . then the elementary republics of the wards, the only tangible place where everyone could be free, actually were the end of the great republic." The basic assumption of the ward system was that *"no one could be called happy without his share in public business, that no one could be called free without his experience of public freedom, and that no one could be called either happy or free without participating and having a share in public power."* Ibid., 255, emphasis supplied. On this point D'Entreves, 17, appropriately compares the work of Evans and Boyte on popular political movements. See Sara Evans and Harry Boyte, *Free Spaces: The Sources of Democratic Change in America* (Chicago: University of Chicago Press, 1991); also Sheldon Wolin, "Contract and Birthright," *Political Theory* 14/2 (1986): 179-93; Harry Boyte, "Populism and Free Spaces," in Harry Boyte, ed., *The New Populism* (Philadelphia: Temple University Press, 1986), 305-18.

closely linked with the past. Authority brings the past into relationship with the present and helps to assure the future of the political context within which people's power of action can continue to be generated. Those who "hold authority" do so in trust; they hold it not in their own names, and not by force, but because authority has been rendered to them by the people's consent or because in some way they embody the force of an authoritative past. Authority, in short, is for Arendt one dimension of the *structure* which is needed to house the public space in which human *action* or agency occurs.[89] When they actively engage in institutions and practices of direct democracy, citizens make concrete the normative link and distinction between authority and power Arendt so persuasively defines.

Power-to and Oppression

In order to probe the difference Hannah Arendt's theory of power might make for thinking about concrete social ethical questions, let us briefly consider what light her thought sheds upon the issue of social or political oppression. Arendt gave political oppression extended attention in her first book, *The Origins of*

---

[89]Tolle notes that Arendt's abiding interests in revolution and in tradition reflect her recognition of the indispensability of both action and structure for human affairs. "Arendt's normative theory recommends we build a political order in which political participation is possible and continues long after the initial upthrust of foundation." Her advocacy of the spirit of revolution (beginnings) arises from her commitment to humanness as requiring public freedom and great action. Her advocacy of authority and tradition arises from her concern for the establishment of "a stable public arena in which the volatile, fleeting, and unpredictable human action can take place." *Human Nature Under Fire*, 110-112.

Totalitarianism, originally published in 1951.[90] What becomes dramatically clear in this complex work is the penetrating perspective that Arendt's developing political philosophy affords her on the events surrounding the rise and fall of the Third Reich. Arendt's notion of power as a capability springing from and fostering communal connection informs her interpretation both of the predicament of German Jews in the 1930s, and of totalitarianism system as the perverse triumph of violence over power-to.

In the first instance, Arendt links the Jewish community's susceptibility to Nazi oppression with German Jews' peculiar power situation in the 1930s. Contrary to the common assumption that Jews were resented because they had gained too much power, she seeks to show that insofar as Jews became a group who retained *wealth*, but wielded little or no genuine *power*, they became targets of anti-Semitism. This is so, she contends, because private wealth unaccompanied by public power prompts even greater resentment than public power that is used to oppress or exploit. Though in Arendt's later writings her usage of "power" is more precise, one can discern here a working understanding of genuine power as shared capacity available only in the public realm:

> What makes men obey or tolerate real power and, on the other hand, hate people who have wealth without power, is the rational instinct that power has a certain function and is of some general use. Even exploitation and oppression still make society work and establish some kind of order. Only wealth without power or aloofness without a policy are felt to be parasitical, useless, revolting, *because such conditions cut all the threads which tie men together.* Wealth

---

[90]Hannah Arendt, *The Origins of Totalitarianism* (Cleveland and New York: Meridian Books, The World Publishing Company, 1951). Canovan argues that it is this book, and not her more frequently analyzed later works, that reveals the foundations of Arendt's theoretical agenda. See Canovan, *Hannah Arendt*, 17-62. See also, Wayne Allen, "Hannah Arendt and the Ideological Structure of Totalitarianism," *Man and World* 26 (1993): 115-29.

which does not exploit lacks even the relationship that exists between exploiter and exploited; aloofness without policy does not imply even the minimum concern of the oppressor for the oppressed.[91]

In Arendt's eyes, public power can protect people not because it shields them from others, but because it creates and maintains connections with them. Though Arendt respects the great complexity of the events surrounding the genocide perpetrated by Hitler's Third Reich, she argues that it was least in part because, in the absence of public power-to, these connections had worn thin or become severed, that European Jews proved so uniquely vulnerable to the horrors Nazi anti-Semitism would wreak.

Arendt's more general analysis of totalitarianism further highlights the pivotal importance of connection and collaboration to power. The perverse genius of modern totalitarianism lies in its perfection of a range of techniques whereby the public realm is obliterated, and persons are effectively isolated one from another. Terrorism, deceit, and ideology conspire to produce an atomized citizenry who are helpless in the face of the regime. The powerlessness wrought by totalitarianism's thoroughly violent rule thus highlights, by contrast, the profound significance of Arendt's simple description of power as the capacity that springs forth when people act in concert.

Anthony Giddens

Michel Foucault's theory portrays power-over not only as constitutive of social relations, but also as the source of power-to.

---

[91]Arendt, *Totalitarianism*, 5, emphasis supplied. Arendt goes on to reject portrayals of the Jews as simply historical victims or scapegoats. Arendt's provocative statements reflect her concern that historical interpretation not deny the existence of the power of action, and hence, responsibility, that was constitutive of the Jewish community. Ibid., 5-9.

Hannah Arendt argues the converse: that power-to is constitutive of political life, and the necessary condition for all communal action, including coercive rule.   Arendt would regard the constraining and antagonistic features of Foucault's relations of force as extrinsic to the power that such relations might bear. Foucault might concur with those of Arendt's critics who claim that by writing coercion and hierarchy out of her definition of power, she simply closes her eyes to the asymmetry and force that are in fact intrinsic to all social and political power. In the face of the two alternatives represented by Arendt and Foucault, British social theorist Anthony Giddens provides a theory of power which aims to rectify the imbalances and deficiencies their comparison reveals.

Giddens has written prolifically and constructively on the theme of power and its place in modern society. In an analysis of society he calls "the theory of structuration," Giddens critically appropriates the contributions of Karl Marx, Max Weber, and Emile Durkheim. Besides being informed by an impressive grasp of social, economic and behavioral theory, Giddens's discussion of power reveals a philosophical expertise influenced by the thought of Ludwig Wittgenstein, Martin Heidegger, and Paul Ricoeur.

Giddens's work attempts to integrate two contemporary streams of thought on the subject of power. One in the field of philosophy centers on action theory; the other, in the social sciences, has tended to focus upon forms of domination and authority.[92] He finds this split indicative of an analytical problem that marks the majority of modern treatments of society and power. That problem is a tendency to dualistically separate the notion of action from the notion of structure, and to view them as antinomies.   Social theoretical versions of this standpoint most often operate with the

---

[92]See, e.g., Anthony Giddens, *Central Problems in Social Theory: Action, Structure and Contradiction in Social Analysis* (Berkeley: University of California Press, 1979), 49-51, 88. Giddens notes that both philosophers and sociologists have tended to define action and structure as antinomies, with philosophies of action focusing on the abilities of actors, and sociology concentrating on structures of domination.

assumption that action has to do primarily with enablement or freedom, while structure is connected with domination and constraint. Within this dualistic view, Giddens claims, power gets misconstrued. Depending on whether action or structure is given greater weight, theorists inaccurately describe power as, predominantly, either enablement (as do Talcott Parsons and Hannah Arendt) or constraint (the tendency of social theorists from Marx and Weber through the Frankfurt school and French structuralists).

Society, Structuration, and
the Political Sphere

Giddens's theory of society attempts to provide a framework in which the two kinds of social experience designated by "action" and "structure" can be integrated. He argues that instead of assuming a *dualism* of action and structure, we ought to speak of their *duality*. The duality of action and structure refers to "the essentially recursive character of social life: the structural properties of social systems are both medium and outcome of the practices that constitute those systems."[93]

Having made this claim, Giddens specifies his terms. *Society*, defined as "the patterning of social interaction reproduced across time and space," has an event-like character. "A society ceases to exist if it ceases to function."[94] *Structure*, in Giddens's parlance, refers to "rules and resources, organized as properties of social systems." Strictly speaking, there is no such thing as a structure,

---

[93]Giddens, *Profiles and Critiques*, 36-37. Also, Anthony Giddens, "On the Relation of Sociology to Philosophy," in Paul F. Secord, ed., *Explaining Human Behavior: Consciousness, Human Action, and Social Structure* (Beverly Hills, CA: Sage Publications, 1982), 184.

[94]Ibid., 182.

only structural properties.[95] A *system* is "reproduced relations between actors or collectivities organized as regular social practices," that extend over space and time. *Structuration*, that is, "the conditions governing the continuity or transformations of structures, and therefore the reproduction of systems" is, broadly considered, the object of all social theory.[96]

Rather than opposing action, structure both allows and results from human activity; the two are inextricably bound, and an adequate understanding of the notion of power is dependent upon recognizing this. "The notions of power and domination are logically associated with the concepts of action and structure as I conceptualize them,"[97] Giddens argues, because it is power that actuates and sustains the action/structure nexus in reproduced interactions over time and space.

In light of this study's focus on socio-political power, a look at the way Giddens defines the political sphere is appropriate. All human interaction, he states, involves "the communication of meaning, the operation of power (the use of resources), and normative modes of sanctioning (including the use of physical violence or the threat of its use)." As they interact, agents draw upon corresponding structural elements of social systems: signification (meaning), domination (power), and legitimation

---

[95]Giddens, *Central Problems*, 66. Elsewhere Giddens cautions that using architectural imagery to explain what is meant by structure or by a social system can render too-static understandings of these phenomena. "If we were to use this sort of imagery at all, we should have to say that *social systems are like buildings that at every moment are constantly being reconstructed by the very bricks that compose them.*" Anthony Giddens, *Sociology: A Brief But Critical Introduction* (London: Macmillan, 1982), 14. See also, Giddens, "A Reply to My Critics," in David Held & John B. Thompson, eds., *Social Theory of Modern Societies: Anthony Giddens and his Critics* (Cambridge: Cambridge University Press, 1989), 253-59.

[96]Giddens, *Central Problems*, 66.

[97]Giddens, *Profiles and Critiques*, 197-98.

(sanctions).[98]   Different institutions incorporate their own configurations of these basic structural ingredients. Thus, legal institutions include domination and signification, but highlight legitimation. Economic institutions bring domination of allocative resources to the fore, with signification and legitimation following in lexical order. Political institutions center on the domination of authoritative resources, and involve secondarily, legitimation and sanctions.[99] As for political institutions, Giddens does not confine the political to a separate sphere of social life. Nor does he believe that political practices and institutions always concern the use of force.

> The 'political' aspect of organizations concerns their capability of marshalling authoritative resources or what I shall call *administrative power*. All organizations have political features. But only in the case of states do these involve the consolidation of military power in association with control of the means of violence within a range of territories.[100]

Giddens analyzes political organization and political power as instances of the general pattern of action and structure elucidated in his theory of structuration. In his studies of society and politics, the duality of action and structure acts as a rubric whereby Giddens

---

[98]Anthony Giddens, *A Contemporary Critique of Historical Materialism*, vol. 2, *The Nation-State and Violence* (Berkeley: University of California Press, 1985), 19. Giddens's apparent equation of domination and power in this summary statement signals an ambiguity in his usage, to be discussed below.

[99]Ibid.

[100]Ibid., 19-20. Giddens defines the *state* as "a political organization whose rule is territorially ordered and which is able to mobilize the means of violence to sustain that rule." He notes the similarity between this and Weber's definition, but unlike Weber, Giddens does not accentuate the need for a monopoly of the means of violence or for legitimacy. Ibid., 20.

critically analyzes other interpretations of socio-political power, and advances his own.

Human Agency, Social Structure, and Power

In common with the other theorists considered in this chapter, Giddens rejects the opposition of individual and society, elaborating instead the interplay of their distinction-in-connection. He lays great weight upon the importance of understanding structures, and is skeptical of the introduction of individualized notions of "will" and "intentionality" into definitions of social power; yet at the same time he insists upon the integral place of the notion of human agency in an adequate theory of society.

Accountability, the ability to give account or supply reasons for action, and *freedom*, defined as the ability to behave otherwise, are the basic characteristics of human agency in Giddens's view.[101] Giddens sharply criticizes theories which "derogate the lay actor," and calls for greater recognition of the "knowledgeability" possessed by the people who participate in social patterns. Though thoroughly enmeshed in and radically affected by them, people are not simply reactive pawns of externally imposed structures, but are

---

[101]Here Giddens characteristically attempts to bridge an apparent dichotomy between "actionist" and "structurist" theories of society. He proposes a crucial role for the accountable agent, but neither demonstrates nor explicitly details the workings of freedom or accountability in the minds or actions of individual agents. In this effort to retain the understanding of the agent proposed by *Verstehen* sociology, Giddens's debt to Weber is clear. Yet, as Dallmayr notes, Giddens's formulation of the notion of agency also "undercuts or transcends the customary bifurcation between subjectively intended conduct and externally stimulated reactive behavior--a bifurcation which in large measure permeates Weberian sociology . . . ." Fred L. Dallmayr, "Agency and Structure," Review of Giddens, *Central Problems in Social Theory, Philosophy of the Social Sciences* 12 (December, 1982): 434.

the agents who compose, enact, and reproduce structural properties.[102] Everyday people in society operate with a great deal more practical and discursive knowledge of the processes in which they are involved than most social theories acknowledge.[103]

His insistence on the intelligence of social actors and on the importance of categories of freedom and accountability for accurate social scientific description reflects Giddens's respect for the concrete human beings who compose the social world. Attention to the impact of all agents in a social setting is plainly expressed in Giddens's conceptualization of power, a conceptualization that accords an integral place to transformative capacity, or power-to.

Giddens's theory of socio-political power must be understood in the context of his treatment of key terms such as domination, resources, power relationships, and transformative capacity. This author operates with both a "broad" and more "narrow" definition of power, and his use of the term is at points equivocal. But despite occasional lapses in clarity, Giddens makes a crucial

---

[102]The knowledgeability of actors is bounded by *unacknowledged conditions of action* on one side, and by *action's unintended consequences* on the other. Giddens, "On the Relation," 180. Cf. Weber's and Arendt's respective emphases on action's unpredictabilities.

[103]Giddens's theory of the knowledgeability of social actors emphasizes the importance of the reasons people have for their actions as these are enmeshed in "the chronic reflexive monitoring of conduct that social actors routinely carry on." Institutions "do not just work 'behind the backs' of the social actors who produce and reproduce them. Every competent member of every society knows (in the sense of both discursive and practical consciousness) a great deal about the institutions of that society. Such knowledge is not *incidental* to the operation of society, but is necessarily involved in it." Ibid., 185. The distinction between practical and discursive knowledge is analogous to the difference between one's ability to employ the rules of grammar and syntax (practical knowledge) and one's ability to explain or state those same rules (discursive knowledge). Giddens gives examples in relation to social "rules," in "Reply to My Critics," 255-56.

contribution by seeking to outline a notion of power that intentionally draws the notions of power-to and power-over into a single, integrated scheme.

Power and Domination

Power in the "broad" or "general" sense is, says Giddens, a logical component of the very idea of action. Action or agency has to do with the intervention of an individual or group in a course of events in the world, such that one may say that "they could have done otherwise." So defined, action involves the application of means to secure outcomes, and these outcomes constitute "intervention" into ongoing courses of events.[104]

As an element of action, "power refers to the *range* of interventions of which an agent is capable. Power in this broad sense is equivalent to the *transformative capacity* of human action: the capability of human beings to intervene in a series of events so as to alter their course."[105] Power considered most generically refers to transformative capacity embodied and expressed by agents and in structures. There is no agency without power in this sense, as the ability to make a difference.

> At the heart of both domination and power lies the transformative capacity of human action, the origin of all that is liberating and productive in social life as well as all that is all that is repressive and destructive.[106]

---

[104]"Remarks on the Theory of Power," in Anthony Giddens, *Studies in Social and Political Theory* (New York: Basic Books, 1977), 347.

[105]Ibid., 348. Giddens goes on to say that in this sense, power is closely bound up with the notion of *praxis*, as related to the historically shaped conditions of social and material existence.

[106]Giddens, *A Contemporary Critique*, 1:49.

Power in this power-to sense is a constitutive dimension of both agency and society.[107]   In enacting transformative capacity, however, interaction with others and the ability to command and disburse resources are indispensable. Thus is domination, power-over, brought into play.

When one turns from power's role in action to consider power's role in interaction, says Giddens, a sub-definition of the preceding one is required. "The production and reproduction of interaction of course involves power as transformative capacity: but in interaction we can distinguish a narrower, 'relational' sense of power. . . . Power here is domination."[108] This narrower notion of power is asymmetrical with respect to control over varied resources. The resources may be material or human; or, in Giddens's terms, *allocative*--referring to dominion over material facilities, including material goods and the natural forces that may be harnessed in their production; or *authoritative*--referring to means of dominion over the activities of human beings themselves.[109]

Such resources are sources of transformative power; but employing them almost inevitably requires relations of domination. Domination here means a mode of power that springs up insofar as "action taken with intentions of securing particular outcomes then

---

[107]While he regards power as indispensable to agency and society, Giddens resists reducing either to power relations alone. This, he thinks, is the error of the so-called "new philosophers" of France, including Foucault and others. These writers replace Marx--who did not attend sufficiently to the role of political power and the state--with Nietzsche, who viewed dominative power as the essential social force. Giddens, *Profiles and Critiques*, 215-30.

[108]Giddens, "Remarks on the Theory of Power, 348. Here Giddens follows Weber in claiming that a broad definition of power as the ability to secure outcomes must be narrowed to focus on domination. This formal similarity with Weber, however, is offset by Giddens's quite different development of the notion of domination.

[109]This definition occurs many times in Giddens's works. It is taken here from Giddens, *A Contemporary Critique*, 2:7-8.

involves the responses, or the potential behavior, of others (including their resistance to a course of action that one party wants to bring about)."[110]   Although he deems them essential to most any actualization of power-to, Giddens does not regard dominative relationships as necessarily zero-sum, conflictual,[111] or in opposition to the interests of those subordinated.[112]

Domination occurs when "structured asymmetries of resources" are drawn upon and reconstituted in the power relations (that is, in the sustained and regularized practices consisting of "reproduced relations of autonomy and dependence in interaction") that constitute social systems."[113]   Besides involving dominion over resources, this mode of power includes an expectation of asymmetry. If power relations are ongoing patterns of autonomy and dependence, the lopsidedness intrinsic to domination dictates that the superordinate will be more autonomous and the subordinate more dependent.

Yet Giddens stresses that these patterns are never completely unidirectional. The presence of agents on both sides of a domina-

---

[110]Giddens, "Remarks on the Theory of Power," 348.

[111]Giddens commends theories such as that of Talcott Parsons, which focus upon the communality and non-conflictual nature of power, yet faults Parsons for failing to conceptualize satisfactorily how structures of domination as well as capacity are implicated in power relations. See, e.g., Anthony Giddens, "'Power' in the writings of Talcott Parsons," *Studies in Social and Political Theory*, 332-346.

[112]Here Giddens parts ways with those who define power as the exercise of domination against the interests of the ruled. This definition is advocated by Steven Lukes in *Power: A Radical View* (New York: Macmillan, 1974) and assumed by a range of social theorists (e.g., Dennis Wrong, critical theorists as described by Raymond Geuss, C. Wright Mills). Giddens notes that Max Weber's famous definition of power (as the chance of an agent to secure his will even against the resistance of others) is usually cast as making conflict, if not conflicting interests, inherent to power. Our author rejects this view, and further claims that this is not what Weber himself intended his definition to convey. See Giddens, *Central Problems*, 93.

[113]Giddens, *A Contemporary Critique*, 1:50.

tive relationship means that there is always give and take of freedom and dependence among the parties. This fact Giddens names "the dialectic of control."[114]

By the dialectic of control Giddens means "the capability of the weak to turn their weakness against the powerful."[115] Just as action is intrinsically related to power, so the dialectic of control is built into the very nature of social systems. "However wide the asymmetrical distribution of resources involved, all power relations express autonomy and dependence 'in both directions.' An agent who does not participate in the dialectic of control in some minimal fashion ceases to be an agent."[116] Every agent retains some capability of making a knowledgeable difference in a relationship; that is, retains some modicum of power-to or power-over. As an example of a group actively engaging the dynamics of the dialectic of control, Giddens points to the modern labor movement.

> The "free" labor contract introduced with the advent of capitalism, as Marx showed . . . served to consolidate the power of employers over workers. But the workers succeeded in turning this position of disadvantage into a new resource of their own through the collective withdrawal of labor, and from this the labor movement was born.[117]

Yet Giddens's sociological vocabulary leaves some confusion regarding the precise relationship among the notions of "power," "domination," and "transformative capacity." In a review of the first volume of Giddens's *A Contemporary Critique of Historical Materialism*, Fred Dallmayr notes that Giddens places "power"

---

[114]Noticeable once again is the care Giddens takes to account for the impact of all actors in a social system, not just the most prominent.

[115]Giddens, "On the Relation," 187.

[116]Ibid., 186-87. This insight is borne out in James C. Scott's study, *Domination and the Arts of Resistance* (New Haven, CT: Yale University Press, 1990).

[117]Giddens, "On the Relation," 187.

between structure and social practices. Power is said to intervene "'conceptually between the broader notions of transformative capacity on the one side, and of domination on the other' and to operate 'through the utilization of transformative capacity as generated by structures of domination.'" Dallmayr expresses surprise that Giddens goes on to state that "power" will be used as "a sub-category of 'transformative capacity,' to refer to interaction where transformative capacity is *harnessed to actors' attempts to get others to comply with their wants.*"[118] Elsewhere, Giddens adds, "Power, in this relational sense, concerns the capability of actors to secure outcomes where the realization of these outcomes depends upon the agency of others."[119]

The ambiguous usage here is indicative, I believe, of a degree of uncertainty about the place of power-to in Giddens's theory. On the one hand, he repeatedly insists that power in the sense of effective capacity is intrinsic to human agency.   Is, then, transformative capacity the most general meaning of power? If so, domination must either be a subcategory of power as transformative capacity, or else, as for Arendt, something that is not power. At points, Giddens suggests the former. Yet at other times Giddens portrays transformative capacity (linked to action and practices) and domination (linked to interaction and to structures) as twin, broad categories "between" which power emerges. Power "intervenes conceptually between domination and transformative capacity" because it names the intersect at which securing outcomes involves gaining the cooperation or acquiescence of other agents.

Depending on which version of the relation between effective capacity and domination is the decisive one for Giddens, two different classifications of his theory of power are possible. We may

---

[118]Dallmayr, "Agency and Structure," 434.

[119]Giddens, *A Contemporary Critique*, 2:93. For an insightful critique of the ambiguities in Giddens's theory of power, and a reconstructive alternative, see Hiekki Patomäki, "Concepts of 'Action,' 'Structure' and 'Power' in 'Critical Social Realism': A Positive and Reconstructive Critique," *Journal for the Theory of Social Behavior* 21/2 (1992): 221-50, esp. 240-42, 245.

read this, on the one hand, as an overwhelmingly power-to approach, which relegates domination to a subsidiary role in the wider social plot to secure outcomes. But this would seem to place Giddens's theory in the company of those of Parsons and Arendt, thinkers he criticizes for insufficiently attending to domination. If, on the other hand, we take most seriously Giddens's placing of power at the intersection between transformative capacity and domination, we may interpret his as a genuine attempt at a comprehensive social theoretical rendering of the notion. This second interpretation not only avoids the problems of the first, but it coheres well with Giddens's methodological propensity for taking ideas commonly divided and showing how in fact they work as two dynamic sides of a single, complex, social experience.

About one point there is no ambiguity: Giddens is convinced that when one speaks of power, both transformative capacity and domination must be addressed. As he states in several places, domination and transformative capacity imply and require each other. Both must be accounted for if the phenomenon of power is to be adequately described.[120]

Critical Sociology and Transformative Practice

One of the questions that concerns us here is whether and how a thinker's notion of socio-political power affects the manner in which social injustice is described, and its remedies suggested. Terms like "justice" or "injustice" are virtually absent from Giddens's large corpus. Yet, with Foucault, he speaks of a "critical" social theory that exposes and dissects patterns of social oppression, and which can make significant contributions toward emancipatory courses of action. To this end, Giddens advocates a sociological standpoint that is at once historically, anthropologically, and critically sensitive.

---

[120]Giddens, *Central Problems*, 92.

Historical and anthropological acumen enable the sociologist to regard the present from a wider perspective, and to "appreciate the diversity of modes of human existence that have been followed upon this earth."[121] Such sensibilities "make it possible to break free from the straitjacket of thinking only in terms of the type of society we know in the here and now."[122] This leads Giddens to the crucial issue of the sociological imagination, which he connects with possibilities for the future. Sociology differs from a natural science because the subjectivity and freedom of its objects--people--assure that social processes will resist neat categorization or prediction. Yet, a critical social theory can assist in the task of assessing present social arrangements, contributing both data and impetus to efforts for ameliorative social change.

> As human beings, we are not condemned to be swept along
> by forces that have the inevitability of laws of nature. But
> this means we must be conscious of the *alternative futures*
> that are potentially open to us. In its . . . [critical] sense,
> the sociological imagination fuses with the task of sociology
> in contributing to *the critique of existing society.* [Such]
> critique must be based on analysis.[123]

The critical function of sociology admitted by Giddens accords social theory an intrinsically normative, as well as descriptive and analytic, dimension. He states this explicitly,[124] and focuses

---

[121]Giddens, *Introduction*, 24.

[122]Ibid., 26.

[123]Ibid., 26-27. Giddens's treatment of these same themes in *The Constitution of Society* (Berkeley: University of California Press, 1984) is probingly evaluated by Richard J. Bernstein, "Social Theory as Critique," in Held & Thompson, eds. *Giddens and His Critics*, 19-33. Equally important is Giddens's response, in "A Reply to My Critics," ibid., 288-93.

[124]Giddens speaks of abandoning an "orthodox" conception of sociology that attempts to mold it as closely as possible to the features of a natural science. Instead, a correct understanding of the sociological enterprise

especially upon the implications of critical sociology for social transformation:

> As critical theory, sociology does not take the social world as a given, but poses the questions: what types of social change are feasible and desirable, and how should we strive to achieve them?[125]

Plainly, Giddens regards social theory as the potential servant of a powerful transformative practice. By showing that what appears to be inevitable and fixed is in fact historically produced, sociology can play an emancipatory role in human society. Yet Giddens cautions that knowledge, while an important adjunct to power, is not the same as power; to those hungry for liberating change, critical sociology thus serves up sobriety as well as hope.[126]

Power and Social Oppression

Giddens's general theory of society treats the specific issue of social oppression only obliquely. The topic is explicitly broached in his critique of classical Marxism. Giddens's relationship to the intellectual legacy of Karl Marx is that of "reconstructed heir." He advocates and develops a social theory that is loyal to Marx's critical and emancipatory interests, but seeks to correct lapses and fill in lacunae in Marx's original formulations. One weakness of Marxist theory perceived by Giddens is its inadequate treatment of

---

requires that we "reject the notion that sociology can be restricted to description and explanation." The fact that sociology is a *critical* enterprise means it is both specially implicated in its own subject matter, and that it is involved in normative assessments of that subject matter. See Giddens, *Introduction*, 166-67.

[125]Ibid., 166.
[126]Ibid., 15.

oppression other than class domination. Marx's class analysis, says Giddens, must be augmented by critiques of sexual, racial, and ethnic oppression, of the nation-state and violence, and of the ecological implications of technological rationality. Such social problems must be examined on their own terms, not reduced to epiphenomena of the operations of economic class.[127]

In each of these cases, the issue of oppression, or--to use the term Giddens more often employs--exploitation, is brought to the fore. Giddens defines exploitation as domination which is harnessed to sectional interests in a society.[128] Exploitation represents power-over exercised against the interests of those subordinated, and buttressed symbolically by social ideology. Through ideology, dominant groups mobilize structures of signification to legitimate the advance of sectional interests, that is, "to legitimate exploitative domination."[129]

If domination tied to sectional interests is exploitation, a non-exploitative domination would serve universal or generalizable interests. "All forms of domination can be adjudged in terms of how far they are harnessed to the sectional interests of particular social categories, collectivities, or classes, and how far they serve the universal (generalizable) interests of broader communities of which they are a part."[130] Giddens is cognizant of the normative implications of this point, and admits that his theory of structuration and of power may be highly suggestive for the development of certain directions in ethics. However, here and

---

[127]Ibid., 166-78. See also, Giddens, *A Contemporary Critique*, 1:59-60.

[128]"Exploitation, I want to propose, is most aptly conceptualized in relation to domination or *power*." Ibid., 59.

[129]Ibid., 60-61. Giddens contrasts "sectional interests" with "general" or "universalizable" interests of the broader communities and societies of which dominant groups are a part. He does not, however, regard sectional and universal interests as mutually exclusive categories. Ibid.

[130]Ibid., 60.

elsewhere, he stops short of explicitly treating the ethical dimensions of his conceptualization.[131]

We are left with scattered hints about the directions that normative thought and practical programs based on Giddens's sociological approach might take. For instance, in discussing Marx, Giddens alludes to transformative programs whose aim is the total elimination of all domination. Undoubtedly, his theory of structuration would deem such a goal unrealistic; yet, with Foucault, Giddens also rejects the opposite conclusion, that present dominative relationships are unalterable.

> Specific forms of domination, as historically located systems of power, are in every instance open to potential transformation. [However,] since power, according to the theory of structuration, is held to be intrinsic to all interaction, there can be no question of transcending it in any empirical society . . . .[132]

Giddens goes on to make tantalizingly undeveloped remarks pertinent to the concerns of many contemporary social movements.

> It would be possible to develop a model of emancipation based upon the achievement of equality of power in interaction. But taken alone, this would be quite inadequate. For it does not come to terms with the significance of power, in the guise of transformative capacity, as the *medium of the realization of collective human interests*. From this aspect, freedom from domination in systems of interaction appears as a problem of the achievement of rationally defensible forms of authority.[133]

---

[131]See his brief comments on moral critique in Giddens, "A Reply to My Critics," 292-93.

[132]Giddens, "Remarks on the Theory of Power," 349.

[133]Ibid., emphasis supplied.

Theories of liberation or programs of social reconstruction that fail to adequately attend to power as transformative capacity are, in Giddens's eyes, descriptively faulty, and thus likely to be practically inadequate. The connection he draws between the goal of *equality of power* and *rationally defensible forms of authority* suggests the need for a complex theory of justice, wherein the distribution of control over allocative and authoritative resources serves, rather than subverts, the genuine interests of all parties. Here, as elsewhere, Giddens seeks to coherently relate the phenomena, interests, and functions encompassed by both the power-to and power-over models.

Contemporary Feminist Social Theory

The literature emerging from the reflection and practice of contemporary North American feminists[134] adumbrates a theory of power that emphasizes transformative capacity, and that seeks ways to foster and enhance the collaborative and efficacious features of social and political relations.[135] Because their thinking about

---

[134]"Feminism" is not a monolithic movement. There is neither a single, undisputed "feminist" understanding of women's situations, nor a homogeneous approach to questions surrounding gender differences, nor a unified "feminist" agenda for change. Most basically, feminists are those working to end the subordination of women, and to promote their well-being. See, e.g., Allison M. Jaggar, *Feminist Politics and Human Nature* (Sussex: Rowman & Allenheld, 1983), 7; Iris Marion Young, "Humanism, Gynocentrism and Feminist Politics," *Women's Studies International Forum* 8/3 (1985), 177-83. My focus here is feminists occupying a "radical transformationist" political stance. See n. 135 below.

[135]Broad methodological and political distinctions exist among "liberal," "radical," and "socialist" or "Marxist" feminists. See, e.g., Carol Robb, "A Framework for Feminist Ethics," in B. Andolsen, C. Gudorf, and M. Pellauer eds., *Women's Consciousness, Women's Conscience: A Reader in Feminist Social Ethics* (Minneapolis: Seabury Winston, 1985), 219-31; Jean Bethke

power is oriented by an acute awareness of the reality of sexual oppression, feminists have also been constrained to give careful attention to power-over. This simultaneous sensitivity to power-over and power-to poises feminist social theorists to contribute to a comprehensive reformulation of traditional thinking about socio-political power.

Feminists of varied backgrounds and schools unite in their opposition to sexist or patriarchal ideology, practices, artifacts, and social structures. "Patriarchy" is the term used especially by radical and socialist feminists to refer to systemic devaluation, subjugation, or exploitation of women in historical societies.[136] Some feminists consider sexism, carried and maintained by patriarchy, to be the primal form of social oppression. Most assert that critique of patriarchy is both indispensable for women's liberation, and illuminative of other kinds of dominative relation.

Feminist writers underscore the connections among structural and psychological oppression, normative views of the human, and understandings of the realities and possibilities of political and social life. Working in various scholarly fields, feminists pursue anthropology, sociology, and politics from points of view explicitly concerned with, and informed by, women's circumstances and

---

Elshtain, *Public Man, Private Woman: Women in Social and Political Thought* (Princeton, NJ: Princeton University Press, 1981), esp. ch. 1; Marilyn French, *Beyond Power: On Women, Men, and Morals* (New York: Summit Books, 1985), 446-73; Jaggar, *Feminist Politics*, introduction. I designate the writers considered here "radical transformationists." In contrast to liberal feminists, who envisage gender equity in terms of inclusion into present social structures, these *radical* feminists expose and denounce patriarchy's deeply rooted and multifaceted effects. Simultaneously, (vs. radical "separatists") they place critique at the service of *transformative* engagement that aims to renovate oppressive patterns. Finally, while agreeing with socialist feminists about the significance of economic analysis, they place economic concerns in the context of a more encompassing cultural analysis of women's situation.

[136]Gerda Lerner, *The Creation of Patriarchy* (Oxford: Oxford University Press, 1986), offers an historical analysis of the term and the cultural patterns it connotes. See also, French, *Beyond Power*, chs. 2-4.

experiences. In so doing they intend to provide a corrective (some would say replacement) to mainstream approaches in fields historically controlled by males and reflecting primarily male-centered perspectives.[137]

The Relational Self, Community, and Power

As they seek a non-patriarchal understanding of human agency and community, many feminists are re-interpreting the basic self-other relation. Philosopher Caroline Whitbeck, for example, makes a case for a feminist ontology or metaphysics, at whose heart is a conception of the self as essentially in relation rather than in

---

[137]What is meant by "women's experience", its sources (nature or nurture), its relation to the experiences of men and to descriptions of "human experience," and its significance for descriptive and normative discourses are hotly debated issues both within and beyond feminist ranks. The diverse answers given to such questions serve to define some flexible yet distinguishable schools of thought within feminist theory and practice today. The authors highlighted here agree in the main with political theorist Kathy Ferguson's framing of the issue:

"The source of feminist discourse is in the characteristic experiences of women as caretakers, nurturers, and providers for the needs of others. Not all women have these experiences equally, of course, but most women have some access to them and nearly all women have far greater access to them than do nearly all men. Out of the lie that women are all the same . . . there has been a truth created about women: in many ways we *are* the same, we have come to be the same, we have been produced at least partially within the patterns of femininity and femaleness that bureaucratic capitalism requires. Divided by lines of class, race, ethnicity, and so on, most of us nonetheless encounter a characteristic set of linguistic and institutional practices constitutive of the life experiences of the second sex." Kathy E. Ferguson, *The Feminist Case Against Bureaucracy* (Philadelphia: Temple University Press, 1984), 158-59.

opposition to others.[138] Modern Western thought is characterized by a dualistic ontology which posits the self as a monad in basic opposition to other selves, and sets the social and political task as bringing individuals into some tolerable order and relationship. Whitbeck's alternative, relational ontology (which bears affinities to the understanding of self promoted by pragmatic philosophers like George Herbert Mead, and process philosophers like Albert North Whitehead)[139] regards relationships, past and present, realized and sought, as constitutive of the self. Since on this view relations of selves to others are relations among analogous rather than opposed beings, differentiation is not dependent on opposition.[140] Rather than issuing in a perception of reality in terms of opposed dualisms (e.g., self-other, male-female, mind-body, egoism-altruism, theory-practice, culture-nature), "the self-others relation generates a multifactorial interactive model of most, if not all, aspects of reali-

---

[138]Caroline Whitbeck, "A Different Reality: Feminist Ontology," in Carol C. Gould, ed., *Beyond Domination: New Perspectives on Women and Philosophy* (Totowa, NJ: Rowman and Allanheld, Publishers, 1983), 64-88.

[139]On pragmatists' relational view of the self, see G. H. Mead, *Mind, Self, and Society* (Chicago: The University of Chicago Press, [1934] 1962). For feminists engaging pragmatism, see Kathy E. Ferguson, *Self, Society, and Womankind: The Dialectic of Liberation* (Westbury, CT: Greenwood Press, 1980); Charlene Haddock Seigfried, "Shared Communities of Interest: Feminism and Pragmatism," *Hypatia* 8/2 (Spring, 1993): 1-14. Feminists' and process thought's relational understanding of the self are compared in Sheila Greeve Davaney, ed., *Feminism and Process Thought*, The Harvard Divinity School/Claremont Center for Process Studies Symposium Papers (New York, NY: E. Mellen Press, 1981).

[140]Whitbeck, "Feminist Ontology," 69. Nancy C. M. Hartsock discerns a similar move in Hannah Arendt's reinterpretation of the Greeks' agonal understanding of self-other relationships in terms of plurality. She paraphrases Arendt to the effect that "plurality is the condition of human action because we are all the same, that is, human, in such a way that nobody is ever the same as anyone else who ever lived, lives, or will live." Nancy C. M. Hartsock, *Money, Sex, and Power: Toward a Feminist Historical Materialism* (Boston: Northeastern University Press, 1985), 215.

ty."[141] Their counterposition of a relational to an oppositional notion of the self undergirds feminists' advocacy of power-to versus mainstream power-over models.[142]

The Feminist Critique of Power-Over

Feminist theorists are keenly aware of the prevalence of power-over in social life, quintessentially embodied in the patriarchal domination. Flowing from their opposition to patriarchy is a general critique of dominant-subordinate relationships. Even purportedly benign exercises of power-over (such as certain approaches to parenting, or to social welfare) which focus on the superordinates' setting and executing ends for the benefit of their charges, are viewed with suspicion by these writers. Such a strong anti-hierarchical bias may be explained at least in part by women's historical positions within such arrangements: persons traditionally denied power-over are less likely to look favorably upon dominative patterns than those for whom hierarchy has assured privileged status.

Equity and mutuality among women and men can be accomplished, feminists contend, only by a dual response to the

---

[141]Whitbeck, "Feminist Ontology," 76. See also Drucilla Cornell and Adam Thurschwell, "Femininity, Negativity, Intersubjectivity," in Seyla Benhabib & Drucilla Cornell, eds., *Feminism as Critique* (Minneapolis, MN: University of Minnesota Press, 1987), esp. 157-62.

[142]A psychoanalytically-oriented analogue to Whitbeck's philosophical treatment, which focuses on female-centered child rearing practices as equipping women to experience selfhood as relational, is the widely-cited work of Nancy Chodorow, *The Reproduction of Mothering* (Berkeley: University of California Press, 1978). Isaac D. Balbus draws on Chodorow to argue that shared parenting is critical to men's apprehension of the relational features of self, in *Marxism and Domination: A Neo-Hegelian, Feminist Psychoanalytic Theory of Sexual, Political, and Technological Liberation* (Princeton: Princeton University Press, 1982).

problem of power. First, dominative power over women and over all other oppressed groups must be refused and defused. Domination does not promote human well-being; it therefore must be resisted and to the extent possible eliminated.[143]

Feminists contend that in order to successfully confront and overcome subjugation, women and other oppressed groups must shed the identity of powerless, insignificant "other" foisted upon them by androcentric society, and instead begin to claim, develop, and express their own power as power-to. Women do not wish to duplicate the relations of power under which they have suffered. If old dominative patterns are to be rooted out, and new, non-oppressive relations forged, different theories and practices of power are needed.

An Emerging Feminist Theory of Power

This different way of understanding and enacting power is variously described. Political scientist Nancy Hartsock speaks of "the widespread adoption of an understanding of power as energy and competence rather than dominance, an understanding referenced by the term, 'feminist theory of power.'"[144] Psychiatrist Jean Baker Miller holds that for women today, power may be defined as "the capacity to implement." Women need to put into action capabilities they already have and the new ones they are developing. This understanding contrasts with the meaning given to "power" in the past. "Power," says Miller, "has generally meant the ability to advance oneself, and, simultaneously, to control, limit, and if possible destroy the power of others." In other words, power has been seen as including two components: effective capacity

---

[143]As we shall see, these feminists do not contend that power-over can be expected to disappear. They do argue that uses of power-over must be oriented by a commitment to promoting the expression of power as effective capacity without dominance. See, e.g., French, *Beyond Power*, 502-512.

[144]Hartsock, *Money, Sex and Power*, 224.

[power-to] for oneself and control over [power-over] others.[145] In this context, the capacity to implement of other persons or groups was generally seen as dangerous; therefore, others must be controlled, or they would control you.

But Miller points out that in the realm of human development, this is not a valid formulation. Quite the reverse, in fact, is true. Seen from the perspective of human development, the greater the development of each individual the more able, more effective, and less in need of limiting or restricting others she or he will be.[146] Recognizing that power does not require the diminishment of others, "women do not need to take on the destructive attributes which are not necessarily a part of effective power, but were merely a part of maintaining a dominant-subordinate system. Women need the power to advance their own development, but they do not "need" the power to limit the development of others."[147]

Besides the crucial task of limiting dominations, feminists seek to foster forms of collective life that enable members to actuate their potentialities, to the mutual benefit of themselves and the community. Authority, on this view, ought to involve non-

---

[145]Jean Baker Miller, *Toward a New Psychology of Women*, 2nd Edition (Boston: Beacon Press, 1986), 116.

[146]Ibid. Miller and others claim that human development is an arena with which, because of their historical ties with caretaking and parenting, women have been especially familiar. Cf. Sara Ruddick, *Maternal Thinking* (Boston, Beacon Press, 1989).

[147]Ibid., 117. A weakness of this position in its various forms is its inadequate treatment of the question of scarcity. I may not need the power to stunt others' development, but in developing my own capacities, I may, by my use of scarce resources, limit or prevent the growth of others. If empowerment is imagined in terms of a non-zero sum resource such as knowledge, maturity, or love, the problem of scarcity is obscured. But to the extent that education or a loving family assume the meeting of basic physical needs, even here we encounter the question of how to evaluate situations in which my power--either directly or indirectly--creates, promotes, maintains, or requires another's powerlessness. In Christian parlance, scarcity draws attention to finitude, and its complex connections to structures of sin.

oppressive, empowering relations whose aim is the interdependent flourishing of all.[148] Many feminists connect this appreciation for empowerment to women's historical experiences with positive nurturance, especially in good parenting, where germinal agents are helped to mature into interdependent and creative adults. In this vein, Miller speaks of a feminist notion of "the powerful act of empowering others," which she sees as the core meaning of nurturance.[149] Power-over, to the extent that it is employed in a feminist society, would need to reflect this nurturing, empowering, pattern.

Nancy Hartsock suggests that although a "feminist theory of power" is still in the process of clarification, its general lineaments can be discerned. These include a stress on power as capacity for effective action, a collective and expansive rather than a conflictual and zero-sum notion, and a refusal to equate power with domination.[150] Radical transformative feminists recognize that this orientation toward power can be credible only within the context of a reformulated understanding of human agency and community, and a practical possibility only if social and political institutions can be fundamentally reworked to support these different understandings.

Hartsock, among others, makes much of the consistently strong bond drawn between power and community by feminists and other

---

[148]Precisely what "authority" is to mean in a reconstructive feminist political ethic is a debate still in its early stages. See, e.g., Jean Bethke Elshtain, "The Power and Powerlessness of Women," in Elshtain, *Power Trips and Other Journeys: Essays in Feminism as Civic Discourse* (Madison, WI: University of Wisconsin Press, 1990), 134-48; Lynne Tirrell, "Definition and Power" Toward Authority without Privilege," *Hypatia* 8/4 (Fall 1993): 1-34.

[149]Miller quoted from conversation, and papers on "Women and Power," and "The Construction of Anger in Women and Men," in Suzanne Gordon, "Anger, Power, and Women's Sense of Self," *Ms.* 14 (July 1985): 42.

[150]Hartsock, *Money, Sex, and Power*, 224-225.

women theorists.[151]   Feminists' interactive, relational understandings of self and community call for specific forms of practice.
Social and political theorists now face the challenge of clarifying the
normative and strategic implications of feminist anthropology and
sociology for political structures and action. This is in addition to
elucidating the impact that individualistic and hierarchical models
of self and society have had on practices of power, an impact often
concealed by the aura of neutral objectivity those descriptions have
enjoyed.   Although feminists proffer a range of responses to the
challenge for transformed praxis implied by renovated images of self
and society, most urge collaborative political action to shape
institutions more supportive of "agency in community," and more
expressive of power as effective capacity.

Countering Power-Over Critics

In response to the notion of a society operating through
effective capacity without domination, one can imagine power-over
theorists issuing a collective sneer. Feminist suspicion of hierarchy
evokes the counterposition summarized in Max Weber's dictum,
"All ideas aiming at abolishing the dominance of men over men are

---

[151]Hartsock's studies of women's social theories of power lead her to
suggest that women in western society have a strong tendency to envision
power differently than men. Hannah Arendt, Dorothy Emmett, Hannah
Pitkin, and others, strongly link power and community, and, in seeking to
elucidate the workings of power, stress power-to. Hartsock, *Money, Sex, and
Power*, ch. 9. See also, e.g., H. C. Metcalf and L. Urwick, eds., *Dynamic
Administration: The Collected Papers of Mary Parker Follett* (New York:
Harper Brothers, 1941).   I thank Prof. Stewart Herman for calling my
attention to Follett's work in this regard. For criticisms of Hartsock's and
Ruddick's claims about women and power, see Thomas Wartenberg, *The
Forms of Power: From Domination to Transformation* (Philadelphia: Temple
University Press, 1990), 195-200.

'utopian.'"[52] Many secular and religious scholars judge theories which highlight power-to and spurn power-over inadequate to actual social experience, and therefore impractical as guides for transformative action. Yet feminist authors are committed to nothing if not to fostering concrete, practical steps toward social amelioration. Short of pushing their proposals off into some quasi-eschaton, or advocating the pursuit of new, sectarian communal forms at the margins of an irredeemably patriarchal socio-political scene, how do feminists counter this predictable retort to their formulations about power?

They do so in a number of ways; we will mention four. Beyond their relevance to feminist theory and practice, these responses to power-over thinkers offer more general insights into ways that power-to emphasis in social and political discourse may be defended.

First, feminists challenge the adequacy of power-over critics' accounts of social experience. These feminists join thinkers like Arendt to charge that power-over theories confuse power with violence, missing its real essence, communal agency. Weberians, Marxists, and other power-over theorists reply that power-to approaches slice away the precise feature that has made power such an intense and perennial human concern.[53] For power-over theorists, the power-to model may be a statement about what power ought to be, but it is an inaccurate depiction of what *experience* tells us that power is, in fact. To make transformative capacity central to one's notion of power is, they conclude, theoretically inaccurate, and practically unrealistic, if not dangerous.

Feminists take issue with the power-over school precisely on this point. It is the power-over interpretation, these feminists claim, which expresses a skewed and deficient notion of experience, from the level of the self to that of political structures. This is so

---

[52]See Chapter I, 34, n. 50.

[53]As has been mentioned, this is Steven Lukes's criticism of Arendt in his *Power: A Radical View*, one echoed by other power-over theorists against other power-to thinkers.

because the power-over vantagepoint cuts away the range of experiences that involve power without domination, experiences found particularly in the realms of human development and caretaking to which women have been traditionally assigned. Far from being unrealistic, they contend, the power-to starting point rectifies a long-standing and debilitating lacuna in mainstream accounts.[154]

A second criticism to which feminists respond concerns the question of conflict. On the face of it, conflict seems inimical to a heavily power-to approach. Hannah Arendt, for instance, has been accused of rewriting classical history along lines that conceal the importance of competition and conflict in ancient political thought and practice.[155] The feminist literature reviewed here embraces power-to as the descriptive and normative heart of power, yet concomitantly aims to uncover and "reclaim" conflict as necessary to the health of both interpersonal relationships and society. Miller, Ferguson, Audre Lorde and others recognize that women under patriarchy have been socialized to fear and avoid conflict, thereby discouraging challenges to an unjust status quo. Conflict is, in fact, intrinsic to the process of growth and development, but conflict has a different look when perceived from a relational feminist rather than a dualistic patriarchal perspective. Pursued from a standpoint that acknowledges the interdependence of the disputants, and that aims for the well-being of all participants (rather than one which sees conflict as a zero-sum game pursued by wholly separated parties), conflict can become an avenue toward greater justice,

---

[154]Jean Bethke Elshtain probes the implications of this feminist claim for a reconsideration of the history of women's roles in relation to war in *Women and War* (New York, NY: Basic Books, 1987).

[155]See, e.g., Hartsock, *Money, Sex, and Power*, ch. 9. Other critics, however, fault Arendt for glamorizing an "agonal" or competitive ideal of public life. See, e.g., Seyla Benhabib's nuanced critique in "Models of Public Space," Hannah Arendt, the Liberal Tradition, and Jürgen Habermas," in Calhoun, ed., *Habermas and the Public Sphere*, 74-81.

clearer relationships, and more genuine accords.

Kathy Ferguson elucidates feminists' expectation that conflict will persist under the best of social conditions, but that, in a feminist society, the context and methods for engaging in conflict would be revised:

> Feminist discourse does not envision some underlying unanimity in political life, but it does envision a polity in which modes of conflict and definitions of interests are worked out within a context of general concern for the humanness of others. . . . Presumably there would still be conflict in a feminist society, but there would be a public space available for the ongoing process of conflict resolution. . . . The accommodative strategies of conflict resolution that women typically use would be encouraged and legitimated, calling on the cooperative and respectful processes of talking and listening that express care and maintain connection.[156]

A third point of contention between feminists and power-over theorists is the question of whether hierarchy and domination ought to be or can be wholly eliminated. Despite their emphatic refusal to tender relationships of hierarchy or domination central or normative political status, most feminists do not foresee a time when every relation of domination and subordination will have disappeared. Many would echo Marilyn French, who asserts:

> Coercion--domination--is not eradicable. It is impossible

---

[156]Ferguson, *Feminist Case Against Bureaucracy*, 198. This feminist rendering of an interdependent and mutually respectful approach to social conflict has affinities with Arendt's depiction of the nature and function of the public realm. Power-over thinkers would not agree that feminists sufficiently take into account cases of zero-sum, antagonistic conflict. Christian power-over theorists like Niebuhr might further chastise feminists for inadequately attending to the division and egoism wrought by social sin.

to envision a world in which some form or degree of domination is lacking. At the same time, the urge to dominate is responsible for most of the ills humans impose on themselves. Political theorists discuss the problem of how to construct a society in which domination is not possible, but the solutions devised invariably involve a set of checks and balances which in fact create a new level of domination.[57]

The challenge to feminist theorists is, in the face of this, how to relegate social and political domination to minimal and instrumental status, keeping center stage the main goal: the maximum empowerment and development of all participants.

In cautioning about the use of power-over, Ferguson says, "the point is not that no one should ever turn to such channels, but that those avenues are inherently and severely limited in what they can accomplish."[58] This means that a deep and effective suspicion of power-over, and a recognition of its limitations, must be maintained at all times. Other feminists suggest that domination, coercion and hierarchy ought to be seen as marking the limits of the political process, while political life is much more and, indeed, other than those limits.[59] Seeing the limitations of both thoroughly power-to and strictly power-over models, many radical transformationist feminists are working to stake out a mediating, comprehensive alternative.

A final issue on which these feminists encounter criticism both among and outside their ranks concerns the problem of co-optation. As we have seen, this sector of the feminist movement accepts certain sorts and degrees of conflict and superordination as social

---

[57]French, *Beyond Power*, 506.

[58]Ferguson, *Feminist Case Against Bureaucracy*, 180.

[59]See, e.g., Elizabeth Janeway, *Powers of the Weak* (New York: Morrow Quill, 1980), 234-35. Arendt makes a similar point when she insists that once violence and domination become the means of effecting ends, we have left behind the realm of the political in which argument and cooperation prevail.

and political "facts of life." Feminists work for change within a society that still counts power-over as the only genuine power. This being the case, how can feminists avoid being simply co-opted into the presently dominant ethos of power-over? This is a problem to which feminists are sensitive, and to which they acknowledge their movement to have been historically vulnerable.[160] Besides recommending the preventive medicine of ongoing self-criticism, a number of these writers urge women to seek communal contexts wherein concrete practices of power-to may be clarified, cherished and embodied. Feminists so engaged will be better equipped to expose and counter the mistaken and destructive understandings of power that orient current social and political practice.

French reminds her readers that, despite its present hegemony, power-over is the source of untold misery in the lives of people. "Power-to is one of the greatest pleasures available to humans; power-over is one of the greatest pains."[161] Power-to is, she judges, the real, legitimate goal of those who purport to "need" or

---

[160]Some authors lift up the racial and class corruption and co-optation of white, middle class women in both the first and second waves of U.S. feminism. See esp., Barbara Hilkert Andolsen, *Daughters of Jefferson, Daughters of Bootblacks: Racism and American Feminism* (Macon, GA: Mercer University Press, 1986); Nancy Caraway, *Segregated Sisterhood: Racism and the Politics of American Feminism* (Knoxville, TN: University of Tennessee Press, 1991). Related are efforts by a range of scholars to prevent the contemporary feminist agenda from being confined to the sectional concerns of affluent, white, first world women. See, e.g., Cherrie Moraga & Gloria Anzaldua, eds., *This Bridge Called My Back: Writings by Radical Women of Color* (Watertown, MA: Persephone Press, 1981); Patricia Hill Collins, *Black Feminist Thought: Knowledge, Consciousness, and the Politics of Empowerment* (Boston: Unwin Hyman, 1990). On other fronts, communitarian and radical feminists contend that their "liberal" sisters have been deluded by a falsely individualist vision that constricts feminist analysis and distorts its transformative agenda. See, e.g., Elshtain, *Public Man, Private Woman*, 228-55; Dorchen Leidholdt & Janice G. Raymond, eds., *The Sexual Liberals and the Attack on Feminism* (Elmsford, NY: Pergamon Press, 1990).

[161]French, *Beyond Power*, 509.

"want" to dominate. The difficult work for feminists is to convince themselves and their interlocutors of the practical difference this distinction makes. If this can accomplished, the danger of co-optation will be greatly lessened. Alluding to the fact that the disagreement between power-over and power-to thinkers is rooted in a clash of normative anthropologies, French summarizes the brunt of her view:

> Domination is not eradicable, but we can lessen its attraction for humans if we can learn to see it for what it is—a desperate shift, made in the belief that humans are predators and incapable of felicity. The need to dominate is a substitute for faith in affection and other satisfactions.[162]

Such a conviction, variously elaborated, provides a compass which can enable women to keep their bearings as they manage in "the tension between living/surviving in the world as it is and making the world into what it should be."[163]

Feminist theories of power emerge directly from within, and are meant to serve, a liberative agenda whose aim is to overcome social oppression. Increasingly, that agenda has been widened to include not only women, but all systemically subordinated groups.[164]

---

[162]Ibid., 512.

[163]Ferguson, *Feminist Case Against Bureaucracy*, 180.

[164]Besides challenging a women's movement that has tended to be predominantly white and middle class (see n. 160 above), radical transformationist feminists are attending to the "interstructuring" of racism, classism, and sexism, and the consequent double and triple oppression of third world women, poor women, lesbian women, and women of color. See, e.g., Miller, "Foreword to the Second Edition," *Toward a New Psychology of Women*, xii-xvi; Andolsen, et al, eds., *Women's Consciousness*, xv, xix; Andolsen, *Daughters*, vii, 108-110, 124-25; Patricia Hill Collins, *Black Feminist Thought*; Audre Lorde, *Sister Outsider* (Trumansburg, NY: Crossing, 1984); and essays by Claudia Card, Maria C. Lugones, Christine Pierce and Allison

Social and political arrangements are sought that will promote an "affiliative context" where cooperative traits can be fostered, and the best of the supportive and generative values traditionally relegated to the female gender may become cherished and effective in the public sphere. In the judgment of these scholars, a society in which the importance of having power over people is diminishing must simultaneously increase the opportunities for exercising transformative power with and for others. "The question is how to create a way of life that includes serving others without being subservient."[165] Creating such a way of life involves renovating every facet of collective interaction. As feminists and others struggling against oppression face this challenge, articulating an accurate theory of power will continue to be essential.

Conclusion

The diverse group of theories examined in this chapter illustrate different ways that the notion of power as transformative efficacy, or power-to, gets incorporated into contemporary social and political thought. Michel Foucault and Hannah Arendt represent two ends of a spectrum in which power-to is increasingly stressed. Foucault argues that the transformative, relational, collaborative dimensions of power-to are spawned by a complex network of antagonistic relations of force. Arendt wishes to rescue power from its entanglements with violence and hierarchy and to restore its pristine meaning as pure, collaborative efficacy. Attempting to construct mediating positions are Anthony Giddens and the feminist social thinkers we have considered. While both Giddens and the feminists explicitly seek to account for both power-over and power-

---

Jaggar in Claudia Card, ed., *Feminist Ethics* (Lawrence, KS: University Press of Kansas, 1991), 3-104. The struggle for a feminism that is both collaborative and respectful of diversity remains in its early stages.

[165]Miller quoted by Gordon, "Anger, Power, and Women," 44. Notice the rich possibilities for relating this insight to Christian theological ethics.

to in political life, Giddens puts relations of domination to the fore, while feminists struggle to find ways in which power-to can orient all social interactions.

All four contributions reveal connections between theories of power and understandings of personhood and society. Amidst descriptive arguments about power, all four--Arendt and the feminists explicitly, and Giddens and Foucault more implicitly-- harbor normative assumptions about social flourishing, which their talk of power reflects. Finally, to the extent that each attempts to take into account the features of social and political experience captured in both the power-over and power-to models, these thinkers move toward a comprehensive approach to socio-political power.

In Chapter Two, we considered the impact of the power-over model on the Christian political thought of Jacques Maritain and Reinhold Niebuhr. The present chapter has investigated the power-to discussion in recent social theory. We now turn to the task of identifying sites of power-to emphasis in recent Christian ethics.

CHAPTER IV

POWER AS TRANSFORMATIVE CAPACITY:
DIRECTIONS IN THEOLOGICAL ETHICS

The preceding chapter explored resources for transformative paradigms of power in contemporary social theory. We saw that attention to power-to takes various forms. Some scholars, like Michel Foucault, highlight the positive transformative capability afforded by power, but envisage such capability as emerging from within basic configurations of super- and subordination. Theorists who more fully embrace power-to, such as Hannah Arendt, reject the majority's assumption that hierarchy and domination are essential or normative features of power. We have also noted contemporary social theorists who strive to describe power in a way that is comprehensive, by incorporating in some integrated fashion both the power-to and the power-over paradigms. All these treatments of power, we have seen, are rooted in specific descriptive and normative visions of the human person and of society.

This chapter will demonstrate a similar range of emphases in recent Christian theological and social ethical writings. Paul Tillich's ontological analysis of power features a complex intertwining of power-over and power-to. The ethics issuing from process theology clearly gravitates toward the power-to approach. For contemporary liberation-oriented theologies, empowerment is a central concern. Yet the ardent commitment to confront and resist injustice that motivates Latin American, feminist, African American, and other representatives of this latter approach also prompts distinctive treatments of power-over. Predictably, many of the religious scholars considered here rely less on mainstream philosophies, social theories, and theologies, which tend to make power-over central in their treatments of social and political relations, and turn instead to alternative traditions that accent effective energy as a basic meaning for power. Liberation writers, whose thinking about power emerges and proceeds amidst concrete social struggles, also find in the particular experiences of their constituencies both a vital resource and a demanding test of adequacy.

Ontological Approaches to Power

Among the twentieth century Christian thinkers who have explicitly considered power-to and its relevance for ethics are some of those engaged in contemporary retrievals of metaphysics or ontology. A commanding figure in this arena has been Paul Tillich. Also representing this approach in North America have been process theologians such as Charles Hartshorne, Henry Nelson Weiman, John B. Cobb, and Bernard Loomer. Process thinkers are particularly indebted to the thought of Alfred North Whitehead. Tillich's theology is less bound to one philosophical mentor, and draws insight from an array of classic Greek and Christian, and more recent existentialist sources[1] to synthesize an ontology of religion for a modern world.[2] A brief analysis of the ontological

---

[1]Among the classical sources, Plato and Augustine are probably most important for Tillich. A useful summary of Tillich's perception of his debts to existentialist philosophy is given by James Luther Adams in the introduction to Paul Tillich, *Political Expectation*, James Luther Adams, ed., (New York: Harper and Row, 1971; Macon, GA: Mercer University Press, 1981), ix-x.

[2]Tillich's ontological approach is evident in the way he raises the question of power: "In what way is power rooted in being-itself? The question of being-itself *is* the ontological question. This approach, then, attempts to

notion of power presented by Tillich, followed by a look at process theologians' treatments, will reveal their significance for discussions of power-to in Christian social ethics.

Paul Tillich

Paul Tillich's theory of power is embedded in a system that unites a sophisticated philosophical stance with an encompassing theological vision.[3] Within the ambit of an ontological analysis of being, Tillich develops understandings of the Christian doctrines of creation, sin, and redemption; these, in turn, influence his description and evaluation of socio-political life.

Christian Doctrines and Socio-Political Relations. As the public arena wherein human creatures actualize their God-given potentialities, socio-political life participates, first, in the order of

---

answer the . . . simple and infinitely difficult question, What does it mean to *be?* What are the structures, common to everything, that is, to everything that participates in being?" Paul Tillich, *Love, Power, and Justice: Ontological Analyses and Ethical Applications* (London: Oxford University Press, 1954), 19. Tillich regards ontology as a descriptive method that attempts to identify the structures which are presupposed in any encounter with reality by analyzing concrete encountered realities, and seeking to "separate those elements of the real which are generic or particular from those elements which are constitutive for everything that is and therefore are universal." Ibid., 23. There is no experimental way of verifying ontological judgments, but there is the possibility of an experiential way, which involves "intelligent recognition of the basic ontological structures within the encountered reality, including [within] the process of encountering itself." Ibid., 24.

[3]Kyle Pasewark provides a fine, detailed analysis and critique of Tillich's theology of power as the climax of his own constructive argument that power is, at heart, the communication of efficacy across boundaries. See *The Theology of Power* (Minneapolis MN: Fortress Press, 1993), chs. 5 & 6; and on developments in Tillich's treatment of power, 237-45.

creation. Life is a process whereby potentiality is actualized; as such life at the most basic level is a push toward transformative efficacy. Life is also characterized by a "centeredness" which is, for each existent, both reality and task.[4] Each person--and in a more limited sense, each society--actualizes itself according to what Tillich identifies as the three functions of life: self-integration, self-creation, and self-transcendence.[5]

Self-integration is the activity by which a center of self identity is established, is drawn out into life processes involving self-alteration, and then, in a sort of circular movement, is re-established along with the outcomes of the changes that it has undergone.[6] This is "self" integration because it is not achieved by outside forces but rather by an inner dynamic of movement. Self-creation, the second function, refers to a process of creating new centers of the self which proceeds in the context of historical time.   In self-creation the actualization of potential "goes forward in a horizontal direction,"[7] as one focuses, not on consolidating present identity, but on growth and development.[8] *Praxis*, which Tillich defines as "the whole of cultural acts by centered personalities who as

---

[4]See Paul Tillich, *Systematic Theology*, vol. 3, *Life and the Spirit; History and the Kingdom of God* (Chicago: The University of Chicago Press, 1963), 33-34, for a discussion of the meaning of "centeredness."

[5]Ibid., 30-106. Tillich's dynamic portrayal of humans' historical self-actualization highlights the fact that his is a historically conscious ontological approach. Cf. Pasewark, *Theology of Power*, 239-42.

[6]Tillich, *Systematic Theology*, 3:30.

[7]Ibid., 31.

[8]Growth is dependent on the basic polarity of dynamics and form. "Growth . . . is the process by which a formed reality goes beyond itself to another form which both preserves and transforms the original reality." Ibid., 50. Tillich also insists that self-creation is never *ex nihilo*, but is growth that works within the parameters of divinely given life. Furthermore, self-creation always requires form as well as dynamism. Neither a simple series of changes nor a simple series of forms constitute self-creation, but both are present in the creative process. Cf. Niebuhr, *Nature and Destiny*, vol. 1, ch. 2.

members of social groups act upon each other and themselves," constitutes the self-creation of life in both the personal and the communal realms.[9] The third of life's functions is self-transcendence, whereby the potentiality of life is actualized in a "vertical" direction as it presses beyond itself as finite, and toward the sublime, the great, the ultimate: in Christian terms, toward God.

These life functions are basic to human self-actualization, and can only occur in the context of encounters with others. Such encounters require and produce a social matrix. Only in community can individuals fully realize the foundational relations of love, power, and justice. These relations mark divine life and are, in turn, intrinsic to humans' essential identity as *imago dei*.[10]

Due to the creaturely limitations of living beings, each life function is continually threatened by its opposite: self-integration with disintegration and loss of identity;[11] self-creation with destruction and death;[12] and self-transcendence with finitude and profanization.[13] As the Genesis myth of the fall recounts, humanity responds to the anxiety attending finitude by sinfully misusing freedom. This response causes the threats against life functions to be realized in ways more acute, more perverse, and more tragic than would otherwise be the case.

Tillich calls the effects of this conspiracy of finitude and sin the human condition of estrangement. Persons and groups pursue the basic life functions and seek to actuate their essential identities, but in so doing they persistently experience themselves as separated or cut off from the dynamic relatedness that would accompany genuine flourishing. Tillich draws on existential philosophical categories and the Christian theological tradition to suggest that estrangement has both ethical and tragic elements. Humans bear responsibility for

---

[9]Tillich, *Systematic Theology*, 3:65-66.

[10]Through the *imago dei*, the human is related to the divine ground and origin of all power. On this see, e.g., Tillich, *Political Expectation*, 116.

[11]Tillich, *Systematic Theology*, 3:32-50.

[12]Ibid., 50-86.

[13]Ibid., 86-107.

the havoc wrought by their alienation from God, self, others, and cosmos; yet, tragically, estrangement could not be avoided in the movement of humanity from essence to freely self-actualizing existence.[14]

Since, unlike individuals, social structures lack full-fledged centers of freedom or decision, Tillich does not believe that social groups as such experience either estrangement or reconciliation. Nonetheless, the conflict and the abuse of power marking all facets of collective existence testify to the fact of estrangement. In social as in personal life, "the relationship between love and power and of both of them to justice is in reality not what it essentially is, and therefore ought to be in human existence."[15]

For Tillich, redemption concerns the accomplishment of the eschatological goal of human life, a goal described as the reconciliation of self with self and with all other beings in the whole of being, a condition of final "reunion of the separated," or, love. Genuine reconciling love also encompasses relations of justice and the perfection of the power of being. In Tillich's system, Jesus Christ stands as the "New Being" who unlocks the possibility of reconciliation. Christ provides the ultimate criterion for every healing and saving process,[16] and the effects of Jesus as the healing presence of the New Being continue to be worked out in history. In the third volume of his *Systematic Theology*, Tillich offers an analysis of the reconciling, justifying, and regenerating processes wrought by the "Spiritual Presence" amidst the ambiguities of

---

[14]Paul Tillich, *Systematic Theology*, vol. 2, *Existence and the Christ* (Chicago: The University of Chicago Press, 1957), 36-39. On this point, Tillich's theology has drawn criticism for apparently adopting a theory of the "necessity" of the fall. Traditional formulations of this issue, such as Augustine's, view the fall as inevitable, but not necessary.

[15]Tillich, *Political Expectation*, 119.

[16]Tillich, *Systematic Theology*, 2:167-68.

historical life.[7] Here we find an exposition of the implications of salvation for socio-political life, revolving around the pivotal symbol of the Kingdom of God.

Because Tillich understands power ontologically, he finds power implicated in all facets of the creative, sinful, and redemptive processes that make up human history. Tillich's specific definition of power, and the impact that his interpretations of creation, fall, redemption, and eschatology have on his thinking on socio-political power, will become clearer as we examine his treatment more closely.

Power in Relation to Love and Justice. Tillich regards power, along with love and justice, as rooted in the basic structure of reality, that is, in being. He begins his analysis in *Love, Power, and Justice* by focusing on love as the dynamic drive of all being toward reunion of the separated. Yet, power is arguably even more fundamental than justice and love in Tillich's conception, since for him, being itself *is* "the power of being," a power ultimately identifiable as God.[18] This terse formula requires further analysis.

By "power of being" Tillich means the capacity of all that is to affirm itself in spite of the forces of non-being that threaten it. "Non-being" refers to a state in which "what is" is no longer, or to the external and internal forces that tend to produce this state.[19] The condition of finitude, insofar as it signals incomplete and non-

---

[7]By "Spirit" Tillich means the divine presence and activity as it is both immanent in, and transcendent to history. He discusses the Divine Spirit in relation to the notion of "spirit" as a constitutive, *power-bearing* dimension of life in *Systematic Theology*, 3:21-30.

[18]Tillich, *Love, Power, and Justice*, 35-40, esp. 37; *Systematic Theology* 1:235-36, 261. Cf. Pasewark, *Theology of Power*, 245-46.

[19]For Tillich's description of "non-being" and its relation to finitude, see Paul Tillich, *Systematic Theology*, vol. l, *Reason and Revelation; Being and God* (Chicago: The University of Chicago Press, 1951), 186-204.

eternal being, is one in which non-being is an ongoing threat.[20] For persons and societies, power is the ability to combat non-being through participation in the basic life functions of self-integration, self-creation, and self-transcendence. The power that constitutes personal and social being is, most basically, transformative efficacy-- power-to. Power of being also includes elements of power-over insofar as efficacy requires that threats to non-being be resisted or overcome.[21]

Tillich's wide-ranging treatment of power is oriented by his description of its ontological relationship to love and justice. The power of being drives and sustains love and justice. Conversely, power relations must be formed by justice and put in the service of love if power is not to degenerate into oppression or subjugation. These interrelations play an important role in Tillich's social analysis and social ethics.

Tillich believes that most religious social ethicists do not properly construe the relationship between power and love. In the absence of an ontological analysis, power tends to be regarded with distrust, and love is reduced to its emotional or ethical dimensions. Religions which emphasize love are then inclined to belittle political relations for their absorption with power, and to view their own concern with love as utterly distinct from the political. This leads to the separation of the political from the religious and the ethical. Too frequently, the outcome is a politics "of mere compulsion." For Christian social ethics, this will not do.

---

[20]"'Finite' means carrying within one's being the destiny not to be. It designates a limited power of being, limited between a beginning and an end, between non-being before and non-being after . . . ." Tillich, *Love, Power, and Justice*, 39.

[21]So, Richard Grigg argues that the experiential center of Tillich's theological system is in the "phenomenon of empowerment" as a process of human consciousness. "The Experiential Center of Tillich's System," *Journal of the American Academy of Religion* 53/2 (Summer 1985): 251-58.

Constructive social ethics presuppose that one is aware of the element of love in structures of power and of the element of power without which love becomes chaotic surrender. It is the ontological analysis of love and power which must produce this awareness.[22]

In social life, love is expressed in the bonds that unify a group and produce its "communal spirit." Power is found in the intrinsic "power of being" that such a united community emanates, as well as in the structures of authority and enforcement which the group creates to express, preserve, and expand itself.

For Tillich, "justice" refers to the necessary and adequate form within which the power of being is actuated as the drive toward reconciling love.[23] Each being, simply because it *is*, makes a claim for relations within which it can affirm its existence. There can be no fruitful dynamic of self-actualization without an adequate form, and "justice" refers to the form immanent in any instantiation of the power of being.[24] While the term "justice" can be applied to any formed set of relationships, in human relations, justice involves deliberately ordering power according to reflective criteria.

The justice of a flock or a grove of trees is the natural power of the more powerful ones to force their potentialities into actualization against the natural resistance of others. In a human group the relation of the

---

[22]Tillich, *Love, Power, and Justice*, 12-13.

[23]"If life as the actuality of being is essentially the drive towards the reunion of the separated [i.e., toward love], . . . justice of being is the form which is adequate to that movement." Tillich, *Love, Power, and Justice*, 57. Pasewark analyzes the relation between power and justice in Tillich's thought in *Theology of Power*, 291-99.

[24]Tillich, *Love, Power, and Justice*, 67.

members is ordered under traditional rules, conventionally or legally fixed.[25]

In human collectivities, natural asymmetries of power are not erased by means of such rules. Differences in power are reflected in organizational structures, but, when justice is sought, these differences are ordered according to principles deemed conducive to its accomplishment.

> The interpretation of these principles is endlessly varied, but justice itself is the point of identity in all interpretations. . . . According to the polarity of dynamics and form, a social group could not have being without form. And the social group's form is determined by the understanding of justice effective in the group.[26]

The specifics of justice can never be mechanically deduced from pre-set principles or rules, but must be discerned within the dynamics of particular situations.[27]

The ideal toward which love, power, and formal justice ought to conspire in social relations is described by Tillich as "creative justice," that is, "fulfillment within the unity of universal fulfillment. The religious symbol for this is the Kingdom of God."[28] This definition of justice reveals its relation to reconciling love, and its function as providing the normative form for the power of being.[29] In collective life, justice, so defined, is the goal of social and political praxis in the same way that truth is the goal of theory.[30] Yet, under the estranged conditions of existence, every effort to

---

[25]Tillich, *Systematic Theology*, 3:78-79.

[26]Ibid., 79.

[27]Tillich, *Love, Power, and Justice*, 56. For this reason, discerning what is justice in any given instance requires daring and risk.

[28]Ibid., 65.

[29]Ibid., 66-67.

[30]Tillich, *Systematic Theology*, 3:67.

actuate justice is beset by ambiguity and limitation. We shall return to consider the ambiguities of justice, and how Tillich thinks they ought to be addressed, after describing some other constitutive features of his understanding of socio-political power.

Power, Centeredness, and Hierarchy. We have seen that Tillich conceives of power as the dynamic energy that drives the self-integrating, self-altering, and self-transcending processes of life. As such, it is fundamentally power-to. Yet Tillich does posit an element of compulsion in power, for power must be efficacious in spite of resistance by the forces of non-being. To understand the role played by force in Tillich's treatment of socio-political relations, we must examine two other features of his general theory of power: centeredness and hierarchy.

Like Reinhold Niebuhr, Tillich understands power in any context to require and emanate from an organizing center. The more centered an entity is, the more power of being it may have.[31] Far from creating a static or stagnant order, appropriate centering involves a balance among the constitutive elements in any structure of power.

For Tillich all being is characterized by tensive polarities which are in constantly changing states of dialectical interrelation and

---

[31]Tillich, *Love, Power, and Justice*, 44. Speaking of the self, Tillich asserts, "self-centeredness implies the power which the self exercises through a stable balance of its constituent elements over each of [its] elements. In this sense every self is a power structure." Ibid., 53. Balance is achieved among the elements constituting the center either "by the exclusion from the center of many elements which are present in the self [or] by a union of many elements in the center without the exclusion of most of them. Whether self-control is exercised in the former or in the latter way decides about the *ethical* meaning of self-control, the former way for a more puritan, the latter for a more romantic ethics . . . ." Ibid., 52-53. In either case, the basic structure is the same: a dynamic, yet ordered, balancing of the many elements through an orienting "center."

opposition. Individual and communal power relations are pursued within this matrix. In a vision that bears some resemblance to that proffered by Foucault, Tillich portrays power as at the heart of this dynamic process.

> According to the polarity of individualization and participation which characterizes being itself, everything real is an individual power of being within an embracing whole. Within the whole of power the individual can gain or lose power of being. Whether one or another happens is never decided *a priori*, but is a matter of continuous concrete decisions . . . .[32]

Intrinsic to this complex interplay, and complicating it, is what Tillich calls "the hierarchical structure of all life."[33]

Greater centeredness in an organism, person, or group is correlative to greater power of being. And wherever there is centeredness, there is also a hierarchial structure of power.[34] Speaking of social bodies, Tillich insists:

> Even the most egalitarian societies have centers of power and decision, in which the large majority of the people participate only indirectly and in degrees. These centers are strengthened in the moment in which the fullest development of power by a social group is demanded, in

---

[32]Ibid., 43-44.

[33]Ibid., 44.

[34]This combination of dialectical dynamism, centeredness and hierarchy seems odd, since dialectic is a mode that appears to contradict the stability and form indicated by centeredness and hierarchy. But for Tillich this combination expresses the duality of form and vitality that he discerns in all aspects of life, including socio-political life.

emergency situations. The need for an acting center makes even an egalitarian group hierarchical.[35]

In Tillich's view, inequality in social relations is inevitable, and inequality naturally breeds hierarchy. In the process of encounter of power with power that is group life, there will always be some with more power of being than others. Inequality in this sense is neither unjust nor evil, but a fact which makes for the rich diversity and creativity of life. Ethical criteria do apply, however, to the manner in which those with superior power use their advantage in relation to those holding less.

> It is not unjust that in the struggle between power and power one of the beings involved shows a superior power of being. The manifestation of this fact is not unjust but creative. But injustice occurs if in this struggle the superior power uses its power for the reduction or destruction of the inferior power.[36]

Tillich integrates these themes of centeredness, hierarchy, and justice into his descriptive and normative considerations of social and political power.

Socio-Political Power: Distinguishing Features. Tillich views political organization as basic for historical existence, for it is particularly in and through political relations that historical life takes place. The

---

[35]Tillich, *Love, Power, and Justice*, 44-45.

[36]Ibid., 88. He continues: "This can happen in all forms of personal encounters. Most frequent are those forms in which the personal encounter occurs within the frame of an institutional structure and the preservation and growth of the institution give the pretext for unjust compulsion." Tillich's concern with power struggles and with the ways institutional frameworks conspire to transform inequality into exploitation indicate points of intersection with central themes in the work of Foucault.

bi-dimensional power that marks what Tillich calls "history-bearing groups" is analogous to the internal and external aspects of individual power. On the one hand, there needs to be a unifying, centering force that keeps the political community in existence. On the other, there must be the capacity to resist threats from without and to affirm the community through extension and expansion.[37] To assure the presence of each of these dimensions of power, an institutional apparatus is required, and in modern times this is located in the state.[38]   In any large social group, "A State-like organization cannot be avoided."[39]

Though Tillich acknowledges that a group can be seen as a social organism which has in its decision-making organs a kind of centeredness, he resists the tendency to simply personify the state or the nation. "A group is not a person."[40] The fact that a group must depend for its own center upon rulers who will simultaneously seek to actualize their individual power-of-being is a primary source

---

[37]In a lecture delivered during the last year of his life, Tillich argued that socio-political power requires three conditions: first, centeredness in the political sense, "that is, the possibility of acting with *one* will, even if this will is forced by the ruling powers upon the majority of the members against their own will;" second, the possession of a space and the ability to keep it in the face of both inner disintegration and external aggression; and third, the possibility of growth--though he does not define precisely in what growth would consist. Tillich, *Political Expectation*, 114-15, 118-19.

[38]"History-bearing groups . . . must have a centered power which is able to keep the individuals who belong to it united and which is able to preserve its power in the encounter with similar power groups. In order to fulfill the first condition a . . . group must have a central law-giving, administering, and enforcing authority. In order to fulfill the second condition a history-bearing group must have tools to keep itself in power in the encounter with other powers. . . ." Tillich, *Systematic Theology*, 3:309.

[39]Tillich, *Love, Power, and Justice*, 97.

[40]Ibid., 94.

of political power's ambiguity.[41] One consequence of this ambiguity is that oppressive relations of varied sorts pervade even the most "liberal" political systems. Conversely, "a powerless liberalism or anarchism" are often the unintended outcome of efforts to make oppression impossible by constructing social and political orders wherein every chance for domination is removed.[42]

Despite the difficulties and dangers power structures inevitably entail, Tillich rejects the claim that an ideal society is one that abolishes them. Since every socio-political power structure interweaves elements of compulsion with a tensive distinction between the group and those who represent the group as its leaders, injustice is always a threat. But dismantling power structures also leads to injustice, for, "being without a power structure means being without a center of action. It means an agglomeration of individuals without a united power of being and without a uniting form of justice . . . ."[43]

Is socio-political power as Tillich describes it primarily superordination, or communally shared transformative capacity? On many counts, his treatment seems to fit the parameters of our power-over model. Yet several factors qualify this impression, and consonance between Tillich's theory of socio-political power and the basic thrust of his ontological description of power as

---

[41]The leader raised up by the community "represents the center, but he *is* not the center in the way in which his own self is the center of his whole being. The ambiguities of justice which follow from this character of communal centeredness are rooted in the unavoidable fact that the ruler and the ruling group actualize their own power of being when they actualize the power of being of the whole community they represent . . . ." Tillich, *Systematic Theology*, 3:263-64; also, 3:81-83 on the ambiguities of leadership. Maritain's notion of the tensive relation between personality and individuality in pursuit of the common good represents another formulation of this point.

[42]Tillich, *Systematic Theology*, 3:264.

[43]Tillich, *Love, Power, and Justice*, 97. See also, Ibid., 92-93, and Tillich, *Political Expectation*, 117, on the limits of the analogy between individual and social organisms in relation to these matters.

transformative energy. For one thing, the external and internal power of the state, though wielded directly by rulers or ruling groups, nonetheless depends upon and expresses the unity ("eros relations") between group members and the rulers, and among the members of the group. Further, power which imposes, administers and enforces the law--power-over--presupposes a central, ruling group, but rulers' authority must be at least silently acknowledged by the citizenry. "A withdrawal of such silent acknowledgement by the supporters of a power structure undercuts it."[44] In short, power-over relations are derivative of a more basic strength.

> [That strength resides in] unity, an experience of belonging, a form of communal *eros*. Blood relations, language, traditions, and memories create many forms of *eros* which make the power structure possible. Preservation by enforcement and increase by conquest follow, but do not produce, the historical power of a group.[45]

The "power-of-being" of a group plainly includes the manifestation of power-over, but power-of-being can neither be identified with nor be reduced to its coercive or superordinating features. Also fundamental to power are the bonds of union Tillich associates with love. "The element of compulsion in every historical power structure is not its foundation but an unavoidable condition of its existence. It is at the same time the cause of its destruction if the *eros* relations disappear or are completely replaced by force."[46]

---

[44]Tillich, *Systematic Theology*, 3:309.

[45]Ibid.

[46]Ibid. See also, Tillich, *Love, Power, and Justice*, 98: "The silent acknowledgement received by a ruling group from the whole group cannot be understood without an element which is derived . . . from love." Every organism, whether natural or social, "is a power of being and a bearer of an intrinsic claim for justice because it is based on some form of reuniting love. It removes as organism the separatedness of some parts of the world." On the power-over of ruling groups, see *Political Expectation*, 108-11, 118-19,

A third factor mitigating Tillich's contention about the inevitability of hierarchical power-over is his insistence that rulers retain their power--indeed, the social body can continue to exist--only as long as they act on behalf of the whole, and not on behalf of themselves.

> The center of power is only the center of the whole as long as it does not degrade its own centrality by using it for particular purposes. In the moment in which the representatives of the center use the power of the whole for their particular self-realization they cease to be the actual center, and the whole being, without a center, disintegrates.[47]

Certainly, he continues, it is possible for a ruling group to force its will against the desires or good of the community. But this eventually leads to the demise of both leaders and group. "Finally, the loss of the power of the whole, through internal or external causes, is unavoidable."[48] And, in Tillich's formulation, such a loss of power is equivalent to the loss of being/existence itself. A notion of the well-being of the whole, or the "common good", as the legitimating goal of any ruling center is thus entailed in Tillich's conception of the dynamics of hierarchy. Common good, in turn, entails some measure of common power, or power-to.

Finally, Tillich's understanding of authority lends itself to inclusion in a power-to model of social relations. He makes a distinction between authority in fact and authority in principle, or between actual and established authority. Actual authority--authority in fact--tends to be converted into established forms of

---

and 123. "Force serves power;" (123) but power properly construed serves the reconciling aims of love, and does so in the form and measure of justice.

[47]Tillich, *Love, Power, and Justice*, 45. See also, Ibid., 98, on ruling groups' need for acknowledgement by their subjects.

[48]Ibid. 45. The similarities between Tillich's and Hannah Arendt' views on this point are striking.

authority in principle, whereby submission is demanded simply due to the position of the authority holder. Herein lies the ambiguity of authority and its vulnerability to corruption. But authority in fact is a reflection of the cooperative and interdependent nature of human life, and bespeaks the reality of a network of mutual empowerment.

> Authority in principle means that a person has authority by the place he occupies and that he is beyond criticism because of this place. [Examples include the position of the pope as pope, and the authority held by parents over children.] . . . All this "authority in principle" is unjust authority. It disregards the intrinsic claim of human beings to become responsible for ultimate decisions. Quite different is the "authority in fact" which is exercised as well as accepted by each of us in every moment. It is the expression of the mutual dependence of all of us on each other; it is an expression of the finite and fragmentary character of our being, of the limits of our power to stand by ourselves. For this reason it is a just authority.[49]

Power and Democratic Structures. Tillich regards modern democratic forms of government as best suited to fostering common flourishing and to countering the harmful tendencies of social hierarchy and centeredness. In considering the problem of achieving justice through structures of political power, he recognizes the limits set by the need for both consent and enforcement.[50] Within any power structure, sin and finitude pose ubiquitous threats to justice. Yet, under the impact of what Tillich variously calls theonomous forces, "the Spiritual Presence," or the forces of the kingdom of God,

---

[49]Ibid., 89-90.

[50]"You cannot remove silent acknowledgement [consent] and you cannot remove manifest enforcement [force] from any structure of power." Ibid., 94. See also, 96.

members of the ruling group are . . . able to sacrifice their subjectivity in part by becoming objects of their own rule along with all other objects and by transferring the sacrificed part of their subjectivity to the ruled. This partial sacrifice of the subjectivity of the rulers and this partial elevation of the ruled to subjectivity is the meaning of the "democratic" idea.[51]

As valuable as democracy is, its pursuit becomes destructive if it is not clearly recognized that any actual social arrangement requires maintenance, surveillance, and guidance. Tillich considers historical democracies prone to naiveté concerning the dynamics of power structures and ruling groups. In modern western society, there is a widespread assumption that leaders are merely functionaries who wield only that power allotted them by the people. The frequent result is a climate wherein "all the structuring powers of society are denied . . . and repressed."

Nevertheless, they are not absent. For reality is organized structurally, it is not egalitarian and structureless. Even in the most extreme democracies, the state is borne by special groups. Their power is concentrated in special offices. But, in a democracy . . . this . . . remains hidden. It is realized indirectly, without consecration and without law, but therefore no less emphatically.[52]

It would be contrary to the essence of the political community as a justice-bearing body (that is, one that provides a *form* within which common flourishing may be pursued), Tillich asserts, simply to condemn structuring powers. What ought to be condemned are

---

[51]Tillich, *Systematic Theology*, 3:264. This democratic idea is, we should note, neither necessarily identical with any historical democracy, nor necessarily excluded from other forms of government, such as monarchy or aristocracy.

[52]Tillich, *Political Expectation*, 109.

circumstances in which such powers are allowed to operate, "unseen, irresponsibly, and indirectly. Concealed by democracy, they utilize it and undermine it, they bear it and at the same time destroy it."[53] Power-over ignored or denied can be neither criticized nor properly regulated; as such it may exercise a hegemony all the more suffocating for being covert.

God's Kingdom, Political Empire, and Justice. As the final "response" and "solution" to the ambiguities of history, the Jewish and Christian symbol of the Kingdom of God includes an intra-historical or immanent, and a trans-historical or transcendent dimension. Both the transcendent and immanent dimensions of the Kingdom have relevance for politics and historical societies.[54] Tillich argues that God's Kingdom provides hope for resolving the ambiguities of socio-political power inherent in the internal processes of centralizing control, and in the external extension of "empire" that every great society manifests. In keeping with the double thrust of the kingdom symbol, the resolutions Tillich detects reveal both intra-historical and trans-historical dimensions.

A brief look at Tillich's discussion of empire will illustrate his perception of the impact of the theonomous forces of the kingdom on one concrete instance of socio-political power.[55] "Empire" refers to a political community's drive toward universality and totality as it engages in the process of historical self-integration. Though it is never fully achieved, the aim of any historical empire is all-inclusiveness. This drive toward empire is morally ambiguous, however, for it is always motivated at least in part by a will to subjugate and dominate. History attests to any empire's tendency to dehumanize and objectify through violent force the groups it seeks to bring within its sphere of influence. Yet, Tillich contends,

---

[53]Ibid., 110.
[54]Tillich, *Systematic Theology*, 3:385-87.
[55]Ibid., 339-51.

to simply call it a will to power (whether power-to or power-over) does not wholly explain the drive to empire. Another ingredient in this drive is "the vocational self-interpretation of the historical group."[56] Despite its potential for distortion and abuse, this sense of calling has impelled the great empires toward accomplishments redounding to the common good. Amidst empire building, a vocational sense has at times mitigated nations' drive to dominate and provided the impetus for genuine collaboration or inclusivity.[57] Nonetheless, ceaseless vigilance is needed to prevent the quest for empire from degenerating into self-serving power mongering, for "the disintegrating, destructive, and profanizing side of empire-building is as obvious as [many would say more obvious than] the integrating, creative, and sublimating side."[58]

In another discussion of similar themes, Tillich explains that the power of a group resides both in physical force, and in the symbols and ideas, or "spiritual substance," through which the group expresses itself. Consciousness of the latter can become a "feeling of a special vocation" arising out of the group's identity, which in turn gets expressed in ways that unite the group's basic "power drive" (a thrust to expand influence and control based on the ability to compel) with a "vocational consciousness."[59] The implication is that when properly combined with a group's basic power drive, vocational consciousness can mitigate the worst temptations of power and put power in the service of more universal or inclusive goals.

As Tillich describes it, this combination seems to produce a more domesticated or beneficent version of power-over, rather than

---

[56]Ibid., 340.

[57]Tillich argues that the Roman empire's zeal to represent and preserve the law, and the sense of a mission to represent the principle of liberty that has animated the United States' thrust toward empire, are two examples of the positive effects of linking power drive with vocational consciousness. See Tillich, *Systematic Theology*, 3:340; Tillich, *Love, Power, and Justice*, 101-104.

[58]Tillich, *Systematic Theology*, 3:340.

[59]Tillich, *Love, Power, and Justice*, 101-106.

a modification that gives equal priority to the inclusive and collaborative features of power-to. Yet there are plausible grounds for arguing that Tillich believed that the theonomous intrahistorical impact of the kingdom made possible just such modifications. Employing both the power-to and power-over lenses illumines the complex relations between domination and transformative efficacy at work in Tillich's analysis. Regarded from a concern for power-to, however, it must be admitted that the whole notion of "empire" is problematic, inasmuch as Tillich joins it with "conquest" to connote the taking of other lands and peoples by dint of sheer force. Tillich seems ready to deem such taking by force legitimate, especially if the vocational consciousness motivating empire-building is "genuine," or beneficent in its side effects. Peoples who have been on the receiving end of colonial expansion, with or without the aid of a Marxist analysis, might regard the linkage of vocational sense and thirst for conquest in quite a different light.

As we have noted, Tillich perceives the impact of the Kingdom of God on history as double edged, owing to the duality between its political, immanent connotation, and its transcendent, futuristic thrust. On the one hand, the Kingdom means that every social structure is required and enabled to better approximate the essential unity of love, power, and justice that marks human nature and destiny.[60]   On the other hand, within the confines of human existence, social groups will never completely overcome the debilitating effects of estrangement and must therefore see, judge, and act in light of these effects. This means that in concrete situations, tension and conflict will persist among the values of power, love, and justice, and that power will never be wholly separated from the tragic necessity of coercion.[61]

---

[60] In human existence there is estrangement "from that unity of power and love in the form of justice which is the basis for all valuation of justice." Tillich, *Political Expectation*, 119.

[61] Discussing power in light of the Kingdom, Tillich clearly assumes a norm of power without compelling force. Yet elsewhere, he just as clearly argues that a compulsory element is basic to the very meaning of power.

Whenever power of being encounters power of being, compulsion of some sort is inevitable. Tillich deems coercion tragic because to the extent that persons are coerced, they are denied the personhood, the power of being, and the freedom due them. Force only appears non-tragic if we disregard the personal worth and identity of those who are forced. This is exactly what occurs in instances of oppression. But such an interpretation distorts and makes power inauthentic, since, "Genuine power knows the tragic, though unavoidable, character of coercive force."[62]

Does the coercion inherent in social encounters and relations mean that injustice is inevitably implicated in the exercise of socio-political power?

> The answer must be: it is not compulsion which is unjust, but a compulsion which destroys the object of compulsion instead of working towards its fulfillment. . . . It is not compulsion which violates justice, but a compulsion which disregards the intrinsic claim of a being to be acknowledged as what it is within the context of all beings.[63]

This apparent inconsistency might be resolved if we construe Tillich to mean that, while power always includes the *possibility* of coercing, in the ideal conditions of the Kingdom, that possibility would never need to be actuated. This interpretation also seems to cohere with Tillich's understanding of Divine power.

[62]Tillich, *Political Expectation*, 121.

[63]Tillich, *Love, Power, and Justice*, 67-68. He continues: "A power structure in which compulsion works against the intrinsic justice of its elements is not strengthened but weakened. The unacknowledged, justified claims, although suppressed, do not disappear. They . . . may ultimately destroy a power structure which is neither able to accept them as participants, nor able to throw them out as strange bodies. The intrinsic claim in everything that is cannot be violated without violating the violator."

The upshot of this for ethics is that force as an element of power must always be acknowledged, and at the same time every effort must be made to assure that force is curbed, and applied only for the sake of the communal good.

Concluding Remarks. We may conclude with some evaluative comments on the contribution and legacy of this influential twentieth-century theologian. Tillich's use of the term "center"--rather than a term like "head" or "ruler"--to describe the controlling "organ" of the self or of society is intriguing, particularly in light of recent theological efforts to re-conceive notions of social power and authority using images of circles and centers, rather than of pyramids and hierarchies. "Center" imagery may allow a clearer sense of relatedness between center and other dimensions of the circle; it can imply varying degrees of participation in, rather than exclusion from, the coordinating activity of the center.[64] Yet the fact that Tillich employs the center metaphor in tandem with a stress on the hierarchical nature of all complex entities[65] allows more than one potential reading of Tillich on this matter. Since any social encounter involves a meeting of power with power and presupposes some minimal degree of mutual participation, power for Tillich is never a wholly zero-sum and asymmetrical relation between exerciser and recipient. Yet, along with Niebuhr and Foucault, Tillich does perceive reality as a vast, dynamic field of power

---

[64]One example of a Christian feminist who employs "circle" and "center" imagery is Letty Russell, *Household of Freedom: Authority in Feminist Theology* (Philadelphia: Westminster Press, 1987). More on this below.

[65]Tillich's use of "organism" is telling here. Other thinkers who favor organic imagery also assume a link between organic unity and hierarchy. This seems to be the case in strands of romantic philosophy, in certain Pauline texts, and in certain ecclesiological models. Connections between organic bondedness and hierarchy are, however, neither self-evident nor necessary.

struggles, in which "winning and losing" are continual and ever-shifting occurrences.[66]

The multivalent interaction between power-over and power-to in Tillich's thought helps explain the influence his work has had both on Christian thinkers who emphasize superordination, and on those who stress transformative efficacy. Tillich's analysis of the power of being is taken up and transformed into more explicit statements of power-to by some religious feminists, notably by the early Mary Daly. Martin Luther King, Jr.'s delineation of love, power, and justice, and Reinhold Niebuhr's theorizing about power and society both show clear debts to Tillich's thought on these matters.

In Tillich's complex religious vision, power joins love and justice to form the metaphysical matrix within which intrapersonal, interpersonal, socio-political, humanity-cosmos, and humanity-God relationships take place. As essential structures, power, love, and justice are also norms for these relationships. Their presence in all relationships assures analogous features to power's appearance in different arenas, whether intrapersonal, interpersonal, or socio-political. Furthermore, to violate the normative structures of justice, power, or love is always in the end to contravene the necessary conditions for flourishing of the party who so violates. This is so because of the unity of being within which Tillich situates all particular existents. In this ontological web, the coherence of the whole realm of moral activity with respect to power depends,

---

[66]Jack A. Keller, Jr., in "Niebuhr, Tillich, and Whitehead on the Ethics of Power," *American Journal of Theology and Philosophy* 7:3 (September, 1986): 134-148, argues that Tillich's treatment of power supersedes that of Reinhold Niebuhr by more adequately focusing on power's intrinsically valuable and non-competitive features. However, Tillich's insistence on centeredness renders his perspective on inter-group relations problematic. "Tillich is committed to an ontology that tends to absolutize centeredness and that makes difficult a pluralistic concept of the good world as a harmony of diverse groups." Ibid., 139. Keller suggests a Whiteheadean corrective to this deficiency in Tillich.

finally, upon "the Spiritual Power," or "the Spiritual Presence," that is, God as the Power of Being, the source and ground of love, and the sustainer of justice.

Process Theologies of Social Power

Paul Tillich's ontologically founded interpretation of socio-political power has been enormously influential among Christian social ethicists. Contemporary process philosophy, especially the writings of Alfred North Whitehead, have provided some North American theologians and ethicists with a different ontologically-based way to envisage power as something other than domination. One process-oriented social ethicist is Bernard Loomer, who presents a theory of power animated by the thesis that, "the nature and role of relationships determine both the level of human fulfillment that is possible and the conception of power that is to be practiced."[67]

Bernard Loomer. Loomer believes that the common portrayal of power in popular and scholarly contexts is based upon a unilateral understanding of the relationships involved, and that a more adequate, relational theory is required for social and religious theory and ethics.

"Unilateral power" is one-directional and makes the other a function of one's own ends. The one exercising unilateral power aims to have the largest possible effect on others while being minimally influenced by them. Power and self-worth are measured

---

[67]Bernard M. Loomer, "Two Kinds of Power," Inaugural Lecture of the D. R. Sharpe Lectureship on Social Ethics. *Criterion* 15 (Winter 1976): 13. John B. Cobb, Jr. places Loomer within the context of process theology and the "Chicago school" in *Process Theology as Political Theology* (Philadelphia: Westminster Press, 1982), 36-38. Keller elaborates the Whiteheadean metaphysics of Loomer's theory of power in "The Ethics of Power," 139-41.

by how much one can do "a" as compared to how much others can do "a." One party's gain in power is thus experienced as a diminishment of the other's self-worth. Since power is seen as the exercise of influence or control, to be on the receiving end of such influence is the very definition of weakness.

What Loomer describes fits very well our model of power-over. This prevalent view, he avers, is philosophically inadequate, for it rests on a faulty anthropology. It is theologically inaccurate because it is rooted in a misguided apprehension of the power of God and God's commerce with the world. And, because it orients action on the basis of perverted theology and deficient philosophy, the unilateral view of power is ethically deleterious. It both presupposes and promotes the alienation of persons from each other, and as such it promotes the corruption of humans and their relationships. A relational view of power, Loomer contends, proves a better way to unravel the descriptive and normative dimensions of power in social relations.

The core of "relational power" is the capacity to both give and undergo effects. Recalling that one of the classic philosophical definitions of power is *the ability to receive an influence*, Loomer insists that both receptivity and activity characterize genuine power.[68] "Power is the capacity to sustain a mutually internal relationship."

This is a relationship of mutually influencing and being influenced, of mutually giving and receiving, of mutually making claims and permitting and enabling others to make their claims. This is a relation of mutuality which embraces all the dimensions and kinds of inequality that the human spirit is heir to. The principle of equality most profoundly means that we are all equally dependent on the constitutive relationships that create us, however relatively unequal we are in our various strengths, including our ability to

---

[68]Keller attributes this dual description of power as both active and receptive to Plato, *Sophist* 247D-E. Ibid., 139-40.

exemplify the fullness and concreteness of this kind of power.[69]

Loomer notes that a particular anthropology and sociology underlie the notion of power as relational. The foundation of relational power lies in the "constitutive role of relationships in the creation of individuals and societies. The individual is a communal individual."[70] Relational power presumes a communal conception of the self that contrasts sharply with the "non-relational or substantive" view of the self that has dominated the history of western thought, and that undergirds notions of unilateral power."[71]

Loomer's relational view of power offers a fresh perspective on two related issues: the common good, and inequality. Loomer argues that a dimension of equality or mutuality is indispensable to relational power. At the same time, he acknowledges that inequality is a "bed-rock condition" decisive for human relationships. With Tillich, Loomer regards concrete inequalities among persons as ineradicable, and even necessary, although they are the source of ambiguity and the context for potential injustice. "The general condition of inequality . . . is a necessary component in the division of labor and in the variety of creative capacities."[72] Loomer deems this fact part of the meaning of human finitude.

In cases of unilateral power, inequalities are inevitably exploited at the expense of those who are less advantaged in any particular situation; the result is injustice. The practice of relational power involves the hope that we may learn to interrelate inequalities so that, rather than being competitive and zero-sum, they can become mutually enhancing.[73]

---

[69]Loomer, "Two Kinds of Power," 23.

[70]Ibid., 21.

[71]Ibid., 21-22.

[72]Ibid., 25.

[73]Ibid.

Turning to the Christian tradition, Loomer discovers in the biblical figure of the suffering servant a model for relational power's response to inequality. As a bearer of relational power, the suffering servant is not one who passively undergoes the effects of sinful, exploitative forms of unilateral power, but rather the one--person or community--who develops the "stature" or "size" to absorb and creatively respond to hate and evil in ways that might enable their transformation.[74]

Even in communities that struggle for mutuality, inequalities will persist, along with the temptation to exploit them. This means that there is an unfairness to life that even our best efforts cannot overcome. Our way of responding to this unfairness will depend on whether we have embraced a unilateral understanding of self, community, and power, or a relational one.

> In the life of unilateral power the unfairness means that the stronger are able to control and dominate the weaker and thereby claim their disproportionate share of the world's goods and values. In the life of relational power, the unfairness means that those of larger size must undergo greater suffering and bear a greater burden in sustaining those relationships which hopefully may heal the brokenness of the seamless web of interdependence in which we all live. "Of those to whom much is given, much is expected."[75]

Loomer's words about brokenness and the need to rediscover a "seamless web of interdependence" reflect his acknowledgment, in accord with the Christian doctrine of sin, that the present order is ambiguous and estranged. Relational power is seen as a way to and a sign of a renovated world, one symbolized in Christianity as the kingdom of God. Those with the courage and "size" to pursue the

---

[74]Ibid., 28.
[75]Ibid.

way of relational power practice an eschatological ethic that carries no guarantee for success under the conditions of historical existence.[76] The Christian symbol of the cross evokes the price in pain and suffering paid by those who consistently practice relational power amidst this-worldly values and structures. Relational power is an eschatological norm, whose demands can never be perfectly fulfilled in history.

John B. Cobb.   Unfortunately, Bernard Loomer leaves this provocative discussion of power without specifically addressing how the relational model ought to affect the exercise of power in social and political structures.   John B. Cobb, in *Process Theology as Political Theology*, gives more direct attention to the implications of process theological thinking for political theory and practice. Cobb's picture of power's operation in the concrete circumstances of historical life bears similarities to the portrayal offered by Tillich. In a chapter entitled "The Politics of Political Theology," Cobb examines basic Christian affirmations about the person and society, and their implications for political and economic theory and practice, in light of a process theological viewpoint informed by Whitehead.   For our purposes, Cobb's discussion of the communality of human life and of the role of coercion in political life are most pertinent.

While acknowledging the value placed on the individual in Christian theology, Cobb insists that in fact, Christian teaching falls more heavily on the side of human solidarity.[77]   Nonetheless, a purely collectivist theory does not properly illumine the Biblical meaning. Cobb suggests that the conception offered by Whitehead is more useful. For Whitehead, the individual is constituted by its relations and exists solely as a creative synthesis of these relations. In any usage or sense, the idea of an individual apart from relations

---

[76]Ibid., 29.

[77]Cobb, *Process Theology*, 95-96.

to community is nonsensical. "Persons are communal beings. Rich experience is possible only in community with others whose experiences are rich."[78]

Cobb points out that contemporary western political economies obscure the communal nature of the self by positing *homo economicus* as the disconnected individual who constantly seeks competitive advantage over his or her fellows. Cobb agrees that competition is a fact of life, but argues that it is damaging to elevate it, as standard economic theory and practice are wont to do, to *the* fact of life. To do so falsely universalizes the standard economic assumption that to be a rational agent is always to seek to maximize one's gains, and that the gains of one person are acquired generally at the expense of other persons.[79]

Cobb urges that relational thinking be substituted for the atomistic and zero-sum assumptions that prevail in standard economics, and which then spill over into understandings of political life. A relational lens uncovers previously concealed connections between agents, and the fact that individual well-being is deeply linked to the well-being of others. Once this recognition dawns, it can begin to influence social theory and practice in salutary ways. At work in Cobb's argument is a process version of the common good which contains a claim that genuine flourishing resides in "richness of experience," a richness only possible for the most deeply related among us.

> The point here is simply that since the richness of our experience depends upon the richness of the experience of others with whom we associate, the growth of our good is a function not primarily of competitive advantage but of communal well-being.[80]

---

[78]Ibid., 96-97. Cf. Keller, "The Ethics of Power," 146-48.
[79]Cobb, *Process Theology*, 97.
[80]Ibid., 98.

The implications of Cobb's position for a theory of socio-political power are not difficult to surmise. The economic notion of the self that he is criticizing most often incorporates a notion of power as power-over. Conversely, the relational view that he judges most descriptively accurate and evaluatively fruitful for Christian political and economic practice implies an understanding of power as communally generated and mutually exercised, ideas congenial to the power-to model. Cobb does not deny the realities of scarcity, conflict and opposition, and, with Whitehead, he is attuned to the existence of power-over in socio-political relations. Nonetheless, power-to rests at the heart of his process-oriented anthropology and sociology.

The normative priority Cobb accords to power-to is reflected in his treatment of a Christian response to coercion and violence in social life. Notwithstanding a long history of the conditional approval of violence and coercion by the Christian community, the weight of Christian teaching has fallen on the value of human life and the undesirability of violence against persons. No society, Cobb assumes, can exist "without some measure of coercion and some measure of persuasion."[81] On this matter, Cobb again urges a Whiteheadean reformulation for Christian social ethics.

Whitehead's view, restated by Cobb, is that dominance and coercion cannot be completely eschewed, but that the worth of a particular social arrangement increases to the degree that coercive elements are minimized and persuasive elements maximized:

> The compulsory dominance of men over men has a double significance. It has a benign effect so far as it secures the coordination of behavior necessary for social welfare. But it is fatal to extend this dominion beyond the barest limits necessary for this coordination. The progressive societies

---

[81]Ibid., 106.

are those which most decisively have trusted themselves to [the] way of persuasion . . . .[82]

The normative status given to persuasive power reflects process theology's apprehension of God's own posture and activity.[83] This norm, Cobb claims, sets the agenda for socio-political practice: to continually work toward social relationships and policies oriented by persuasion rather than coercion.

The only power that is truly creative is persuasive power, and this power is exercised in supreme and ultimate fashion by God. . . . If we would be perfect as God is perfect, then we will undertake vigorously to affect the course of events creatively, and that means by persuasion. We will construct institutions that encourage persuasive relationships and provide a context in which the possibility of such relationships is safeguarded. We will also realize that this entails the construction of a society in which the natural necessities of life are provided for all as easily and freely as possible so that the needs of survival will not dominate human activity.[84]

---

[82]Alfred North Whitehead, *Adventures of Ideas* (New York: The Free Press, 1933), 108-109. Quoted in Cobb, *Process Theology*, 106. Lois Gehr Livesey agrees, and provides a feminist development of the Whiteheadean "paradigm of persuasion as the normative expression of power" in "Women, Power, and Politics: Feminist Theology in Process Perspective," *Process Studies* 17:2 (Summer 1988): 73.

[83]Following Whitehead, process theologians reject the doctrine of divine impassibility "in favor of a doctrine of divine suffering and joy in solidarity with the world." See the elaboration of God as "Holy Advocate" in Livesey, "Women, Power, and Politics," 75-76; also, Sheila Greeve Davaney, *Divine Power: A Study of Karl Barth and Charles Hartshorne* (Philadelphia: Fortress Press, 1986), chs. 5, 6.

[84]Cobb, *Process Theology*, 107-108. Cobb elaborates the economic dimensions of such a society in Herman E. Daly & John B. Cobb, Jr., *For*

Underlying Cobb's last point is the significant insight that in situations where the basic needs of some go unmet, conflict and resort to coercion are more likely. In particular, when the needs of survival "dominate human activity," the pursuit of persuasive power arrangements is impeded. Hannah Arendt incorporates a similar concern in her distinction between labor, by which humans try to dominate or are dominated by the biological necessities of life, and action, in which humans collaboratively generate power-to. Both Cobb and Arendt--along with Marx--recognize that political power that is transformative, mutual, and non-coercive thrives best in conditions of widely distributed material sufficiency. Where such sufficiency is lacking for some or all, greater manifestation of power-over is reliably, if not certainly, predictable.[85]

To conclude, Bernard Loomer and John Cobb are representative of a range of thinkers whose treatments of the theology and ethics of power are influenced by process philosophy. Our brief examination of these two figures suggests that process treatments of power tend toward a theologically-grounded, comprehensive understanding of power that gives central place to power-to, and orients power-over in service to interdependent forms of transformative efficacy.[86]

The Common Good (Boston: Beacon Press, 1989). The authors treat forms of power (both power-to and power-over) in Ibid., 182-89.

[85]The extent to which Cobb perceives power-over as necessary for pursuing material sufficiency is unclear. Arendt judges a sort of power over *the material world* proper and necessary to labor, dovetailing with Engels, who speaks of superseding the domination of men, while continuing to perfect the domination of nature. More recently, feminists and ecological ethicists have questioned the accuracy and morality of a dual standard concerning power-over in the natural and human communities. See Daly & Cobb, *Common Good*, 190-94, 364.

[86]See, e.g., Arthur McGill, *Suffering: A Test of Theological Method* (Philadelphia: Westminster Press, 1982); and the work of feminists influenced by process thought such as Davaney and Livesey.

Among the strengths of process approaches is their systematic attention to receptivity as an element of power. This accent, less explicit in other power-to treatments such as Arendt's, springs from a profoundly relational anthropology and theology. Loomer's description of power as the capacity to sustain a mutually internal relationship also contributes toward a substantive formulation of mutuality, a pivotal notion for many feminist theologians and ethicists.[87] Process formulations may also shed fresh light on the meaning of solidarity, which has emerged as an important ethical category in recent liberationist and Roman Catholic social thought. These distinctive features commend process theological interpretations to the serious consideration of Christian social ethicists concerned with power.

Ontological Theologies of Social Power: Critical Summary

Tillich and process theologians share the conviction that the issue of power is best understood from a metaphysical or ontological perspective, articulated in vocabulary and categories informed by modern philosophy. Both Tillich and process writers distinguish between the normative face of power, which they ground in divine agency, and power relations under the finite and fallen conditions of actual social life, where coercion remains a tragic necessity.

Their approaches also differ. Despite Tillich's elaboration of power as the preserving and transforming capacity characterizing being itself, his political theory more clearly incorporates the features of hierarchy and control characterizing power-over. Process thinkers like Loomer and Cobb acknowledge the inevitability of compulsion in social life, yet make its minimization a primary goal. Tillich is more prone to regard compulsion and hierarchy as natural

---

[87]On this see Dawn M. Nothwehr, OSF, "'Mutuality' as a Formal Norm for Christian Social Ethics," Unpublished Ph.D. dissertation, Marquette University, 1995.

and for that reason positive features of social relations.[88] As a group, these thinkers challenge Christian ethicists to address and clarify the metaphysical underpinnings and implications of experiences and theories of socio-political power. For those developing a comprehensive, power-to focused ethical analysis, their thought offers rich resources.

Liberationist Approaches to Power

"Liberation theology" refers to a diverse literature that has sprung up within Christian scholarship during the past three decades. Here I shall use the term "liberation" and "liberationist" to designate not only third world theologians, but also a range of North American Christian writers who, despite significant differences, share a number of fundamental theoretical and practical allegiances.[89]

First, Christian liberationists depart from the concerns and methodological assumptions that, since the Enlightenment, have shaped the agenda of the theological academy in Western Europe and North America. Mainstream post-Enlightenment theology has sought to respond to the crisis of belief that accompanied the rise of modernity, and to do so in ways sensitive to modern concerns with scientific objectivity and analysis, value neutrality, and

---

[88]Given Tillich's emphasis upon being-itself, the fact that the capacity to compel is an inescapable feature of existence lends it a certain normativity. On this reading, the potential for compulsion is a feature of all power, and therefore a feature of all life, and a capacity of God. Process-oriented thinkers join others who take a different theological tack. McGill, for instance, re-articulates the doctrine of God's omnipotence, claiming that, "Force is no attribute of God." *Suffering*, ch. 4. Cf. Wendy Farley, *Tragic Vision and Divine Compassion* (Louisville, KY: Westminster Press, 1990).

[89]A concise entry into liberation theologians' concerns and methods is Leonardo & Clodovis Boff, *Introducing Liberation Theology*, trans. Paul Burns (Maryknoll, NY: Orbis Books, 1987).

universalizable claims. Liberation theology and ethics is affected by theoretical and practical sources that cast suspicion on each of these concerns.

Liberation thinkers write amidst, and in response to, conditions of systemic, collectively experienced suffering--most often, humanly-wrought suffering--that continue to ravage the life-chances of so many in the contemporary world. It is this crisis, liberationists argue, that ought to animate Christian thought and practice, and to the extent that it genuinely does so, both are irrevocably changed.[90] To do theology and ethics from the perspective of those on the "underside of history" requires attention to the concrete particularities of believers' social, cultural, economic and interpersonal contexts, and especially to the dynamics of domination and subordination that shape them.

At least two methodological ramifications follow from this. First, rather than simply abstracting from the concrete and particular to reach the general or the ideal, the liberation theologian maintains an explicit commitment to doing theology for and in a particular concrete situation and community. This commitment to the particular makes for an irreducible plurality of liberation theologies. Second, theology in this key is by necessity not detached or value-neutral, but an enterprise of advocacy, pursued in solidarity with the suffering community. Transformative

---

[90]Despite liberationism's unabashedly normative tone, a systematic ethics of liberation has been slow to emerge. See Douglas Sturm, "Praxis and Promise: On the Ethics of Political Theology," *Ethics* 92 (July 1982): 733-50. In various streams of Christian liberationism, there has recently been growing attention to elaborating this ethical agenda. See, e.g., José Miguez Bonino, *Toward a Christian Political Ethics* (Philadelphia: Fortress Press, 1983); Enrique Dussel, *Ethics and Community* (Maryknoll, NY: Orbis Books, 1988); Katie Geneva Cannon, *Black Womanist Ethics* (Atlanta, GA: Scholars Press, 1988); Sharon D. Welch, *A Feminist Ethic of Risk* (Minneapolis: Fortress Press, 1990).

praxis is the ongoing source and purpose of theology and ethics seen in this light.[91]

Liberation theologians offer a number of specifically religious warrants for their stance. Their characteristic insistence on the need for solidarity with victims, often called the "preferential option for the poor and oppressed," is grounded in an interpretation of the divine activity and command as embodied in the Exodus God and in Jesus Christ. Christians must be in solidarity with victims because God is so. Solidarity propels believers into a dynamic process that leads from identification and denunciation of sources of victimization (articulated in terms of oppressive power-over), to annunciation of God's demands and promises in the face of injustice, and action to abolish or renovate structures and patterns that create, perpetuate and maintain oppression. Thus is embodied, in the practices of solidaristic communities, the prophetic impulse that vivifies Jewish and Christian biblical faith.

Along with the preferential option for the poor and oppressed, the eschatological symbol of the Kingdom of God is a central religious notion for liberationists. The fullness of reconciliation, justice, and peace denoted by God's reign is depicted as a future possibility that impinges upon every dimension of present human life, requiring practical response. From this perspective, the litmus test for Christian discipleship is less orthodoxy, or correct belief, than orthopraxis, practice that joins believers in the struggle to promote God's kingdom through peace- and justice-seeking activity.[92] This eschatological/prophetic orientation is reflected in

---

[91]See Thomas L. Schubeck, S.J.'s chapters on "praxis" as a central category for liberation theology in his helpful study, *Liberation Ethics: Sources, Models, and Norms* (Minneapolis: Fortress Press, 1993), 37-86.

[92]Liberation theologians have sought to articulate the relationship between human activity and the accomplishment of the kingdom in a way that avoids Pelagianism yet fosters justice-seeking action. Rather than viewing salvation history and secular history as firmly distinguished "planes," these thinkers argue that history is one; hence, such simple separations are neither possible nor desirable. See esp., Gustavo Gutierrez, *A Theology of*

the critical and action-directed features of liberation theology, and in the strong ethical sensibilities that animate it.

Besides religious sources, liberation thinkers rely on social theory and analysis to illumine the particularities of their situations. Here the direct or indirect influence of Marxism is frequently evident, especially in liberationists' use of ideology critique, their emphasis on the material and economic dimensions of victimization, and their acknowledgement of systemic conflict and the need for struggle and confrontation in the face of oppression.

The distinctive outlook we have been describing is summarized in the complex meaning attributed to "liberation" by these Christians. The definition of liberation offered by Gustavo Gutierrez in his groundbreaking work, *A Theology of Liberation*, has become a *locus classicus*, and expresses an understanding echoed by the writers considered here.[93] Liberation, Gutierrez urges, is the most appropriate way to apprehend the meaning of the Christian doctrine of redemption for today. Liberation/redemption is constituted by three distinct but interlocked and interpenetrating dimensions of meaning: a spiritual dimension, an institutional dimension that encompasses social, political, and economic structures, and an anthropological or historical dimension. Each of these involves both individual and collective components. For a genuinely redemptive or liberative process to occur, all three dimensions must be addressed. In each, one can discern a normative stance against power-over insofar as it is the instrument of exploitation and division, and in favor of power-to that expresses solidarity and justice.

Liberation: History, Politics, and Salvation, Sister Caridad Inda and John Eagleson, tr. and ed. (Maryknoll, NY: Orbis Books, 1973), chs. 5 & 11. Cf. Dean Brackley, "Salvation and the Social Good in Maritain and Gutierrez," (Ph.D. dissertation, University of Chicago: 1980).

[93]Gutierrez, *Theology of Liberation*, 36-37, 176-78. Schubeck elaborates Gutierrez's meaning in relation to praxis, and to the wider literature of Latin American liberation theology in *Liberation Ethics*, 52-57.

The first aspect of liberation, the spiritual, is described in traditional doctrinal language: humanity is freed from the bondage of sin and reconciled with God, self, and others through the gracious action of Jesus Christ. Since sin affects not simply individuals but whole cultural patterns and institutional structures, spiritual liberation assumes a collective and public dimension as well as an individual sense. Jesus Christ, liberator, is the essential foundation for all other facets of liberation.

Social, political and economic meanings of liberation are intertwined with spiritual meanings since, for liberationists, human beings and their history can not be divided into asymmetrically valued material and spiritual compartments. "History is one," so the gospel message of freedom from sin and its effects necessarily includes the renovation of warped social, political, and economic relations.[94] Gutierrez emphasizes that liberation cannot be reduced to the political or economic, but it cannot fail to include them and still be genuine.

The third dimension of liberation, called the anthropological or historical, serves as a hinge between the first two, for it highlights the persons involved in the emancipatory process. It also brings liberationists' concern with empowerment of people more clearly into focus. Anthropological liberation consists of the transformation of victims from the status of objects of history to that of subjects. It involves the movement of persons and groups from passivity, isolation, helplessness, and despair, to activity, solidarity, competence, and hope. The empowerment envisaged here is not simply power to resist and destroy unjust structures, though it includes that. It is also the discovery and actuation of the efficacy of individuals in community, power-to.

Taken together, these three dimensions form a picture of liberation that is encompassing and complex. It is one that catches up modern concerns for freedom and reshapes them in deeply biblical and communal ways. Though not explicitly acknowledged

---

[94]Gutierrez, *Theology of Liberation*, 153. See n. 93, above.

by Gutierrez or others, their portrayal of liberation also implies and requires the multifaceted, nuanced and comprehensive approach to power being advanced here.

Along with its formulation of redemption in terms of empowering liberation as presented by Gutierrez, several issues and problems characteristic of Latin American liberation theology are instructive for understanding the discussions about power in liberationist Christian social ethics generally.

First, a strong emphasis on empowerment is undermined at points by an insufficiently differentiated use of the term, power. This is, in part, reflective of still-developing state of liberation ethics.[95] Douglas Sturm notes that Latin American liberation theologians view the central moral problem of the modern age as the crippling dependency of the oppressed on dominative social, political, and economic arrangements. Liberation involves breaking free from this dependency and pursuing the genuine moral purpose of human existence, community in which is made present "the active solidarity of love."[96] Liberation theologians like Gutierrez and José Miguez Bonino reveal considerable moral sophistication in their engagement with political movements, in their specifications of central political and moral crises, and in setting forth alternative political orientations in general terms. "But one can fault [liberation theology] for its failure to formulate principles out of its praxis from which concrete historical options might be identified and developed, even if such options are held to be always in some tension with the ultimate moral purpose of universal solidarity."[97] Sturm puts his finger on the challenge faced by a liberationist ethics of socio-political power: to develop norms and practices whereby an

---

[95]Sturm, "Praxis and Promise," 736-38. To give only one example of this undifferentiated usage, see José Comblin, *The Church and the National Security State* (Maryknoll, NY: Orbis, 1979), ch 4. See also, n. 91 above.

[96]Jose Miguez Bonino, *Christians and Marxists: The Mutual Challenge to Revolution* (Grand Rapids, MI: William G. Eerdmans Publishing Co., 1976), 158. Cited in Sturm, "Praxis and Promise," 747.

[97]Sturm, "Praxis and Promise," 748.

eschatological vision of healed power relationships can effectively inform transformative engagement with the power dynamics of a history affected by sin.

The struggle for liberation, these authors imply, involves finding concrete ways to replace antagonistic power-over with shared empowerment. Gutierrez's very definition of liberation signals this close bond between emancipation and empowerment, especially on the second, historical-anthropological level of liberation. Genuine emancipation, it would seem, implies a redistribution of power whereby dominant minorities no longer hold power over all others, but instead power is widely diffused and cooperatively exercised. Among the liberationists he studies, Sturm detects a preference for some form of democratic socialist political economy, which many regard as offering the greatest hope for wedding empowerment with freedom in community.[98]

Power-related questions that continue to vex Latin American liberation theologians are relevant in varying degrees to all the liberationist views we shall consider. First, there is the question of precisely how a Christian ethic is to relate and distinguish freedom and power. In the context of struggle for change, the appropriate relations between emancipation and resistance, freedom and communal efficacy, constitute pressing practical as well as theoretical issues.

Liberationists also need to clarify an ethics of the use of power for social change that addresses the relation between means and ends, and, in this vein, the question of the legitimacy of violence. This problem is felt especially keenly by people in situations of extreme political instability or repression, or harsh divisions between material and social privilege and deprivation. What specific sorts of social goals with respect to power does liberation require? What uses of power constitute legitimate means to such

---

[98]See, e.g., Gutierrez, *Theology of Liberation*, 237; José Miguez Bonino, *Toward a Christian Political Ethics* (Minneapolis: Fortress Press, 1983), 77-78. Forms of democratic socialism are also frequently recommended by North American liberation theologians, e.g. Cornel West, Rosemary Ruether.

change? For too many suffering people, these questions are literally matters of life and death. The ways particular liberationist treatments of power cast such questions may in part depend on the intensity of the crisis of suffering being experienced by their people, and the availability of peaceful avenues for transformation. So, in North America Martin Luther King, Jr. and many feminists attempt to wed radical reform and non-violent resistance, while in other circumstances, some liberationists argue that empowerment must entail social revolution, accompanied by justifiable uses of violence.

African American Liberationists

The treatments of power found in selected writings of James H. Cone and Martin Luther King, Jr. provide a window on the teeming upsurge of reflection and action among African American Christians that began earlier in this century and reached a watershed in the 1950s, '60s and early '70s. As is well known, the Rev. Martin Luther King, Jr. became the acknowledged leader of the civil rights drives in the southern United States during the later 1950s and 1960s. King's public life was marked by three orienting commitments: to Christian love, to the principles of U.S. constitutional democracy, and to non-violent methods for bringing about justice, defined in terms of empowered freedom and substantive equality, for black Americans.

After impressive success with this approach in the southern United States, in the 1960s King and such organizations as the Southern Christian Leadership Conference (SCLC) and the Student Non-violent Coordinating Committee (SNCC) moved on to confront racist structures, especially in the areas of education and housing, in the north. To the shock of many, and the profound disillusionment of many more, the previous decade of legal and political progress in the south had little impact on the intransigent combination of *de facto* institutional segregation and racist attitudes that King and his movement encountered in northern cities like

Chicago and Detroit.[99] One response to frustrations encountered in the drive for civil rights during the latter half of the 1960s was a growing conviction, particularly among some of the younger followers of King, that black *power*, not black freedom, was the appropriate theme for this new stage of their struggle. Armed with the battle cry, "Black Power Now!", an increasingly militant wing emphasized black identity and black rights over against white power and oppression.[100] Those advocating "black power" defined it variously, but James Cone captures the heart of the matter when he says that black power means, "complete emancipation of black people from white oppression by whatever means black people deem necessary."[101] A comparison between Cone's religious-ethical concept of black power and that put forth by King illuminates an important and historically significant instance of the struggle to define liberative notions of power in the North American setting. For purposes of focus and because of their chronological proximity, this analysis will concentrate upon King's 196 work, *Where Do We Go From Here: Chaos or Community?*, and Cone's first book, *Black Theology and Black Power*, published in 1969.

Martin Luther King, Jr. King's last full length book devotes a chapter to the issue of black power. There King proposes a positive

---

[99]For an in-depth analysis of the history of the civil rights drives in Chicago during the 1960s and their aftermath, see Alan B. Anderson and George Pickering, *Confronting the Color Line: The Broken Promise of the Civil Rights Movement in Chicago* (Macon, GA: University of Georgia Press, 1987).

[100]Both King and Cone chronicle these developments. See Martin Luther King, Jr., *Where Do We Go From Here: Chaos or Community?* (Boston: Beacon Press, 1968), 23-32; James H. Cone, *For My People: Black Theology and the Black Church* (Maryknoll, NY: Orbis Books, 1984), 54-59.

[101]James Cone, *Black Theology and Black Power* (New York: Seabury Press, 1969), 6.

meaning to the notion that explicitly seeks to counter what he viewed as the negative and destructive tendencies of the "black power" ideology emerging among disaffected members of his non-violent movement in the later 1960s. Interestingly, King recounts (as does Cone) the eruption of the new symbol for black justice with the rejection of the movement's battle cry, "freedom now," in favor of the "black power now" slogan by some of the participants in the March for Freedom through Mississippi, following the shooting of James Meredith in the summer of 1966. For black power advocates, to speak of freedom without clear reference to power no longer adequately expressed the goals toward which racially marginalized persons were pressing. This rearticulation of the agenda for racial justice provoked consternation and fear among many in the white community, who read separatist and violent connotations into the change of emphasis. Far from denying such implications, many proponents of black power embraced them.

King sympathized with the frustration that he believed had prompted the militant version of black power then being touted by Stokely Carmichael and others. He also acknowledged the need for Afro-Americans to think and act in terms not simply of freedom, but also of power. Yet he stridently disagreed with the militants' interpretation of power in terms of separation, dominance, and even violence. In *Where Do We Go From Here?*, King sets forth a picture of black power that reveals his understanding of genuine power as collaborative, non-violent transformative energy.

King's interpretation of black power includes three interrelated features: prophetic denunciation of injustice perpetrated by a white power structure against African Americans; the amassing by African Americans of communal strength to achieve goals; and self-affirmation and self-assertion of black communal identity and worth. He speaks, first, of deep disappointment with, and prophetic condemnation of, the failure of white power-over to achieve justice on the political, cultural, economic, religious and social fronts.[102]

---

[102]King, *Where Do We Go?*, 32-36.

To this extent, black power pits itself over and against the evils of whites' historical hegemony over all these areas.

But this denunciation is grounded in a second, more substantive understanding of black power as the amassing by Afro-Americans of communal strength in order to attain shared goals--in our terms, power-to. "Power, properly understood, is the ability to achieve purpose. It is the strength required to bring about social, political, or economic changes. In this sense power is not only desirable but necessary in order to implement the demands of love and justice."[103] For King, love involves persons in a network of mutual concern and interdependence that provides the matrix for individual and social flourishing. In a formulation bearing the imprint of the thought of Paul Tillich, King argues that love requires the dynamic energy of power to be effective, and power needs the discipline of love in order to be just. "Power at its best is love implementing the demands of justice. Justice at its best is love correcting everything that stands against love."[104]

In King's estimation, there is nothing essentially wrong with power; problems arise when power is maldistributed, for then those with greater power-over can achieve goals without concern for the community, and those without power-over are constrained to rely on persuasion and ineffectual appeals to love in their efforts to attain their legitimate aspirations. This sort of collision of "immoral power" with "powerless morality" constitutes the major crisis of our times.[105] Yet to think about power solely in terms of a struggle for dominance, King declares, betrays a misunderstanding that yields a morally deficient framework for addressing socio-political problems.

To overcome this deficiency, a theory of power that unites a

---

[103]Ibid., 37.

[104]Ibid. King's encounters with the thought of Tillich, Reinhold Niebuhr, and forms of personalist philosophy during his studies at Boston University are traced in John J. Ansbro, *Martin Luther King, Jr.: The Making of a Mind* (Maryknoll, NY: Orbis Books, 1984).

[105]King, *Where Do We Go?*, 37.

moral concern for love and justice with practical efficacy is needed. King was convinced that the appropriate means for wedding power with love and justice in the public arena was the organized application of non-violent pressure. Non-violent direct action was a method that allowed people to exercise power for the sake of liberation, while paving the way toward reconciliation among oppressors and oppressed. This made it the essential strategy on the way to justice for Afro-Americans. Justice, King repeatedly stressed, would be served neither by separation from the white community, nor by black domination or violent destruction of whites. In *Where Do We Go From Here* King works to dissuade his readers from these latter strategies, especially the recourse to violence.

King raises two objections against the use of violence: it is impractical and it is immoral. On the first count, King makes the prudential point that since blacks are greatly outnumbered, any attempt at violent rebellion would be summarily quashed, and only result in worse oppression.[106] King further argues that nothing of positive moral value can be found in resort to violence, no matter how just the cause. Violence and its emotional counterpart, hatred, simply cannot appeal to conscience. When power is linked with morality, as King argues it must be, violence is never its means. "Nonviolence is power, but it is the right and good use of power."[107] Nonviolent expressions of power, by eschewing hatred, effect goals while reducing one's opponents' fears and holding forth the possibility of reconciliation based on forgiveness and rectification of injustices. "Violence is the antithesis of creativity and wholeness. It destroys community and makes brotherhood impossible."[108] Conversely, nonviolent applications of power promote the values of creativity, wholeness, community, and neighborly solidarity.

---

[106]Ibid., 56-59.

[107]Ibid., 59.

[108]Ibid., 61.

King does allow pressure and coercion a part in moral power. In battling the entrenched strength of what he calls structures of evil in society--and the multifaceted phenomenon of racism is a prime example of such a structure--persons of good will must couple ethical appeals with forms of nonviolent pressure, or "constructive coercive power."[109] "True non-violence is more than the absence of violence. It is the persistent and determined application of peaceable power to offenses against the community."[110]   To this end mass non-violent action must be supplemented by the creation of more long term organs of power through the organization of grassroots groups, as well as by accumulating legitimate political and economic strength.[111]

Since nonviolence is so central to King's normative vision of power, it is worth examining key criticisms of his nonviolent position, summarized in John J. Ansbro's helpful study.[112] First, critics frequently charged King with increasing hatred and instigating violence by his mass protest techniques. To this King's response was always the same: his movement did not create violence, but surfaced the latent hatred and violence society directed toward its black citizens. His movement only exposed and drew out this systemic hatred and violence so that progress could be made toward addressing and eradicating it.[113]

Second, some claimed that King engaged in subtle hypocrisy by relying upon peoples' fear of violence to wrest blacks' demands from white society. King and other black leaders accomplished this, these critics contended, by issuing repeated warnings that, if demands were not met, leaders could not guarantee the continued nonviolence of all their followers. King's reply reflects his characteristic combination of principled vision and realistic

---

[109]Ibid., 129.

[110]Ibid., 184.

[111]Ibid., 36-38, 129-30, 137-41.

[112]Ansbro, *Making of a Mind*, ch. 7.

[113]Ibid., 243-45.

assessment of people. On the one hand, he vehemently denounced the morality and practicality of resort to violence whenever such was advocated or practiced by members of the black community. Even as he warned intransigent whites that black patience would have its limits, he warned blacks that rioting or other violent tactics would only redound to their own disadvantage. To those who interpreted King's predictions of violence as invitations to it, King insisted that to the contrary, such warnings sprang from a sincere intention to avert violence. Ansbro adds that King felt a moral obligation to alert the nation to of the possibility of violent outbreaks should movements toward social justice be frustrated. Hence King's words in the wake of the 1965 riots in the Watts section of Los Angeles:

> Those who argue that it is hazardous to give warnings, lest the expression of apprehension lead to violence, are in error. Violence has already been practiced too often, and always because remedies were postponed. . . . This is not a threat, but a fact of history."[4]

Finally, another version of the charge of hypocrisy came from critics who discerned in King's methods a rejection of violence among his protesters, yet an expectation of support from the coercive power of the police or military. King did admit the value of restrained and lawful use of police action in the protection of justice, as evidenced by his approval of the use of Federal marshals to protect the freedom riders in Alabama in 1961, and of the involvement of marshals and military troops in securing the admission of James Meredith to the University of Mississippi. Ansbro cites King's comments on the latter instance in a 1962 editorial published in *The Nation*:

> Whereas I abhor the use of arms and the thought of war,
> I do believe in the intelligent use of police power . . . .

---

[4]Martin Luther King, "Beyond the Los Angeles Riots," *Saturday Review* (Nov. 13, 1965): 35. Quoted in Ansbro, *Making of a Mind*, 249-250.

Mississippi's breakdown of law and order demanded the utilization of a police action to quell the disorder and enforce the law of the land. Armed force that intelligently exercises police power, making civil arrests in which full due process is observed, is not functioning as an army in military engagement, so I feel the presence of troops in Oxford, Mississippi is a police force seeking to preserve law and order rather than an army engaging in destructive warfare."[5]

Now, in his fight against segregation laws, King had decried the use of the issue of law and order as an excuse for police enforcement of what he regarded as an unjust code. From one perspective, his support for police force in the Meredith case does suggest a willingness on King's part to give up nonviolent principles when it suited the interests of his movement. On closer inspection, however, King appears to have consistently admitted the need for peaceful, yet *coercive* measures for achieving and preserving justice against an historically unjust system. Nonviolent direct action was judged the most moral and, in the long run, the most practical path to justice. Yet in a world where evil remains a reality, at the limits of nonviolent action a police or military force committed to upholding human rights and to the prevention (or at least strict minimization) of violence was never rejected by King. King was keenly aware of the active reality and strength of the evil of social injustice, and of the need to fight and struggle against it."[6]

---

[5]Martin Luther King, Jr., "Who Is Their God?," *The Nation* 195 (Oct. 13, 1962): 210. Quoted in Ansbro, *Making of A Mind*, 245-46.

[6]Ansbro documents King's convictions about the aggressive nature of collective evil and the need for intense and systematic resistance to it. He notes that King wrote on various occasions, "Evil is stark, grim, and colossally real . . . . Evil is recalcitrant and determined, and never voluntarily relinquishes its hold short of a persistent, almost fanatical resistance. . . . Evil must be attacked by a counteracting persistence, by the day-to-day assault of the battering rams of justice." Ibid., 160-61.

In both domestic and international affairs, King argued that expanded awareness of and commitment to nonviolent action would diminish reliance upon police and military violence for combatting social evil. He recognized that such a commitment to nonviolence required a revolution in values which would not soon, or perhaps ever, be shared by the whole populace.[117] Given this indisputable fact of experience, King accepts the occasional need for strictly law-bound and limited uses of military and police force.[118] But, in line with his allegiance to power-to, King's normative vision and strategic commitments remained firmly fixed on nonviolence. "Occasionally in life," he wrote during the year before he died, "one develops a conviction so precious and meaningful that he will stand on it till the end. That is what I have found in nonviolence."[119]

The last dimension of King's construal of black power is the self-affirmation and self-assertion of the black community in terms of group identity and a "rugged sense of somebodyness."[120] In this sense, the black power movement can be seen as "a psychological call to manhood."[121] Black self-assertion and self-esteem, expressed in ways ranging from a stress on "black is beautiful," to the appreciative retrieval of African-American history and culture, is an indispensable antidote to the pervasive ideology of slavery and racial inferiority to which the black citizen is heir.[122] Effective, collaborative action for the sake of individual and group betterment

---

[117]See King, *Where Do We Go?*, ch. 6, esp. 184.

[118]Here we see at work King's realism, reflecting perhaps the influence of his study of Reinhold Niebuhr coupled with his own experience.

[119]Ibid., 63-64.

[120]Ibid., 122.

[121]Ibid., 38.

[122]Cornel West delineates the history of the aesthetic and anthropological degradation of African Americans in *Prophesy Deliverance! An Afro-American Revolutionary Christianity* (Philadelphia: Westminster Press, 1982), ch. 2, esp. 53-63. Cf. Dwight N. Hopkins, *Shoes That Fit Our Feet: Sources for a Constructive Black Theology* (Maryknoll, NY: Orbis Books, 1993), 177-79, where King's view is compared with Malcolm X's.

both expresses and nourishes this sense of worth. Here we see King's recognition of the psychic dimensions of power and powerlessness in his own version of what Gutierrez would call the anthropological meaning of liberation: the ability of those who have been victims to join in celebration of and active participation in their own history and identity-making. His sensitivity to the need for overcoming generations of negative psychic conditioning also allows King to understand, though not to condone, the more harshly defiant, militant, and separatist elements in the rhetoric of some proponents of black power in the 1960s.[123]

Clearly, King understands power to be a constitutive element in the justice sought by the American black community, and indeed in any substantive situation of justice. Integration, the stated goal of King's civil rights movement, cannot be achieved merely by removing long-held legal constraints such as slavery or segregation laws. Black liberation is not merely "freedom from" such external bonds.[124] Nor is integration merely the presence of blacks and whites in the same setting. For King, integration has a full-bodied meaning: it is "true intergroup, interpersonal living," a state of affairs which requires "the mutual sharing of power." "I cannot see how the Negro will be totally liberated from the crushing weight of poor education, squalid housing, and economic strangulation until he is integrated, with power, into every level of American life."[125]

We must not leave this discussion of King's power-to focused theory without remarking that this conception of power springs from a keen awareness of the interdependence of individuals and of groups in society. King rejects violence and separatism in large part because these fail to acknowledge the fact of social interdependence among blacks and whites, an error which, in his eyes, simply repeats one of the worst offenses of those who have historically been oppressors. "In a multiracial society," King insists, "no group can

---

[123]King, *Where Do We Go?*, 39-44.

[124]Ibid., 79.

[125]Ibid., 62.

make it alone."[126] He favors nonviolent struggle and integration (again, defined in terms of vital interrelationships and shared power) because these methods and these goals, by acknowledging the "facts of--interdependent--life," offer the only viable alternative to the destructive patterns of oppression that his movement seeks to terminate.

> In the final analysis the weakness of Black Power is its failure to see that the black man needs the white man and the white man needs the black man. However much we may try to romanticize the slogan, there is no separate black path to power and fulfillment that does not intersect white paths, and there is no separate white path to power and fulfillment, short of social disaster, that does not share that power with black aspirations for freedom and human dignity. We are bound together in a single garment of destiny.[127]

It is because of this interdependence that King can claim that effective freedom requires participation in power: not its complete usurpation from others, but a sharing on equal footing with other groups in the community. King calls for a nation in which a multiracial people are "partners in power," and where power is mutually exercised for the benefit of each and all.[128] This shared power entails economic, as well as civil and social aspects.[129]

The ongoing work of actuating mutual power requires that both black and white citizens undergo a difficult education in creative

---

[126]Ibid., 50.

[127]Ibid., 52.

[128]Ibid., 53.

[129]Hopkins insightfully examines the increasing emphasis on economic aspects of racial justice in King's later thought in *Shoes That Fit Our Feet*, esp. 175-79, 182-87. This evolution brought King closer to the more radical critique and analysis of African American social critics such as Malcolm X, James Cone, and Cornel West.

interdependence, for a history of racism has bequeathed to both groups strong tendencies toward fragmentation, conflict, and egoism--and the perverted notions of power that accompany these. The particular scars that mark oppressor and oppressed differ, but the challenge to forge collaborative unions for the common good of the nation, and the international "world house," is issued similarly to all.

James H. Cone. With the 1969 publication of his book, *Black Power and Black Theology*, James H. Cone became the most widely known spokesperson for black power among Christian theologians in the United States.[130] This work delineates a stance on power and black power that is specifically committed to the view, shared with other proponents of black power, that gentle suasion and peaceful admonition will not suffice to bring about the genuine revolution in the status of black American citizens that justice demands. Further, Cone mounts an argument for the appropriateness of black power as a Christian theological theme. In his treatment of black power, one can detect similarities to the constructive notion developed by King, but one also finds elements that King would undoubtedly question, if not reject. In his later works, Cone describes the approach that he and other black theologians have struggled to develop as a creative synthesis of elements of the democratic-Christian position enunciated by King with the militant-African posture of black power advocates such as Malcolm X.

> As long as Martin King was the acknowledged symbol and standard-bearer of the movement, it remained Christian, emphasizing love, integration, and nonviolence. But the emergence of Malcolm's philosophy through black power meant the introduction of a radicalization that excluded

---

[130]West situates Cone's work within the history of black theology in the U.S. in *Prophesy Deliverance!*, 101-108. See also, Hopkins, *Shoes That Fit Our Feet*, 210-212.

Christianity.

Black theology arose as an attempt to stem the tide of the irrelevance of Christianity by combining both Christianity and blackness, Martin and Malcolm, black church and black power, even though neither side thought it was possible. The early interpreters of black theology were theologians "on the boundary" . . . between integration and separation, nonviolence and self-defense, "love our white enemies and love our black skins." They refused to sacrifice either emphasis; they insisted on the absolute necessity of both.[131]

Black Power and Black Theology expresses Cone's early effort to forge this synthesis in a style that emphasizes differences with King more than similarities. With respect to the treatment of socio-political power, these differences are seen in Cone's emphasis on separation and separatism, his stress not on love but on justifiable hatred for white racists and racist society, and his refusal to embrace nonviolence as the only method for achieving black goals. Striking too, in contrast to King, is Cone's argument that black power so defined is not in contradiction with the principles of Christianity, but in fact, the heart of the gospel for our time and place. "Black power, even in its most radical expression, is not heretical or the antithesis of Christianity--it is, rather, Christ's central message to 20th century America."[132] This claim rests on an assessment of the corruption wrought by white racism in this country, the depth of which convinces Cone that only by the harshest prophetic

---

[131]Cone, *For My People*, 58.

[132]Cone, *Black Theology*, 37. Cone's later writings nuance this claim. In *God of the Oppressed* (New York: Seabury Press, 1975), for instance, Cone cautions, "Unless we black theologians can make an adequate distinction between divine revelation and human aspirations, there is nothing to keep Black Theology from identifying God's will with anything black people should decide to do at any given historical moment." 84-85.

denunciation and fiercest struggle will social redemption be possible. Thus, the object toward which black power must point is "complete emancipation of black people from white oppression by whatever means black people deem necessary."[133]

> Simply stated, Black Power is an affirmation of the humanity of blacks in spite of white racism. It says that only blacks really know the extent of white oppression, and thus only blacks are prepared to risk all to be free. Therefore, Black Power seeks not understanding but conflict; addresses blacks and not whites; seeks to develop black support, but not white good will. Black Power believes in the utter determination of blacks to be free and not in the good intentions of white society. It says: if blacks are liberated, it will be blacks themselves who will do the liberating, not whites.[134]

Cone understands the emergence of black power to require a genuine withdrawal and separation of black persons from the expectations, values, culture, and ideology of white America. Here we see a radicalization of the point made by King about group identity and self-affirmation, and expressed by Gutierrez as the anthropological dimension of liberation: the oppressed group must cease to be objects and victims, and take charge of its own history. Cone's explicit rejection of integration as a civil rights goal,[135] and

---

[133]Cone, *Black Theology*, 6.

[134]Ibid., 16-17.

[135]Ibid., 17-20. "If integration means accepting the white man's style, his values, or his religion, then the black man must refuse. There is nothing to integrate. The white man, in the very asking of the question, assumes that he has something which blacks want or should want, as if being close to white people enhances the humanity of blacks . . . . [Whites] . . . also ignore the beastly behavior of the "devil white man." Ibid., 17. "Integration, at this stage, too easily lends itself to supporting the moral superiority of white society." Ibid., 19.

his antagonistic tone toward his white audience[136] attest to the deep, recalcitrant evil he perceives in all aspects of white society.

Quite simply, Cone argues, integration is an improper goal because it implies that white culture is the normative context into which blacks should aim to be included. Cone would never pen the lines King wrote about the black movement being one that aimed for inclusion. There is, Cone acknowledges, a positive interpretation of integration that black people could accept. This understanding involves the mutuality of power-to without domination:

> [I]f integration means that each man meets the other on equal footing, with neither possessing the ability to assert the rightness of his style over the other, then mutual meaningful dialogue is possible. Biblically, this may be called the Kingdom of God. Men were not created for separation, and color is not the essence of man's humanity . . . .[137]

But, he immediately adds, we do not live in the consummated Kingdom, and so must cope with conditions as they actually exist. Those conditions are such that the dominant white culture degrades all those not sharing its racial features. In the face of this, "oppressed blacks . . . must affirm the very characteristic which the oppressor ridicules--blackness. Black people must withdraw and form their own culture, their own way of life."[138]

Connected with this exhortation to create, foster, and celebrate black heritage, culture, aesthetics, and values is Cone's vehement insistence that black power requires that blacks unilaterally set the

---

[136]"[T]his book was written in anger and disgust. . . . This is a word to the oppressor, a word to Whitey, not in the hope that he will listen (after King's death who can hope?) but in the expectation that my own existence will be clarified." Ibid., 3.

[137]Ibid., 17.

[138]Ibid., 18.

agenda for their own liberation. Whites, even well intentioned "white liberals," have no right to dictate or even to suggest what the posture or program of blacks should be. The menace of white intellectual arrogance lies in "the dangerous assumption that the structure that enslaves is the structure that will also decide *when* and *how* this slavery is to be abolished. . . . The time has come for white Americans to be silent and listen to black people."[139]

Fueling Cone's stress on black separatism, or at least on a separatist moment within black cultural development, is his conviction that social power involves social self-determination. Historically, black people have been peculiarly victimized by institutions and ideologies which have contaminated their undertakings with the dominant group's racism. There is thus a pressing need to move apart in order to rediscover authentic black identity, history and future.   In this process, whites may be spectators, but blacks themselves are the central actors.[140]

We have mentioned that Cone's description of black power includes more tolerance for violence and hatred against oppressors than does King's. This bears a bit more analysis. The differences between the two thinkers are illustrated by their respective assessments of the views of Frantz Fanon, the Algerian psychiatrist whose revolutionary writings had a strong impact on many militant black power advocates in the United States during this period.[141] In direct contrast to King, Cone joins Fanon in designating hatred and anger as healthy and appropriate responses to racist power

---

[139]Ibid., 21. King, *Where Do We Go?*, 88-94, also considers the problem of the white liberal and his/her latent prejudice, though with characteristically milder tone.

[140]Karen LeBacqz helpfully situates the phenomena of anger, resistance, and separationism of oppressed groups in the context of the wider dynamics of justice-seeking in *Justice in an Unjust World: Foundations for a Christian Approach to Justice* (Minneapolis, MN: Augsburg, 1987), ch. 5.

[141]See esp., Frantz Fanon, *The Wretched of the Earth* (New York: Grove Publishing Co., 1963). King critiques Fanon's endorsement of violence in *Where Do We Go?*, 55, 65-66.

structures. Black hatred, which Cone describes as the strong aversion of any reflective black person to white society, is not identical with black power, but nor is it black racism.[142]

Fanon further contends that for the victim of oppression, violent retaliation--besides being understandable, justified, and usually necessary--serves a number of wholesome purposes. Violent action restores initiative to the formerly passive victim, it separates him from crippling dependency on the dominative relationship, and is an expression of existential freedom and self-affirmation. While he does not praise violence, Cone does insist that it is not up to white oppressors to dictate nonviolence to blacks, nor should blacks be wedded to nonviolence in the face of recalcitrant racist evil. Violence by blacks, such as riots, should be interpreted as understandable outbursts of rebellion against white oppression that may not be without some of the benefits Fanon describes.

Despite these and other important differences with Martin Luther King, Jr., Cone sees continuity between a Christian rendering of black power and the legacy of the slain civil rights leader. He reads the later King as moving toward the kinds of radical affirmations that black power represents, and so regards black power advocates as King's legitimate heirs.

> [King] may not have endorsed the concept of Black Power, but its existence is a result of his work. Black power advocates are men who were inspired by his zeal for freedom, and Black Power is their attempt to make his dream a reality. If the black church organizations want to remain faithful to the New Testament gospel and to the great tradition of the pre-Civil War black church, they must relinquish their stake in the status quo and the values in white society by identifying exclusively with Black Power.[143]

---

[142]Cone, *Black Theology*, 14.
[143]Ibid., 109.

Conclusion: Black Power and Socio-Political Structures. This brief look at two African American Christian treatments of "black power" illumines a community's struggle to forge a vital complex of descriptive-normative-strategic affirmations about social power. The tensions between the positions of King and Cone are instructive, for they reveal dynamics at work in other emancipatory movements as well. Their disagreements reflect distinctive, but not inherently opposing descriptions of power. Each description, by highlighting both solidarity and empowerment *and* the capacity to resist evil and oppression, incorporates both power-to and power-over aspects. Yet each thinker advances his notion of power on the basis of a different assessment of the problem of racism and its solutions.

King regards racism as a deviation from the true moral identity of America, whose solution requires a return to that identity in a truly integrated society. Cone, writing in the wake of the frustration of the King agenda, joins those who judge racism to be an all-but-ineradicable, possibly congenital disease afflicting U.S. culture. Given the depth of the problem, the responses Cone favors involve a more antagonistic and separatist understanding of power relationships than do King's. The opposing tacks the two authors take on the question of violent resistance reflect this.

Put another way, power as seen by Martin Luther King, Jr. is expressed within the community through black solidarity, and externally through resistance to oppression whose aim is reconciliation and "true, intergroup, interpersonal living." On the other side of the sin of racism and the necessary struggle against it there remains hope for forgiveness and healing. In the judgment of James Cone, power is also expressed in internecine solidarity and resistance to the forces of racism, but he presumes that the depth of the evil being faced makes separation and confrontation not steps toward reconciliation, but ongoing necessities. Rather than being a serious yet corrigible deviation, racism in fact reveals an ingrained feature of the American identity, a "state of sin" not easily, if ever, to be extirpated. This being so, black power inevitably entails a significant degree of separation and antagonism.

What, then, are the political structures that these two versions of black power might support? On this the later King joined other black leaders, among them Cone and Malcolm X, in a predilection toward some form of democratic socialism as the most conducive means to the redistribution and sharing of power that justice required.[144] As King's analysis of the links between black economic, cultural, and political disempowerment developed, his references to complete social restructuring and the need for a move toward democratic socialism became more frequent and urgent.[145] For his part, Cone from early on identified his black theology with liberationism's critique of western capitalism, and embraces some form of socialism as a more promising path to communal well-being. While King's appreciation for socialism reflects his exposure to the governments of Scandinavian countries, Cone, like Malcolm X, harkens to socialist practices in Africa as sources for constructing rejuvenated, collaborative practices and structures of power.[146]

---

[144]See Hopkins, *Shoes That Fit Our Feet*, 195-201; West, *Prophesy Deliverance!*, 104-106.

[145]King states in 1967, "[W]e must honestly face the fact that the Movement must address itself to the question of restructuring the whole of American society. . . . [O]ne day we must ask the question: "Why are there 40 million poor people in America?" And when you begin to ask that question, you are raising questions about the economic system, about a broader distribution of wealth . . . [Y]ou begin to question the capitalist economy." King, "August 1967 Speech," quoted in Hopkins, *Shoes That Fit Our Feet*, 195. Hopkins notes the erosion of support for King that occurred as he radicalized his notion of democracy to include the fundamental redistribution and sharing of economic power. Ibid, 195-196.

[146]On King see Hopkins, *Shoes That Fit Our Feet*, 196. In a 1977 essay, Cone states, "The time has come for us to move beyond institutional survival in a capitalistic and racist society and begin to take more seriously our dreams about a new heaven and a new earth." He asks, "Does this dream include capitalism or is it a radically new way of life more consistent with African socialism as expressed in the Arusha Declaration in Tanzania?" In *Black Theology: A Documentary History, 1966-1979*, ed. Gayraud S. Wilmore and James H. Cone (Maryknoll, NY: Orbis, 1979), 355-56; quoted in West,

Christian Feminist Liberationists

Contemporary controversy about women's roles in church and society has been an important catalyst for Christian feminist reflection on the meaning and ethical use of power. As feminists, these Christians oppose the oppressive power-over relations inscribed in patriarchal and sexist thought and practice.[147] As Christians, these feminists provide probing analyses of the religious dimensions of experience, thought and action concerning power.[148] Since the 1970s, Christian feminist scholarship has ceased to be the preserve of mostly white, privileged, European and North American women, and is taking on distinctive and significant manifestations among African American women in womanist theology and ethics, Hispanic women in *mujerista* theology and ethics, and among "third

---

Prophesy Deliverance!, 105. Cf. Cone, *For My People*, ch. 10, esp. 201-207.

[147]Elisabeth Schüssler Fiorenza summarizes feminist theologians' understandings of these two terms: Patriarchy, or patriarchalism, refers to "a social system maintaining male dominance and privilege based on female submission and marginality. The word 'sexism' was coined by analogy to racism. It denotes all those attitudes and actions that relegate women to a secondary and inferior status." *Discipleship of Equals: A Critical Feminist Ekklesia-logy of Liberation* (New York: Crossroad, 1993), 131 n. 2.

[148]As they investigate Christianity's implications for women's flourishing, feminist theologians and ethicists address relations between images of God and understandings of human power; biblical hermeneutics and power relations; the impact of soteriological traditions on construals of women's sin, suffering, and redemption in relation to power; Christian notions of justice and *agape* for women in public and domestic spheres. See, respectively, Elizabeth Johnson, *She Who Is: The Mystery of God in Feminist Theological Discourse* (New York: Crossroad, 1993); Elisabeth Schüssler Fiorenza, *But She Said: Feminist Practices of Biblical Interpretation* (Boston: Beacon Press, 1992); Emilie M. Townes, ed., *A Troubling in My Soul: Womanist Perspectives on Evil and Suffering* (Maryknoll, NY: Orbis Books, 1993); Daphne Hampson, "On Power and Gender," *Modern Theology* 4/3 (1988): 234-50; Bonnie J. Miller-McLemore, *Also A Mother: Work and Family as Theological Dilemma* (Nashville: Abingdon Press, 1994).

world" women in a number of nations.[149]   Amidst real differences, the authors I rely on here share the allegiances to Christian liberationism identified earlier in this chapter, and particular foci-- most notably an interpretive and evaluative lens that centers on the situations and well-being of women--that identify them as "Christian feminists."

These authors employ theological and ethical methods distinguished by critical accountability to three key sources: the biblical texts and theological traditions embedded in the Christian community, the truth and value resident in culture past and present, and women's history and experiences within both these settings.[150] They share theoretical and practical commitments not just to denouncing and dismantling patriarchal structures, but to envisioning and developing new, non-sexist forms of relation both within the churches and in society at large.   There exists a gamut of opinions about the degree and kinds of change required in order to attain women's genuine well-being, and about the best means for accomplishing such changes.   North American Christian feminists

---

[149]See, e.g., Ada Maria Isasi-Diaz & Yolanda Tarango, *Hispanic Women: Prophetic Voice in the Church: Toward a Hispanic Women's Liberation Theology* (San Francisco: Harper & Row, 1988); Katie Geneva Cannon, *Black Womanist Ethics* (Atlanta, GA: Scholars Press, 1987); Hyun Kyung Chung, *The Struggle to Be the Sun Again: Introducing Asian Women's Theology* (Maryknoll, NY: Orbis Books, 1990); Virginia Fabella & Mercy Amba Oduyoye, eds., *With Passion and Compassion: Third World Women Doing Theology* (Maryknoll, NY: Orbis Books, 1988).

[150]On feminist theological method, see, e.g., Anne E. Carr, "The New Vision of Feminist Theology: Method," in Catherine Mowry LaCugna, ed., *Freeing Theology: The Essentials of Theology in Feminist Perspective* (San Francisco: Harper, 1993), 5-30; Pamela Dickey Young, *Feminist Theology/Christian Theology: In Search of A Method* (Minneapolis: Fortress Press, 1990). On method for feminist Christian social ethics, see Carol Robb, "A Framework for Feminist Ethics," in Barbara Hilkert Andolsen, Christine E. Gudorf, & Mary D. Pellaur, eds., *Women's Conscience, Women's Consciousness: A Reader in Feminist Ethics* (Minneapolis: Winston, 1985), 211-34; June O'Connor, "On Doing Religious Ethics," ibid, 265-84.

who embrace a liberationist stance, our focus here, gather at the "radical transformationist" point on this spectrum. These feminists analyze and critique the deep roots and pernicious effects of sexism in western society and western religion. Simultaneously, they are actively committed to confronting and transforming patriarchal structures.[151] To the extent that feminism denotes attention to the roots of sexism, and social ethics accents reconstructive social engagement rather than withdrawal, feminist Christian social ethicists tend to be radical transformationists.[152]

---

[151]As noted in Chapter III, radical transformationists differ from "liberal" or "equity" feminists who more readily assume the overall health of present structures, and look to education and legislation as the means for attaining women's equal rights and privileges. On such differences within Christian ethics, see Christine Firer Hinze, "Christian Feminists, James Luther Adams, and the Search for a Radically Transformative Ethics," *Journal of Religious Ethics* (1993): 275-302. Transformationist feminists also differ from radical separatist feminists such as Mary Daly. The latter judge existing structures so ravaged by patriarchy that the only answer is for women to withdraw from the ruins of present society, and to establish sect-like reserves of truly mutual, female-identified relationships. On some of these feminists' turn to Goddess religion, witchcraft, and other woman-oriented forms, see Carol Christ and Judith Plaskow, eds., *Womanspirit Rising: A Feminist Reader in Religion* (San Francisco: Harper & Row, 1979), Part 4, esp. 259-67; Starhawk, *Truth or Dare: Encounters with Power, Authority, and Mystery* (San Francisco: Harper and Row, 1987).

[152]My designation of the feminists referred to here as "radical transformationists" does not, however, imply their theological, doctrinal, or even ethical univocity. Distinct disagreements exist among these Christian feminists in each of these areas: e.g, between Elizabeth Johnson and Sharon Welch on the transcendence of God and christology; between Elisabeth Schüssler Fiorenza and Rosemary Radford Ruether on "full humanity" as a norm for feminist ethics; between culturally and economically oriented feminist liberationists on strategies for social change.

Beverly Harrison's Christian Feminist Power Analysis. The 1985 publication of a reader in feminist social ethics entitled *Women's Conscience, Women's Consciousness* made essays by a number of representatives of this position widely available. The collection was dedicated to the influential feminist religious ethicist Beverly Wildung Harrison of Union Theological Seminary, whose own volume, *Making the Connections: Essays in Feminist Social Ethics*, appeared in the same year.[153] The decade following the publication of these books has witnessed a spate of writing by feminist liberationists addressing theological, anthropological, and socio-political questions concerning power. As is the case with the feminists examined in the last chapter, these writings draw connections among the psychic, bodily, interpersonal, cultural, economic, and political aspects of both women's oppression and women's empowerment.[154] Feminists' conviction that "the personal is the political," precludes sharp lines between the interpretation and evaluation proper to so-called "private" and "public" spheres. This means that to consider one arena of power relations is, for them, implicitly to engage all the others. To date, though, North American Christian feminists have devoted more systematic attention to the psychic, interpersonal, and cultural workings of power, and to power relations within ecclesial

---

[153]Beverly Wildung Harrison, *Making the Connections: Essays in Feminist Social Ethics*, Carol S. Robb, ed. (Boston: Beacon Press, 1985).

[154]A good example of this multifaceted feminist approach to power is Susan Ross's depiction of women's social and ecclesial empowerment in terms of five basic "feminist principles:" solidarity, marginality, embodiment, knowledge, and transformation. Susan A. Ross, "'He Has Pulled Down the Mighty From Their Thrones, and Has Exalted the Lowly': A Feminist Reflection on Empowerment," in Michael Downey, ed., *That They Might Live: Power, Empowerment, and Leadership in the Church* (New York: Crossroad, 1991), 145-59.

communities, than they have to power in economic or political structures *per se*.[155]

The work of Beverly Harrison stands as an exception to this relative inattention to the workings of political and economic power.[156] A brief look at Harrison's treatment of power, with reference to complementary work by Euro-American feminist theologians on the one hand, and African American womanist liberationists on the other, will illumine the contours of a still-nascent Christian feminist ethics of socio-political power.

Harrison's religious social ethics frequently adverts to questions concerning power. This feminist ethicist locates power at the heart of human identity, action, and relations. The proper understanding and use of power is therefore crucial to moral flourishing. Historically, however, the theory and practice of power--including in Christian theology and ethics--has been deeply disfigured by patriarchy. Invoking a widely sounded feminist theme, Harrison argues that "dualisms of domination" have inculcated assumptions

---

[155]Although they must be approached with discrimination, feminist writings about ecclesial communities provide a legitimate resource for our investigation of socio-political power. Women's encounters with ecclesial authority and polity have sparked much power analysis. Feminist treatments of ecclesiology, moreover, incorporate more general social theoretical *and* theological assumptions concerning social power and authority. An emerging possibility, as yet insufficiently developed, is a reciprocal movement of critique and reconstruction between normative understandings of power in ecclesial and in wider socio-political settings. The works of Schüssler Fiorenza, Ruether, Letty Russell, and others, provide examples of the close, at points insufficiently differentiated, connection these feminists draw between ecclesial and socio-political norms and practices concerning power.

[156]Other North American Christian feminists probing political and economic questions acknowledge the influence and guidance of Harrison. These include the editors of and many contributors to the *Women's Consciousness, Women's Conscience* volume, and more recently published scholars such as Elizabeth Bounds, Pamela Brubaker, and Mary Hobgood.

and ways of relating that value males over females.[57] Embedded in cultural mindsets and patterns, patriarchal gender dualisms legitimate and reinforce other forms of domination as they are passed from generation to generation.

The family, Harrison contends, is the locus for the earliest and most decisive indoctrination into these power-over patterns. Through socialization to gender roles in the family setting, children begin to learn to fear equality, and are taught either to feel "strong" by lording it over others or to feel "safe" by being controlled by them. "By conforming rigidly to 'masculine' or 'feminine' roles, we learn, at a foundational level, to tolerate inequality. Through our earliest experience of family power relations we learn whether superiority or inferiority makes us feel safe."[58]

Reinforcing primordial experiences of inequality within the family is a dominant theological and ethical tradition that views power as power-over. Harrison discusses the impact that theological notions of God as transcendent and ultimate "power-over" have had on the theory and practice of Christian ethics. She castigates 20th century neo-orthodoxy for an overweening and distorting emphasis on God as all-controlling agent, and on humans as properly subject to that control. The problem with this theology

---

[57]See Harrison, *Making the Connections*, 28-29. The distorting and oppressive consequences of gender dualist, "binary" ways of conceiving reality are variously developed by Christian feminists. See multiple references in Johnson, *She Who Is*; Rosemary Radford Ruether, *Sexism and God-Talk: Toward a Feminist Theology* (Boston: Beacon Press, 1983); Ruether, "Motherearth and the Megamachine," in Christ & Plaskow, eds., *Womanspirit Rising*, 42-52; Kathryn Allen Rabuzzi, "The Socialist Feminist Vision of Rosemary Radford Ruether" *Religious Studies Review* 15:1 (January 1989), 6; and Schüssler Fiorenza's effort to press feminist analysis of patriarchy beyond the terms of a "binary gender system" in *But She Said*, 114-32.

[58]Harrison, *Making the Connections*, 148. An influential text for some Christian feminists on this topic has been Alice Miller, *For Your Own Good: Hidden Cruelty in Child-Rearing and the Roots of Violence* (New York: Farrar, Straus, Giroux, 1983).

for ethics is that it engenders a deficient anthropology. "God-relationship displaces and overwhelms images of human self-direction altogether. What [is] really needed, by contrast, [is] a new vision of *both* God and humanity, a vision of holiness or godliness and a vision of humanity as co-capacity in relationship."[159] Notions of relations (to God and to others) articulated within an ideology of male gender supremacy teach "implicit power dynamics" in which power means separation and superordination (power-over), and even "good action," conveyed as a mode of "doing for" others rather than "acting with" them, retains its power-over taint.

Harrison judges this view of action and power not only inaccurate, but destructive. Oppressed persons seeking liberation need "an ethic grounded in images and concepts that affirm reciprocity in action."[160] Citing H. Richard Niebuhr in support of her claim, Harrison insists that "if our moral language is ever to interpret self/other duality in terms that affirm and embrace mutuality and support the whole spectrum of human fulfillment," we must "learn to envision all action as genuine *inter*action."[161]

---

[159]Harrison, *Making the Connections*, 36. For a probative analysis of the relationship between theological affirmations concerning God, and humans'--especially women's--apprehension of their identity and capacities in relation to God, see Johnson, *She Who Is*, esp. 65-75, 124-87. See also Anne E. Carr's analysis of the reconsideration of the doctrine of God and divine power currently underway among feminist theologians in *Transforming Grace: Christian Tradition and Women's Experience* (San Francisco: Harper and Row, Publishers, 1988), ch. 7.

[160]Harrison rejects some radical feminists' efforts to replace patriarchy with matriarchy precisely because it does not refashion the way power is understood. "Such responses to our situation not only reinforce gender dualism but reinforce the 'zero-sum' power perceptions that are distinctive of patriarchy, in which one gender must necessarily rule the other." *Making the Connections*, 31.

[161]Ibid., 39. Harrison likens this to the thesis advanced by H. R. Niebuhr (who was the subject of Harrison's doctoral dissertation) in *The Responsible Self* (New York, Harper and Row, 1963). Ibid., 275 n. 46.

To do this requires that traditional theological images be reconsidered. Images of God as Lord, King, or even Father/Mother "teach us that holy power is not reciprocal power."[162] A God capable of sustaining the cooperative transformation of injustice must be one who sustains and grounds the fragile possibilities of action, and lends the power of co-relation to enhance and enrich human acts aimed at fulfillment, justice, and mutuality[163]. These theological claims are situated within a normative picture of reality as reciprocally and positively related.

> In the web of life in which this lovely Holy One is enmeshed with us, personal fulfillment and mutuality are not inherently contradictions, irreconcilables. The social world that our antisocial corporate actions have constructed and sustained over time is now characterized by injustice, so now our interests often are set in deep opposition. But my well-being and yours are not inherently at odds. As relational beings, we need each other for our common well-being, and in our mutual relation we experience God/ess.[164]

This normative vision leads Harrison to a notion of justice defined, on the one hand, by prophetic denunciation of asymmetries of

---

[162]Harrison, *Making the Connections*, 39. For a sustained, constructive theological treatment of these questions from a Roman Catholic feminist perspective, see Johnson, *She Who Is*.

[163]"Mutuality" is a term widely used by feminists to describe a moral goal toward which relationships should aim. Harrison states that mutuality involves "the simultaneous acknowledgement of vulnerability to and need of the other, the recognition of one's own power to give and receive . . . and to call forth another's power of relation and to express one's own." *Making the Connections*, 150. Cf. Nothwehr, "Mutuality as a Formal Norm," ch. 1.

[164]Harrison, *Making the Connections*, 39. Cf. Johnson, *She Who Is*, esp. chs. 7, 12.

power, and, on the other hand, by an eschatological vision of the possibility of a common good.

> Justice is a praxis that realizes conditions that make my fulfillment and yours possible simultaneously, that literally creates a common good. All moral goods are *inter*related possibilities. They seem irreconcilable to us because the world our freedom has constructed and construed is distorted by the heavy hand of privilege and domination. To say no to that is to say yes to this 'phantasie of possibility,' and, in the process, to encounter God as personal living process and ground of relation.[165]

We see that for Harrison, the ways power is understood and employed directly affect the degree of justice or goodness in a particular community. When social inequities get entrenched in perduring structures, the consequence is disparities of power that both reflect and breed a lack of mutuality. In such situations, injustice and collective evil--the social faces of sin--prevail.

> Evil is the consequence of disparities of power because where disparity of power is great, violence or control by coercion is the dominant mode of social interaction. Evil, on this reading, is the active or passive effort to deny or suppress another's power-of-being-in-relation. When power disparities are great, those 'in charge' cease to have to be accountable to those less powerful for what they do. Societies in which . . . some groups have vast and unchecked power and others are denied even the power of survival, are unjust societies.[166]

---

[165]Harrison, *Making the Connections*, 39-40.

[166]Ibid., 154-55. A very similar point is made by King, *Where Do We Go?*, 37-38. In her emphasis on injustice as the social manifestation of sin, and in her claim that a balance of power is needed to prevent abuse, one also detects affinities between Harrison her early teacher, Reinhold Niebuhr.

Moral action thus entails cooperative effort to resist and dismantle power-over asymmetries, and to create and sustain conditions of power-to conducive to mutual efficacy and flourishing. Participating in this redemptive process, persons generate and foster what Harrison calls "holy power" and reject the power of domination and violence. "We act together and find our good in each other and in God, and our power grows together, or we deny our relation and reproduce a violent world where no one experiences holy power."[167]   Every Christian actor and every Christian ethics is implicated in one choice or the other.

Christian Feminists and Social Transformation. How, more precisely, might this feminist theological rendering of power translate into concrete action for social transformation? Like the feminist social theorists we have examined, Harrison is at pains to rebut critics who see in feminist talk of holy power and mutual efficacy a naive disregard for the actual workings of institutional life. This is a criticism to which Harrison regards religious ethicists in general to have been vulnerable, and she cautions her colleagues concerning it.

Beyond denouncing oppressive power-over and promoting the pursuit of collaborative power-to, religious feminists must figure out ways to effectively engage the asymmetrical institutional contexts in which things are actually getting done. One of the serious failures of much theologically informed ethics, Harrison says, has been a tendency to envision a "salvific ethic" without considering the practical conditions or consequences of implementing that ethic at the level of public policy.[168]   To avoid this, "a feminist approach must incorporate sensitivity to power in the institutional matrix."

---

[167]Harrison, *Making the Connections*, 41. Cf. Arendt's description of the power of action created and sustained in public, discussed in Chapter III.

[168]Harrison, *Making the Connections*, 176.

From a moral point of view, it is insufficient if our analysis
of power deals exclusively with its expressive aspects, that
is, with the capacity of persons and groups to realize shared
goals and values, to attain common social ends. Social
policy always is forged in an institutional context in which
power is inequitably distributed . . . . Therefore, clear
awareness of who gains and who loses from any particular
social policy option [is critical]. The challenge is to gain
political support for morally viable social policies.[169]

Harrison makes it clear that in actual social relations, there are
circumstances of conflict over scarce resources in which power does
become a zero-sum relation.[170] Working for a more just society
requires the ability to select and carry out options that configure
such zero-sum situations in ways most accountable to the
flourishing of everyone concerned. Christian transformative
feminists must cultivate skill and wisdom in managing within and
against existing networks of power-over, even while striving to
reshape such networks to make them more conducive to mutuality
and common flourishing.

Power's role in engagement for social change is rendered
differently by other feminist liberationists. Sharon D. Welch, for
instance, tutored by the social theories of Foucault, Habermas, and
Giddens, and by the writings of African American women, situates

---

[169]Ibid.

[170]"[Political] power becomes a finite resource--a zero-sum quantity--
because some goals and interests cannot be accommodated if other interests
conflict with them. In society, some gain their interests at the expense of
others. In politics, power takes on the character of the capacity to set limits
to others' pursuit of their interests. . . . Since every proposal for social change
emerges in situations where certain organizations and groups are already in
the ascendancy . . . a social ethic must incorporate analyses of these power
realities and their ongoing dynamics. An adequate theological-ethical analysis
must convey this sort of concrete sense of existing power dynamics that work
to prevent the realization of a [just] policy." Ibid., 176-77.

transformative power-to in the context of "communities of solidarity and resistance" who practice "a feminist ethic of risk."[171] Welch finds a predilection in mainstream western theory and practice for "an ethic of control." Caught in the narrow confines of a power-over understanding, the ethic of control perceives moral action as entailing predictable, achievable, and controllable outcomes. Transformative efforts that do not or cannot deliver such results are either eschewed or pronounced failures. Among social-change activists, Welch argues, the influence of this ethics of control has the effect of limiting transformative initiatives, and discouraging long-haul commitment to the struggle for social renovation.[172]

In the history and practices of oppressed groups, however, Welch detects resources for a different social ethic, one grounded in a different understanding of power. An "ethic of risk" can nourish hope and persistence in the face of great evil and seemingly overwhelming odds. This ethic consists, first, in a redefinition of responsible action, not as the certain achievement of desired ends, but as creating a matrix in which further actions are possible, and hence the conditions of possibility for desired changes. Second, an ethic of risk requires a grounding in a "beloved community" spanning both time and space. Such a community serves as both home base and staging ground for the third element, "strategic risk taking" whereby oppressive power is confronted or defied. Here success is measured not by the heroism of the actor or the completeness of the results, but by "the contribution such an action will make to the imagination and courage of the resisting community."[173] The value and enlivening power of these communities and actions neither depend upon nor guarantee structural transformation. They do, however, instigate the hope,

---

[171]See Sharon D. Welch, *Communities of Resistance and Solidarity: A Feminist Theology of Liberation* (Maryknoll, NY: Orbis Books, 1985); *A Feminist Ethic of Risk* (Minneapolis: Fortress Press, 1990).

[172]See Welch, *Feminist Ethic of Risk*, 1-47.

[173]Ibid., 21-22.

renewal, and creative persistence that are the conditions of the possibility of such transformation.

Welch's feminist liberationist articulation sheds a different light on the meaning of "transformative efficacy" by accenting the fact and potential of power-to as resistance and witness from the margins. Loyalty to the radicality of their critique and renovative aims amidst the conditions of a fallen world leads feminist liberationists to cherish and foster this peripheral power, and to seek to understand it better.[174]

Socio-Political Power: An Emerging Christian Feminist Approach.
General features of an approach to power being fashioned by radical transformationist Christian feminists may now be summarized, with an eye toward points that await further development and clarification. We have argued that one's model of power interacts with convictions about the nature and flourishing of persons and society to significantly affect the descriptive, evaluative, and prescriptive moments in the ethical decision-making process. This is certainly true of these Christian feminists, who regard relations of power-over as both symptom and breeder of deficient and perverted understandings of persons and society. Feminism, in their view, entails nothing less than a fundamental paradigm shift, whereby power-over saturated patriarchal images of separation, competition, hierarchy, and domination are replaced by a power-to orientation marked by connection, partnership and mutuality.

---

[174]An appreciation for peripheral power is shared by other liberationists. This form of power acknowledges and makes use of the separation experienced by the radical transformationist community from existing mainstream power structures. Peripheral power is frequently a dimension of strategies of non-violent resistance and struggle. On Christian feminist and womanist understandings of peripheral power, see, respectively, Susan A. Ross, "A Feminist Reflection on Empowerment," in Downey, ed., *That They Might Live*, esp. 150-52; Rosita deAnn Mathews, "Using Power from the Periphery," in Townes, ed., *Troubling in My Soul*, 92-108.

Feminist explorations of the impact of this shift on understandings of God, self, and society are underway. An important task facing Christian feminist ethicists is to more effectively transpose these latter images, and the construals of power they reflect, into normative arguments about political, economic, and structures and practices.

As they make transformative efficacy their focal point, an adequately comprehensive theory of power requires that feminists also address power-over. In their experiences of oppression, conscientization, and liberation, women encounter both types or modes of power, often intensely. Paula Cooey points out that these experiences, and the feelings of ambivalence they elicit, have sensitized feminists to the equivocal nature of power itself.

> Power that transforms persons and bonds them with one another in communities calls into question prevailing conceptions of power as an exercise of control. . . . Nevertheless, the line between power apprehended as *shared energy transcending any specific individual or group* [power-to] and power conceived as *an internal and external exertion of control* [power-over] is a fine one that renders power of any kind ambiguous at least.[175]

Power's ambiguity makes ambivalence a logical and appropriate response to encounters with it. Properly attending to these

---

[175]Paula Cooey, "The Power of Transformation and the Transformation of Power," *Journal of Feminist Studies in Religion* 1/1 (1985): 35. First world, middle class, or Euro-American Christian feminists are liable to feel power's ambiguity by way of their "status inconsistent" social position. As white, first world citizens they are oppressors; as women, oppressed. Privileged women have traditionally known this double experience; privileged contemporary women feel it especially keenly insofar as their status is no longer so derivative of bonds with men. This awareness prods feminists to struggle for solidaristic accountability with women in different class, race, or social situations.

reactions of ambivalence engenders a canny and critical stance toward power, be it one's own or that exercised by others.[176] To Cooey's insightful analysis I add my own claim: feminists' efforts to account for the complexities and ambiguities of power call for a theory that convincingly integrates its superordinating and collaborative dimensions.

We have seen that in attempting to speak effectively about social power, religious feminists accord descriptive and moral priority to power-to. Power-to better reflects the relational ontology feminists embrace,[177] and better lends itself to what they perceive as just practices, structures, and outcomes. Indeed, insofar as it expresses the basic vitality, agency, or what Tillich calls the "power of being" of a person or community, feminists are prone to regard power-to as a moral good in itself, to be pursued for its own sake.[178]

Their approbation of power-to might lend the impression that feminists evaluate power-over in uniformly negative, and power-to in uniformly positive terms. On the contrary, questions about the interests served or the consequences produced are seen as relevant to the moral evaluation of both transformative and dominative power. The actuation of power-to can be marked by narrow exclusivism or naive complicity in patterns of domination, and therefore be immoral. Criticisms of the still largely white, middle

---

[176]Cooey continues, "Ambivalence is an important, and indeed logical, response to this ambiguity and marks an openness to self-critique. It is precisely the *contrast* between the two modes of power, as expressed in ambivalence toward power in general, that provides a theologically [and, it can be added, and ethically] critical principle." Ibid., 33.

[177]As with the secular feminists considered in Chapter III, there is widespread agreement among these religious feminists concerning the need for a reinterpretation of the basic self-other relation. See, e,g., Catherine Keller, *From a Broken Web: Separation, Sexism and the Self* (Boston, Beacon Press, 1986).

[178]Hannah Arendt strongly supports the notion of power as a good for its own sake. See, e.g., Arendt, *Human Condition*, 200-201.

class feminist movement by working class, third world, Hispanic, and African American women have highlighted this kind of failure. An emphasis on power-to also carries typical "occupational hazards", reflected, for instance, in confusion about effective decision making process and models of leadership that has beset some women's organizations and groups.

Conversely, insofar as certain instances of power-over aid or protect a person's or community's survival or flourishing, they are potentially morally praiseworthy. Yet feminists acknowledge power-over's potential beneficence only with caution, and insist that superordination be strictly limited to instrumental status, in service of mutual flourishing. Power-to can fall short of or pervert the collaboration and inclusiveness that characterize its genuine expression. But a power-to starting point highlights and promotes a normative anthropology and praxis of power that is relational and collaborative, rather than one that separates some over-against some others. That is why, for feminists, power-to retains the moral edge.

Authority Reinterpreted. Christian feminist reinterpretations of authority illustrate some of the ways in which this power-to, power-over interplay is being formulated. Discourse concerning authority by radical transformationist feminists reveals a strong emphasis on authority's rootage in relations of collaborative interdependence, power-to. These feminists affirm the need for power-over in the form of authority, but "authorities" are only such if they represent and serve communal flourishing, and remain bonded with the community in so doing.[179] Letty Russell's feminist paradigm of

---

[179]Service, a related notion, is of particular concern for Christian feminists and womanists, who are acutely sensitive to the historical abuses of images of self-expenditure (*agape*, Christian sacrifice, and so forth) in the interest of legitimating sexual and racial subordination. Whether in socio-economic structures or in interpersonal relations, interpretations of service that idealize the relinquishment of power and fulfillment by women for men and children, or by subjects for their masters, are not to be brooked. See, e.g., Jacquelyn

authority, for instance, interprets it as *authorizing* the inclusion of all persons as partners, and understands power as *empowerment* for self-actualization together with others.[180]   On this view, she suggests, "authority might be understood as legitimate power only when it opens the way to inclusiveness and wholeness in the household of faith."[181]

Womanist theologian Emilie Townes treats the question of authority in a like manner, enunciating a collaborative understanding of power-to that leads to a partnership-oriented idea of both authority and obedience. She rejects traditional dominative notions of power and authority in favor of an understanding that centers on mutual respect and cooperation. "The concept of power that comes from decision and responsibility is one that entails the ability to effect change and to work with others. This power requires openness, vulnerability, and readiness to change." In contrast to dominative power, which is experienced as a scarce possession, "power as cooperation and mutual respect is power in process that happens through us." It is activated when people engage in "interactions that produce value." This kind of power, wholly reflective of our power-to model, summons persons to develop their capacities for nurturance and empathy, and their interconnectedness. "Its project is justice."[182]

This understanding of power issues, for Townes, in a concept of shared authority:

Grant, "The Sin of Servanthood and the Deliverance of Discipleship," in Townes, ed., *Troubling in My Soul*, 199-219; Christine E. Gudorf, "Parenting, Mutual Love, and Sacrifice," in Andolsen, et al, eds., *Women's Consciousness*, 175-92.

[180]Russell, *Household of Freedom*, 61.

[181]Ibid.

[182]Emilie M. Townes, "Living in the New Jerusalem: The Rhetoric and Movement of Liberation in the House of Evil," in Townes, ed., *Troubling in My Soul*, 86-87.

The key here is partnership that begets coalitions. Shared authority is a dynamic process in which openness to the future evident in power as cooperation and mutual respect is manifest in the actual living out of movements for change and transformation. Shared authority recognizes the plurality in United States culture and is attentive to the various leadership styles and structures intrinsic in this diversity.[183]

Authority, on this view, occurs in a matrix of accountability to one's own immediate context and to those who represent other, diverse contexts. A pragmatic, pluralist, and consensus-building understanding of conversation and coalition-building is highlighted. Power-over is relegated to mutual power-over one another, in the sense that "Authority becomes the tool for dialogue within partnership. Each participant is recognized and valued as a co-creator of God's kingdom on earth. The views, the experience, the analysis of each person receive full weight, as strategies of transformation and community are constructed and enacted."[184]

Speaking of authority in the church as a Roman Catholic feminist liberationist, Elisabeth Schüssler Fiorenza makes analogous claims:

Authority within the Church as the discipleship community of equals must not be realized as 'power over,' as domination and submission, but as the enabling, energizing, creative authority of orthopraxis that not only preaches the Gospel of salvation but also has the power to liberate the oppressed and to make people whole and happy. . . . Leadership in the community of disciples should not be

---

[183]Ibid., 87.
[184]Ibid.

exercised as domination and power over but as service and liberation.[185]

Each of these feminists' deliberations reveal another feature of this approach to power: a dynamic interaction between an eschatological vision that shapes guidelines for the present, and an acute awareness of the ways in which sin and finitude conspire to entrench destructive patterns of power-over.[186] Short of the eschaton, inequality, conflict, and the tendency to exploit will not disappear from social relations. Feminist liberationist thinking about power and authority reflects this recognition. Yet Christian feminists seek to thwart the typical consequences of conflict and inequality--domination, violence, and conquest or exclusion--by developing strategies of service, nonviolent confrontation, and dignity-restoring reconciliation, all of which aim to expand the circle of interdependence and mutuality.

As mentioned, many Christian feminists have until now focused on patterns of ecclesial power and authority rather than on power in politics and economy. Recently, some authors have embarked upon more sustained analysis of empowering political and social structures. Schüssler Fiorenza, for instance, has analyzed power configurations in classical and modern patriarchal polities, and

---

[185]Elisabeth Schüssler Fiorenza, "Claiming our Authority and Power," J-B. Metz & E. Schillebeeckx, eds., *Concilium, The Teaching Authority of the Believers* (Edinburgh: T. & T. Clark Ltd, 1985), 52. Fiorenza insists that new feminist visions of power and authority are essential, but warns that, in the absence of real possibilities for change and conversion of ecclesial structures, such talk "could have a similar function for women in the Church as soap-operas and romantic novels have for abused women." Ibid.

[186]This religious stance has important analogues in some secular critical social theory. See Marcia Hewitt's incisive analysis of this relation, with special attention to the works of Schüssler Fiorenza, in "The Politics of Empowerment: Ethical Paradigms in a Feminist Critique of Critical Social Theory," *The Annual of the Society of Christian Ethics* (1991) 173-92, esp. 187-90.

advanced constructive directions for a "democratic feminist vision for a different society" and church.[87] In other cases, readers are left to extrapolate from discussions of ecclesial communities to judgments about socio-political power and authority. As Christian feminists continue to hone normative approaches to power in extra-ecclesial social settings, the literature of feminist social theory alluded to in Chapter Three promises to be an important source.

Summary: Paths Toward a Comprehensive Model. Despite the still-developing state of feminist ethical discussion on these matters, a number of normative insights concerning power and authority can be gleaned from the literature surveyed here. Together, these adumbrate a comprehensive Christian under- standing of power at whose heart is power-to.

First, feminists suggest that multiple positions of authority should be recognized in correspondence to the manifold and widely distributed gifts in a community. Such positions should accent the fluidity of authorities across time, place, and persons. Stable offices to which authority "in principle" attaches ought to be accorded to persons who carry such authority "in fact."[88]

Second, relations of power-over, either formally instituted or informally present due to inequalities of gifts or circumstance, are legitimate only insofar as they serve and are accountable to the common good, and are strictly limited by this purpose. Given this, functions of authority might include: to coordinate the actuation of power-to for the benefit of all parties; to enter into relations that

---

[87]See Schüssler Fiorenza, *Discipleship of Equals*, 353-72; *But She Said*, 103-32. In light of the interactions among theological, anthropological, and socio-political affirmations in an ethics of political power, feminists advancing such an ethics will need to attend to the ways their viewpoints differ, as well as intersect, on these various levels.

[88]See, e.g., Russell, *Household of Freedom*, 33-36. The distinction between "authority in principle" and "authority in fact" comes from Tillich, *Love, Power, and Justice*, 89-90.

are initially unequal for the purpose of achieving or better approximating mutuality (e.g. teaching, parenting); and to deter or fight external or internal threats to communal flourishing.

This last function of power-over raises the perplexing question of what place, if any, coercion or exclusion have within a power-to oriented ethics of power and authority. Feminists are wont to decry force and exclusion as patriarchal forms of control. But a feminist ethic must also consider whether intransigent practices of oppression or exclusion qualify as punishable, or "excommunicable" offenses. Russell, whose model of authority replaces the hierarchical pyramid with the image of an inclusive circle of interdependence, hints at one possible criterion for exclusion. In a church of diversified partnership, "all parts are welcome to participate as long as they are willing to work for God's covenant purpose of justice, *shalom*."[189]

Practical moral dilemmas emerge when a community must decide how to identify and respond to those who are not so willing, a problem to which circles of interdependence as well as hierarchical pyramids are vulnerable.[190] Under conditions where

---

[189]Russell, *Household of Freedom*, 35-36. Raising the question of power's resisting or excluding functions underscores the aforementioned need for Christian feminist analysis to more clearly distinguish an ethical theory of socio-political power from church-focused treatments such as the one Russell offers here.

[190] As anyone who has felt the sting of being excluded from an "inner circle" will testify, the images of circle and center are not automatically egalitarian or inclusive. Among third world liberationists, in fact, dependency theory employs images of center and periphery to articulate the oppressive economic and cultural relations between so-called advanced, developed nations and those of the third world. United Nations economist Paul Prebisch writes, "By dependency I mean . . . relations . . . whereby a country is subjected to decisions taken in the centers, not only in economic matters, but also in patterns of politics and strategy for domestic and foreign policies. The consequence is that due to exterior pressure the [periphery] country cannot decide autonomously what it should do or cease doing." Prebisch quoted in Ronald H. Chilcote, *Theories of Development and Under-*

the organizing principle remains the patriarchal paradigm, Russell suggests one avenue of response to evil when she calls on feminists to be "house revolutionaries" within the unredeemed orders of the present, challenging patriarchal powers while caringly hammering out alternative structures of authoritative relationship. As Christian feminists continue to fashion an ethics of power and authority, the question of how, from a paradigm of inclusion, one interprets and justly responds to abuses of power, will require careful consideration.[191]

A final insight emerging from these feminists' multifaceted analysis is this: an adequate Christian social ethics of power must attend to specific dynamics of power-to and power-over both within, and between, various social, political, and economic spheres. This includes the need to probe more deeply and critically the gender and power subtexts operative in standard accounts of the functions and relations of the public and private spheres. Some of the most promising Christian feminist ethical work is marked by this combination of finely-textured analysis of concrete power dynamics

---

development (Boulder, CO: Westview Press, 1984), 26.

[191]Forgiveness, coupled with an insistence on justice, is one response to evil that New Testament traditions illumine. Arendt raises the question of the political meaning and value of forgiveness in *Human Condition*, 236-43. Gutierrez's threefold model of redemption-as-liberation implies an important role for forgiveness by a now-empowered people. Clarifying the power dynamics involved in combining genuinely critical confrontation *and* forgiveness of enemies is a challenging task facing Christian feminist ethicists. Cf. Karen LeBacqz, "Love Your Enemy: Sex, Power, and Christian Ethics," *Annual of the Society of Christian Ethics* (1990): 3-24.

in particular social spheres, and astute interpretation of the larger structural patterns and issues at stake.[192]

From varying directions, Christian feminists are developing resources for an approach to socio-political power that has the potential to be genuinely comprehensive. From their vantagepoint informed by Christian sources and solidarity with women, feminists are seeing God, the cosmos, persons, and society in relational terms. Accordingly, they are fashioning an ethics that requires power and authority to be exercised in the context of solidarity, and in service to the goal of kingdom justice, conceived as inclusive, deeply mutual, interdependence and flourishing--*shalom*--within and among the human, natural, and divine communities. At its best, this still-nascent theory of power takes into account both root meanings of power and interrelates them in a way that facilitates discriminating analysis and transformation of social and institutions and practices. The task facing feminist Christian ethicists now is to continue to illumine the ways in which solidarity, mutuality, and interdependent flourishing may be understood and made practically operative in specific societal contexts.[193]

---

[192] See, e.g., See Pamela D. Couture, *Blessed are the Poor? Women's Poverty, Family Policy, and Practical Theology* (Nashville: Abingdon, 1991). Couture traces the disempowering consequences for women of the "gendered" ideological division in 19th and early 20th century middle class U.S. society. She incorporates a nuanced specification of power-to in her proposals concerning "shared responsibility" (versus "self-sufficiency") as the goal toward which public policies concerning poor women and families should aim.

[193] Along with her definition of mutuality (see n. 163 above), Beverly Harrison offers a description of solidarity that captures its meaning for these feminist Christian liberationists. "Solidarity is continuous relationship, fidelity to relationships, and mutual accountability . . . ." Harrison, *Making the Connections*, 231. Elsewhere, solidarity is described as a mode of life involving reciprocal power and mutuality. Ibid., 224-25.

Conclusion

This survey of theological and ethical writings has illustrated the vitality of the power-to model in important strands of recent Christian social thought. Mainstream Catholic and Protestant social ethicists, heirs to traditions represented by Reinhold Niebuhr and Jacques Maritain, continue to analyze socio-political problems primarily in power-over categories. Yet the burgeoning literature just explored testifies to a movement among some religious thinkers to more explicitly incorporate power-to into Christian social ethics.

Despite the definite and growing emphasis on power-to that this chapter has charted, most Christian social thinkers neither articulate nor employ the nuanced, comprehensive interrelation of power-over and power-to being promoted here. In this, religious ethicists mirror their counterparts in secular social theory. There are those thinkers who recognize the need for an integrated, power-to focused view, and a few who are consciously working to develop one. But, like the ethics of liberation (and that being fashioned on the basis of process thought), a complete Christian ethics of emancipatory empowerment remains a work in progress.

Among Christian ethicists, a comprehensive understanding of power will be advanced both by a more focused analysis of the distinctions and relations between power-over and power-to, and by continued dialogue with social theorists, such as those enumerated in Chapter Three, who probe the meaning and place of power-to in socio-political life. I have repeatedly suggested that a robust social ethics must entail such an understanding and evaluation of power. It is now time to make a more explicit case for a comprehensive approach to socio-political power in contemporary Christian social ethics.

CHAPTER V

POWER IN CHRISTIAN SOCIAL ETHICS:
TOWARD A COMPREHENSIVE APPROACH

Introduction

The preceding chapters have demonstrated the operation of dominative and transformative paradigms of socio-political power in social theory and in Christian ethical thought. In the majority of this literature the notion of power as superordination holds sway; but a second, alternative model of power as transformative capacity has also been detected. Along with theorists who heavily emphasize one or the other model, we have identified others who seek to provide a description of power that incorporates in some integrated fashion both the power-over and the power-to paradigms.

Theorists who press toward exclusive use of either model criticize one another on some typical grounds. Power-over thinkers find power-to approaches inadequate and naive with respect to questions of conflict and inequality in human relations. Conflict entails the inevitability of winners and losers--hence, dominators and subordinates--in the competition for scarce material and non-material goods. Even cooperative efforts, power-over advocates aver, require command-obedience relations of some sort: when a group of people moves a piano, there comes a point where one mover must say--"Go this way"--and the others must comply.

Power-to theorists reject the majority's assumption that hierarchy and domination are essential or normative expressions of power. These scholars perceive the heart of power in the efficacy generated by mutuality and collaboration. Each side regards the other as ignoring or underestimating important dimensions of the complete phenomenon of power.

Building on our preceding analysis, this final chapter opens up directions for constructive development of a Christian ethical theory of socio-political power. What arguments support a comprehensive approach to power in Christian social ethics? How might such an approach look? What constitutes an adequate correlation of power-over and power-to in a social ethics informed by the horizon of a particular Christian tradition? Having analyzed power-over and power-to elements in a spectrum of writings, I now want to make more explicit the case for a comprehensive approach to power in Christian social ethics, and to sketch the lines of one such approach. As a sketch, this proposal purports to be neither completely developed nor fully argued. Yet it does, I think, advance reasonably grounded claims that invite further investigation. It also suggests the benefits of incorporating power-to more explicitly and consistently into the discourse of Christian social ethics.

The Case for A Comprehensive Approach to Power in Christian Social Ethics

A central premise of this study is that understandings of socio-political power are grounded in sociological and anthropological presuppositions, which in turn reflect judgments about and choices among fundamental informing sources. These sources include the broad range of communal and individual experiences to which thinkers have access, organized disciplines of human knowing and doing, and, for Christian thinkers, the wisdom instantiated in their religious traditions. An adequate Christian social ethics exhibits dynamic coherence among these sources, these presuppositions, and basic notions like power.[1]

Because one's description of power clearly does not "come first," only to be followed by value considerations, it is also important that ethicists probe the normative and ideological presuppositions in a given social theory, as well as the presuppositions resident in their own criteria for selection among social theoretical resources. By "ideological" here, I mean--following Marx--presuppositions that serve the beneficiaries of given societal arrangements by explaining and legitimating the way power-over is presently distributed and exercised. Liberation theologians are correct to identify negative ideology as a pernicious manifestation of social sin. The insinuation of ideology into ethical method threatens to make moral knowing and doing inauthentic, or worse, complicitous in power's abuse.

This is not to claim that a *wertfrei* depiction of power is the alternative goal. But the objectivity of a treatment of power will be enhanced to the extent that ethicists make a practice of critically attending to the normative and ideological presuppositions that shape both their own perspectives, and the sources on which they draw. In the case of a Christian ethic, the normative vision of self and society harbored in a given social theory must be critically correlated with the normative vision the Christian standpoint encompasses. To be appropriate, the theory of socio-political power brought into play must cohere with the ethicist's interpretation of primary theological doctrines concerning God, person, and society.[2]

The most adequate Christian social ethics employs a comprehensive understanding of power, and articulates a moral

---

[1]"Our methodological coherence depends on the consistency and convergence of presumptions obtaining in our theo-anthropological, moral, and social perspectives." Beverly Wildung Harrison, *Making the Connections* (Boston: Beacon Press, 1985), 56-57.

[2]See the influential articulation of theological criteria of adequacy and appropriateness, and the method of critical correlation, in David Tracy, *Blessed Rage for Order* (New York: Seabury Press, 1975), and *Analogical Imagination* (New York: Crossroad, 1981).

discourse that reflects this complex integration. By a comprehensive approach to power I mean one that includes and relates power-to and power-over in each moment of the moral process: within a *descriptive model* that informs thought about what socio-political power, in fact, is; within a *normative paradigm* that expresses judgments about the good and the right in relation to socio-political power; and within *programs for action* that determine, in specific cases, what formulations of power-to and power-over best reflect the normative paradigm accepted. An effective social ethics articulates this comprehensive approach to power against a horizon of persuasively backed assumptions about individual and communal nature (anthropology and sociology) and flourishing (ethical notions of personal and common good). This normative horizon shapes not only the manner in which power is understood, but also how it is exercised, for what ends, and for whose benefit.

A comprehensive, Christian approach to socio-political power thus entails three tasks. First, it employs a theory of power that integrates its enabling and superordinating aspects. Second, it locates and warrants its discourse on power in relation to central Christian beliefs. Third, it exercises a critical hermeneutic on the assumptions about power embedded in the sources and circumstances shaping the ethicist's perspective. Such a complex understanding connects insights concerning power across different areas of Christian ethical concern: theological, anthropological, social theoretical, and practical-experiential. From each area, warrants for a comprehensive account may be adduced.

Toward a Theological Case

A model of socio-political power that interrelates power-to and power-over is more theologically satisfactory than alternative views. This becomes clear when the issue is considered in light of Christian affirmations about God, Jesus Christ, and the human situation.

In the first place, a comprehensive approach better captures the multidimensionality of divine power, portrayed in Christian scripture and tradition as both transcendent and immanent to humanity and human activity. Power-over illuminates the superiority, transcendence, and over-againstness of God in relation to creation. God as ultimate power-over is creator, protector, ruler, judge, and ordainer of destinies. The sovereignty and majesty revealed in God's mighty works are highlighted by a conception of power as superordination.[3]

Perceived through the prism of power-to, on the other hand, God's agency is illumined as pure effectiveness, and notions of divine power as operative in concert with human beings, or with and within the processes and patterns of the created order, are suggested. God's effective capacity to engender and sustain creation, and God's ongoing, immanent presence upholding and enabling human existence and human activity are highlighted by this model of power.[4]

Because Christian doctrine conceives of the human person as both dependent creature and in the image and likeness of the Creator, the way in which divine power is envisaged has a direct, albeit complicated, relation to a Christian understanding of human power. From the point of view of divine superordination humans' creaturely power is framed, negatively, as derivative of and subordinate to divine sovereignty. God's transcendent power-over

---

[3]James M. Gustafson's *Ethics from a Theocentric Perspective* (Chicago: The University of Chicago Press, 1981, 1984), e.g., incorporates an emphasis upon the transcendence of God, describing God in terms of "power bearing down upon" human existence. Gustafson's theocentric construal of ethics also accents God's "sustaining and enabling" impact on humans, indicating a comprehensive understanding of divine power.

[4]The confluence of the transcendence and immanence of divine power in human moral experience is distilled in Gustafson's succinct rendering of the basic practical moral question as, "What is God enabling and requiring us to be and to do?" *Ethics from a Theocentric Perspective* vol. 2, *Ethics and Theology*, 1-2. See also Kyle Pasewark's re-articulation of God's power as "the communication of efficacy," in *A Theology of Power* (Minneapolis, MN: Fortress Press, 1993), ch. 4, esp. 199-202.

is seen as independent of and distinct from human powers. The sphere of influence granted to human power remains strictly under the dictate of divine rule. Positively, humankind as *imago dei* is seen to reflect divine power-over in its transcendence over lower orders of creation, and in capacities for rational self-rule in moral judgment and action.[5] Historically, notions of divine power-over have also funded hierarchical images of society and church marked by divinely ordained relations of command and obedience.

When the power-to picture of God is emphasized, an understanding of human power as a kind of mutually exercised partnership with God is promoted. Here the implications of the *imago dei* for human power are perceived in humans' creative--God-like--abilities to engender, sustain, and promote the flourishing of life. The linkages and cooperation, rather than the distinctions and potential conflicts between human and divine power are highlighted from this latter perspective.

Warranted by evidence in scripture, tradition, and the experience of historical Christian communities, recognition of both power-over and power-to in a theology of God leads to a theological analysis of human power that attends to God's transcendence and immanence to human experience and agency. The history of Christian theological reflection upon the Trinitarian God and the divine *oikonomia* reveals an ongoing quest to elucidate and integrate these two distinct dimensions of divine power, and clarify their implications for theological anthropology and ethics.[6]

----

[5]Recall for example, Reinhold Niebuhr's anthropology, or Jacques Maritain's stress on the controlling and ordering influence of spiritual "personality," over material "individuality" in the human, as delineated in Chapter II.

[6]See, e.g., Elizabeth A. Johnson, *She Who Is: The Mystery of God in Feminist Theological Discourse* (New York: Crossroad, 1993), 269-72; Catherine Mowry LaCugna, *God For Us: The Trinity and Christian Life* (San Francisco: HarperSanFranciso, 1991), 382-411; Sheila Greeve Davaney, *Divine Power* (Philadelphia: Fortress Press, 1986). See also Arthur McGill's incisive critique of the soteriological and moral implications of a God of pure

In the second place, a comprehensive approach best illuminates the climactic historical expression of divine power in the life, death, and resurrection of Jesus. The notion of power as superordination is certainly relevant to christology. Jesus' *exousia* is experienced by those who encounter him as transcendent and compelling. In his preaching, activity, and person, the Jesus of the Gospels exudes a power that bespeaks a unique authority. This Jesus dramatically demonstrates power-over when he confronts demonic powers that ensnare and men and women--whether sin, fear, enmity, illness, or death. The resurrection is understood within the apostolic community as the definitive victory of divine power over death and sin. Later, as the nascent church gradually gains insight into the full meaning of the Christ event, God's transcendent power working through Jesus becomes more and more evident to the community, culminating in the Nicaean and Chalcedonian formulations of the full divinity of the man, Jesus as the Son of God.

Yet a purely power-over approach to understanding God's action in Jesus Christ is clearly inadequate. Those who do develop christologies from a strongly power-over focus are forced to interpret Jesus' *kenosis* and solidarity with the human lot as the surrender and rejection of power, or to maintain that the Son's descent into human weakness is in fact a quintessential--if paradoxical--expression of God's majestic power-over.[7]

---

power-over, in *Suffering: A Test of Theological Method* (Philadelphia: Westminster Press, 1982), esp. ch. 4; and James Luther Adams's insightful interrelation of human social empowerment and divine power in "Theological Bases of Social Action," in J. L. Adams, *Voluntary Associations*, J. Ronald Engel, ed. (Chicago: Exploration Press, 1986), 62-77.

[7]E.g., Reinhold Niebuhr, "The Power and Weakness of God," in *Discerning the Signs of the Times: Sermons for Today and Tomorrow* (New York: Charles Scribners' Sons, 1949); Karl Barth, *Church Dogmatics* (Edinburgh: T. & T. Clark, 1956-74), esp. II-I, 517; IV-I, 134, 158-59, 184-87, 417, 419, 533. Cited by Davaney, who analyzes Barth's claim that God's omnipotence is retained and reflected in the incarnation, life and death of Jesus in *Divine Power*, 49-58.

Incorporating power-to into christology helps make better sense of the conjoining of divine and human capacity in Jesus, and especially of the mode of service in which Jesus consistently expresses the capacities and authority given him. Jesus does not "lord it over" but comes "as one who serves" (Mk 10:42-45; Lk 22:24-27). For Christians, this message and this life reveal God's posture toward, and intentions for humanity. A power-to perspective uncovers collaborative, transformative capability with and for others as critical expressions of Jesus' power. As imitators of Christ, disciples are to re-enact this pattern that joins prophetic power over-against evil and effective power with and for the neighbor.

In the third place, situating theological affirmations in relation to a comprehensive treatment of power sheds new interpretive light on various facets of human experience and activity. By way of illustration, I will dwell briefly on two important, and surprisingly interrelated, areas: the relation between suffering and power, and the question of Christians' engagement in political power structures.

Suffering in its most basic sense refers to the experience of being vulnerable to external (frequently negative) influences, and of being affected by forces outside of one's control.[8] In any theological ethical consideration of suffering, engaging a comprehensive theory of power enlarges the perspective from which this perennial human problem may be understood.

From a power-over vantagepoint, one's degree of suffering is inversely proportionate to one's degree of power in a situation. An

---

[8]Notice that this definition of suffering directly intersects with the frequently-ignored, but classical definition of power as "the capacity to undergo an effect." This intriguing confluence suggests profoundly important avenues for further Christian theological and moral reflection. See Christine Firer Hinze, "Power in Christian Ethics: Resources and Frontiers for Scholarly Exploration," *Annual of the Society of Christian Ethics* (1992): 285-87.

omnipotent God, on this view, cannot suffer.[9] Jesus suffers insofar as he abdicates power. Now, in pondering why it is that Jesus eschews power-over to suffer and die, Christians down the ages have reaffirmed the creedal response, "for us and for our salvation." The fact that from a power-over perspective power must be discarded for redemption to occur, suggests that to embrace power is in tension with, if not antithetical to, the path of loving self-sacrifice Jesus blazed and meant his followers to pursue.

Turning the theological power-over lens on social relations highlights what experience confirms, that powerholders face the constant temptation to exercise prerogatives over others in an irresponsible and self-serving fashion. Powerholders also tend to forget that power and authority are given by God and subject to God's prerogatives. Morally, this dual pull toward irresponsibility makes powerholding a situation of perpetual double jeopardy. Given these perceptions, it is no wonder that Christians have frequently argued that to exercise power is to come into contact with, if not sin itself, at least with "near occasions" of sin, corruption, and evil.

Soteriological reflection within a power-over paradigm can thus foster the view that relations of superordination and subordination in the human community are, at best, a dangerous accommodation to a weak and sinful world. Dominative relations, by promoting order and checking evil, have been portrayed as the divinely ordained "left hand of God," as in Luther's two-kingdom theory, or as necessary structures implied in the orders of creation. At worst these relations are themselves expressions of God-defying pride and evil. This latter has led to some Christians to claim that disciples

---

[9]Contemporary theologians who reconsider divine and human power with unflinching attention to the concrete experiences of sufferers include Gustavo Gutierrez, *On Job: God-Talk and the Suffering of the Innocent*, trans. Matthew O'Connell (Maryknoll, NY: Orbis, 1987); Wendy Farley, *Tragic Vision and Divine Compassion* (Louisville, KY: Westminster/John Knox Press, 1990); McGill, *Suffering*; Johnson, *She Who Is*, ch. 12.

best imitate Jesus by keeping clear of any position that confers worldly power or status.[10]

A more prevalent line of thought shaped by power-over assumptions has contended that Christian disciples must not, indeed cannot, avoid involvement in positions of power and authority, insofar as these are part of the divinely appointed orders of creation. In family, society, and church, offices of power-over must therefore be exercised, but in strict obedience to God, before whom the powerful are held accountable. Beneficent paternalism, grounded in the divinely created ordained orders of nature, modeled on God's fatherly care, and conforming to divine law, provides a moral ideal for the Christian exercise of power-over. Like God, the Christian in power is not susceptible to the suffering that the powerless undergo, but, also like God, the leader must do all possible to relieve needless suffering and to enhance the lives of those his or her charge.[11]

A power-to perspective offers Christians strikingly different insights into suffering, socio-political power, and their relations. This view steps away from images of command and obedience to incorporate suffering and receptivity (the inevitability of influence by others, influence which is neither fully controllable by, nor always beneficial for its recipient) into the heart of its understanding of human power, of the redeeming power of Christ, and hence, of the co-redemptive activity of Christians. From this viewpoint, mutual influence is basic to a relational human condition. Sin involves relationships in which this mutuality is denied, unbalanced, or corrupted. In the redemptive activity of Christ, Jesus' vulnerability and suffering are inextricably bound to the power-bearing solidarity

---

[10]For distinguishing various interpretations of the Christianity-culture relation, H. Richard Niebuhr's frequently-cited typology remains useful. See his *Christ And Culture* (New York: Harper and Row, 1951).

[11]St. Augustine provides the classic formulation of this position in his *City of God*, Book 19. Augustine, *City of God*, ed. David Knowles, tr. Henry Bettenson (New York: Penguin Books, 1972).

of God with humankind that the incarnation bespeaks.[12] Jesus does not seek out suffering, yet, like anyone, his particular path of solidarity with God and neighbor renders him vulnerable to the effects, positive and negative, of others with whom he is related. Not only does Jesus accept the inevitability of sufferings due to solidarity; he recognizes and values the personally and communally transformative energy that is unleashed when persons risk the mutual vulnerability of service and love.[13] This, in turn, is the stance he requires of his followers: they are to take up their crosses

---

[12]Focused in a power-to lens, New Testament accounts of Jesus' encounters with suffering and social power are differently illuminated. If powerfulness includes the capacity to undergo effects we normally associate with suffering, then the meaning and mode of Jesus' expressions of power are unexpectedly re-framed. Consider, e.g., the accounts of Jesus' temptation in the desert (Mt. 4:1-11; Lk. 4:1-13); of Jesus' beckoning of the disciples to "suffer the children to come unto me," (Mt. 19:13-14); or of the crucifixion.

[13]Jacques Maritain provides this notion of the inevitability of sufferings due to solidarity. "Given the human condition, the most significant synonym for *living together* is *suffering together* . . .", bearing "the sufferings due to solidarity." Maritain, *Man and the State*, 207. Letty Russell and Rosemary Ruether pursue related tracks by describing Jesus as reconfiguring our understanding of power through his suffering solidarity with humanity. James Gustafson, however, cautions that the mutual infliction or acceptance of *suffering* may not best describe what occurs in relations of solidarity or cooperation. Rather, such relations require that "necessary restraints" be undertaken by relevant parties for the sake of communal flourishing. Perhaps, Gustafson agrees, in the broadest philosophical sense of "undergoing an effect," such restraints constitute suffering. Yet, that I curb my goals, desires, or needs for the sake of common order or the common project (a move which may redound to my own long term benefit) may better be described as a form of restraint than as a form of suffering. (Personal conversation, Chicago, April 4, 1988). The relevant distinction between restraint and suffering may be that the former refers to a limit either imposed or voluntarily accepted, while suffering often refers to the result of being deprived of something essential to one's flourishing or survival. This distinction is relevant for an ethics of power, as different normative judgments and different guidelines for action may pertain in the face of each.

and follow him (Lk. 14:27). The Pauline and pastoral epistles provide glimpses of an early church community struggling to understand and practically relate power-to and power-over in ways that faithfully reflected the authoritative service, and powerful love, modeled by Jesus.

When contemporary Christian ethicists join social justice issues at the theological and moral intersection between power and suffering, new questions for an ethics of social and political power arise. What sorts of vulnerability to suffering does participation in community require of citizens? For those holding power-over, what kinds of exposure may be called for? For the power-overless, what kinds of protection? Thinking about suffering in relation to power also forces attention to the exquisitely personal, concrete pain of the victims of violent social power.[14] Questions are newly posed about the significance for social ethics of theologies of the cross and redemptive suffering, on the one hand, and about how power, the powerful, and the powerless are to be involved in efforts to redress suffering, on the other. To be fruitful, these investigations require the amplitude of a comprehensive understanding of power.

These preliminary theological soundings cannot fail to mention the doctrine of the Holy Spirit. Pneumatology is a potentially fertile context for rethinking divine power-over and power-to and their manifestations in relation to human power, both in church and society. In certain respects, the Holy Spirit may provide a particularly apt symbolic medium for reflection on human and divine power-to. A sufficient treatment of the themes being raised here will give sustained attention to this often under-developed resource for a theology of divine-human power.[15]

---

[14]A probing, original study of the interactions between human suffering and power is Elaine Scarry, *The Body in Pain: The Making and Unmaking of the World* (New York: Oxford University Press, 1985), esp. ch. 2.

[15]Some liberation and feminist theologians are probing the implications for social power and authority of a pneumatological theological and ecclesial focus. See, e.g., Johnson, *She Who Is*, ch. 7; Leonardo Boff, *Church: Charism and Power* (New York: Crossroad, 1983). Boff rejects a dominative

We have barely scratched the surface of the profound significance that a comprehensive approach to power adumbrates for theological interpretation. Such considerations may appear rather remote from the mundane dynamics of socio-political power. Yet, for Christians, theological affirmations establish the matrix for ethical understandings of power's meaning and role in social life. Neither power-to nor power-over by itself adequately comprehends God's creative and redemptive activity, nor can either model fully elucidate the dynamics of power that are prescribed for disciples. To be faithful to its theological roots, then, a Christian ethics must employ both. How precisely basic theological and ethical notions about power get applied to socio-political relations will differ according to the particular theological community, depending upon, among other variables, how that community envisions the relationship of Christian truth to the wider contexts of collective life.

Toward an Anthropological Case

A comprehensive approach to power is best suited to the Christian picture of the human person, for it takes into account both the distinctness of the individual and individual agency, and the knittedness of each one to a wider network of relations. Power-over emphasizes the distinctness of individual agents and their ability to achieve separate and superior levels of control in relation to others, making them "powerful" in comparison to those over whom they hold sway. Power-to, in contrast, assumes the interdependence of all parties in the pursuit of effects, and identifies power as a feature of the acting body as a whole.

This duality of human agency as both individuated and communally bound reflects common experience, is affirmed in the simultaneously individual and social anthropology that animates

---

"christocentric" model for ecclesiology in favor of a pneumatological model that makes collaborative power-to central.

biblical religion, and may be found in some version in most social theoretical interpretations of human agency.[16]   I take it as axiomatic. Given this individual and social nature of the person, a comprehensive notion of power affords a diversified vocabulary for treating the complexities of human agency in relation to other agents. Employed in tandem, the concepts of power-over and power-to shed light on the myriad ways we affect one another and yet rely on each other to be effective.

Social Theoretical and Practical-Experiential Cases

The social theoretical and practical-experiential grounds for a comprehensive approach to power I take to be intrinsically related. Good social theory is grounded in and explanatory of concrete social practice. Optimally, then, practice and theory exist in a dynamic relation of mutual and continuing illumination, criticism, and correction.[17] Earlier chapters have provided grounds for my claim that a comprehensive conception best illuminates the multiple practical dimensions of social and political power, thereby enhancing social and ethical theory. On the level of social action, the comprehensive view captures both the cooperative and

---

[16]Certain modern ideological positions do appear to eliminate one side of the individual-social polarity. Extreme forms of liberalism can veer toward an exclusive emphasis on the individual, while all totalitarian and some socialist ideologies tend to obscure the role of individual agency. By so vigorously targetting either side of the individual-social polarity for criticism or rejection, however, such critics thereby acknowledge it, at least as an aberration to be opposed.

[17]The same is true of the relationship between Christian theological and ethical theory, and the practical experiences of Christians in church and society. Complicating the Christian case are questions about the role of core traditions and doctrines, and of structures of ecclesial authority in this dynamic self-correcting process. Such questions, while beyond the scope of this project, are, in fact, connected to its central concerns.

conflictual experiences involved in the actuation, distribution, and sustenance of power and power relations. Paula Cooey calls ambivalence toward power a fitting reaction to a fundamentally equivocal and ambiguous phenomenon.[18] The contradictory reactions people have to power, the fact that it both attracts and repels, elicits desire and fear, are also better accounted for by this model. A comprehensive approach, then, sheds discriminating light on the tangle of enabling and superordinating practices and structures associated with socio-political power. Dynamics of cooperation and complicity as well as competition and conflict, and relations of mutuality as well as of domination and subordination, are illumined.

Relating Power-Over and Power-To
In a Comprehensive Model

In summary, the main warrant for adopting a comprehensive understanding of power for Christian social ethics is as simple as it is crucial: Because a comprehensive model comprises a more complete, precise, and integrated description of power, it can contribute to better normative theory and more effective moral practice. A comprehensive descriptive theory of power affords a more robust and differentiated field in which to discuss the right and the good in social and political life. By more accurately showing what is going on, such a model affords a richer purview within which to consider both what ought to be going on, and the appropriate means by which those desired end-states may be attained.

Among the implications of my argument in favor of a comprehensive approach to power that await further investigation, there is one that demands immediate consideration. If one grants that an adequate construal of power must incorporates both power-

---

[18]Paula Cooey, "The Power of Transformation and the Transformation of Power," *Journal of Feminist Studies in Religion*, 1, no. 1 (1985): 36.

to and power-over, precisely *how* are these two models to be related in a comprehensive descriptive scheme? Ethicists do not satisfy the requirements of comprehensive view by simply holding up two different lenses and reporting the results. Rather, the ethicist must make explicit and defend the way in which she or he configures the relation between these two formulations of power.

To the ethicist seeking a descriptively accurate way of relating the two modes of power, several possibilities present themselves. One is that there is no relation between power-to and power-over, and that these two labels designate wholly distinct and independent social phenomena. This study has been premised on the opposing view, that there is an inescapable relationship between these two models because they are two ways of analyzing a single, multifaceted phenomenon. It may be, secondly, that effective capacity, power-to, is derivative of and ultimately oriented by relations of super- and subordination, power-over. This appears to be the argument of Michel Foucault. Conversely, power-over may in fact be derived from and oriented by power-to, even though that fact may be obscured to superordinates. Political theorists who stress *potestas in populo* make this claim, as do some Marxian interpreters. In a fourth possible configuration, a dynamic interplay between power-to and power-over can be envisioned, whereby transformative efficacy and domination are interdependent and mutually engendering realities. This may be Anthony Giddens's preferred model. Finally, it could be the case that, depending on certain variables, any one of a number of relations may obtain in concrete social circumstances.

To select one of these conceptual possibilities requires analyzing a variety of empirical situations and events, and asking which formulation best illumines the perceptions and behaviors of the relevant actors and institutional patterns. As has been noted, analysis of this sort is complicated by the interaction of ideology with each of these foci (the perceptions and behavior of actors, and institutional patterns). Critical vigilance is necessary, lest the impact of a dominant ideology on people's perceptions and behavior befuddle attempts to discern the ways power actually works. This "ideological proviso" highlights once again the importance of attendng to ways that values (of observers of, and participants in social power) shape perceptions about power.

Christianity's normative interpretation of experience in terms of creation, sin, redemption, and eschatology has a further impact on efforts to clarify and evaluate the interaction of power-over and power-to in the socio-political arena. For, once the most accurate description of *de facto* power relations is determined, the ethicist must judge if, from the perspective of his or her particular theological tradition, another comprehensive interpretation has special *de jure* weight. Should this be the case, the ethicist faces a further task: persuasively articulating and promoting that normative conception of power in the face of opposing social and political arrangements or practices.

Comprehensive Interpretations and Christian Doctrines

The Christian social ethicist considering power must determine whether a specific formulation of the power-to/power-over relation coheres with the interpretive horizon framed by Christian doctrines, and informed by Christian and secular experience, theory, and practice. The materials we have examined illustrate several ways of making this determination. Each is influenced by how a given author understands, configures, or prioritizes the basic doctrines of creation, fall, redemption, and eschatology.

Among Christian thinkers who emphasize power-over in socio-political life, some, like Reinhold Niebuhr, do so on the basis of the impact of *sin* on social relations. For Niebuhr, power-over is to the fore in all historical relations, and this is directly the result of sinful egoism. The effect of this egoism on historical life is to radically constrict the possibilities for genuine expressions of power-to. While power-to stands as an eschatological norm for Niebuhr, and may be approximable in intimate, interpersonal settings, it is virtually unattainable in social or political relations.

By contrast, what seems a more benign picture--though

liberationists might warn that appearances are deceiving!--of power-over emerges among thinkers who regard hierarchy, superordination, and a certain coerciveness as inherent to the created order, and hence as playing a *de jure*, not simply a *de facto* role in socio-political relations. In these treatments, a particular construal of the doctrine of *creation* is highlighted.

Though I have argued that Jacques Maritain construes power-over in this way, while Paul Tillich makes more of the roots of superordination in power-to, the two are finally very similar in their renderings of political power as the ability to achieve purposes over and against the resistance of others. Both Tillich and Maritain ground their appreciation for power-over in affirmations about the hierarchical and controlling features of divine and created power. As God's power is both enablement and constraint, so human institutions require dimensions that order and control, without which they are not genuinely empowering. At the same time, they recognize that structures of power-over ought to allow the greatest possible freedom (a notion which sometimes includes power-to), compatible with the good of the whole of society.

A further, in my judgment promising, avenue toward a comprehensive Christian understanding of socio-political power is being forged by the feminist and other liberationist thinkers we have considered. Notions of *redemption* and *eschatology* are pivotal for these scholars' interpretations of socio-political life. With Niebuhr, liberationists view the prevalence of constraining power-over in socio-political life as the result of sin. Many (though not all) liberationists also agree with Niebuhr that power-over can, paradoxically, be an indispensable tool for combatting and curbing oppression. But, while Niebuhr, Tillich, and many others judge-- due to sin, or creaturely finitude, or both--that every historically significant instance of power entails a heavy emphasis on power-over, many Christian liberationists disagree. Focusing on redemption and God's eschatological community, these thinkers envision a tensive, transformative relationship between biblical visions of peace and justice and all historical relations, including those involving socio-political power.

Far from merely standing in judgment upon all actual structures of power-over, the eschatological reign of God provides the future point from which the present structures may be re-envisioned, points the way for steps to recreate those power arrangements, and inspires and enables renovative action in the here-and-now. While painfully cognizant of the impact of sin on human interactions, and realistic about the prospects for simply or fully wiping away sin's effect on social structures, liberationist ethicists endeavor to take seriously the difference that God's future, initiated through the redemptive action of Jesus, makes for power, now. Accordingly, theirs is a two-pronged approach.

On the one hand, they unmask and vigorously denounce oppressive or constricting practices of power-over. On the other hand, they labor to articulate and embody a praxis of power rooted firmly in collaborative, transformative efficacy, and oriented toward the mutual increase of such efficacy by a lively notion of the common good.[19] The insight just beginning to be developed by these authors is also my own: socio-political power is about, most basically, power-to; from this starting point, instances of power-over have strictly instrumental value, and are to be allowed only to the extent they are necessary to defend or enhance the common good-- which has the empowerment of each and all as one of its important facets.

Christians committed to emancipation of the oppressed thus must form, in the words of feminist Sharon Welch, communities of solidarity and resistance. Within such communities, relations of power-to found a dynamic common good that is resistant to anarchy

---

[19]How particular interpretations of power-to and power-over interact with understandings of the common good in Christians ethics is a question that invites further study. The present analysis of the receptive, collaborative, and non-oppressive features of power-to underscores the need to incorporate empowerment as well as freedom into into contemporary discourse about the common good.

because it incorporates a just ordering, and resistant to external or internal tyranny because of the collaborative inclusivity that characterizes its practices and institutions. Amidst real differences, there is wide agreement among liberationists both about this way of conceptualizing power, and about the theological warrants for so doing.

An Assessment and Proposal

A comprehensive Christian approach to understanding socio-political power must be in alignment with core Christian doctrines. It would be a mistake, though, to assume any simple correspondence between models of power and Christian doctrines-- for example, that power-over is always linked with sin and is therefore always evil, or that power-to, as a feature of creation or redemption, is always beneficent. And, despite the apparent assumptions of some liberationists, there is certainly no evidence that relations of hierarchy always and everywhere are sinful. Many ethicists find a positive role for power-over in beneficent forms of authority, or in social institutions when they redress the effects of sin. Likewise, one may not assume that a group's exercise of transformative efficacy is morally good without scrutinizing the circumstances, goals and effects of that exercise. The Manhattan Project, which produced the first nuclear weapon, was certainly an effective communal effort, yet the morality of that endeavor is not unimpeachable on the basis of the single-minded collaboration and astonishing efficacy it displayed.

Yet critical examination of experience informed by secular and religious wisdom supports the more modest claim that power-to relations are *generally* more conducive to and reflective of dignified human interaction and flourishing than relations of power-over. Moreover, the evidence we have surveyed suggests reasons for regarding power-to as a good in itself. Christian anthropology, theology, and ethics consistently affirm humans' dignity, sociality and creativity--all of which are expressed in the exercise of transformative capacity--as normative. Yet Christians who affirm power-over associate it most often with conditions wrought by sin and finitude. Efficacy with others has creative and redemptive dimensions that control over others cannot claim. Accordingly, I favor a comprehensive view of power for Christian social ethics that gives descriptive and normative priority to power-to, and limits power-over to secondary, instrumental status.

Their focus on power-over in society and politics notwithstanding, I believe an implicit recognition of the theological and moral priority of power-to is discernable among thinkers as diverse as Augustine, Aquinas, Niebuhr, and Maritain. This recognition is implicitly harbored, for instance, in earlier Christian understandings of the common good. Neither Augustine and Aquinas condemn hierarchical social relations; reflecting their philosophical and cultural milieux, they deem them natural or in some cases divinely ordained. Yet both make it plain that such arrangements are just only when leaders govern for the common good. Power-over must be used in service of the people, not for the selfish gain of the rulers. These classical accounts do not, it is true, explicitly elaborate power-to as an overriding feature of a just society. Yet insofar as "common good" refers to circumstances in which all members are flourishing in their particular situations, and all together effectively and cooperatively contribute to the flourishing of the whole, that notion implies the normativity of transformative, collaborative efficacy.

In the modern period, as we have seen, appreciation for power-to has frequently been redirected into the language of freedom. During this century, Christian ethicists in the west have worked amid a cultural milieu wherein individual liberty and creativity have been especially prized. So, authors such as Maritain, while staunchly loyal to the legacy of Aquinas, focus on persons' maximum attainment of freedom and creativity in communion with others as an explicit feature of the common good. Or Reinhold Niebuhr who, while deeply indebted to the political vision of Augustine, pictures dynamic democratic structures rather than harmonious patriarchal ones as the optimal arena for effective and flourishing individuals and groups. These classical and modern thinkers have numerous disagreements concerning understandings of personhood and society, concerning the possibilities and limits framing historical action, and about the degree to which a genuinely common good can be attained or should be pursued. They also disagree about the precise role that power-over should play in social and political interaction. Yet, however remote from historical attainment it may be deemed, each in his own way recognizes harmoniously actuated communal and individual efficacy, power-to, as a norm rooted in basic religious apperceptions about humanity's God-given, communal nature and destiny.

The comprehensive notion of power that is required for Christian ethics, then, accords power-to descriptive and normative priority. But how can a power-to oriented theory and practice be advanced in a socio-political world where power-over seems indubitably to reign? This question is most clearly grasped, though it is only beginning to be adequately addressed, by the liberationist writers we have considered. By embracing a critically transformative relation between Gospel values and socio-political practice, and developing an ethical posture informed by the doctrines of redemption and eschatology, Christian liberationists are charting a trajectory for the sort of comprehensive understanding and ethics of power I am proposing here. Despite the controversy surrounding it and the charges of incompleteness or ambiguity to which its representatives have been vulnerable, liberationist theory and practice is an important source and, I think, the most promising current context for continuing to develop such an ethics.

Other resources investigated here must also contribute to a reformulated notion of socio-political power.   In fashioning comprehensive theories and practices concerning power, Christian ethicists will benefit from the insights into power-to found in social and political theories. On the other hand, classic and modern articulations of power-over will continue to challenge facile religious formulations of power-to, and prod ethicists interested in social change to sharpen and nuance their theoretical presentations and practical applications.

Finally, as we have insisted in every case, Christian social ethicists fashioning a comprehensive approach to power must accountably and coherently "think with" their basic religious affirmations about God, the world, humanity, and human history. Clarifying fundamental understandings of divine power and its relation to human agency, and elaborating the possibilities and limits of socio-political activity and structures accordingly, remain vast but inescapable background tasks for an adequate Christian social analysis and ethics of power.

Conclusion

This study has examined a wide range of materials in contemporary social theory and Christian thought in order to expose the workings of two basic models for socio-political power. We have uncovered and critically assessed the theological, anthropological, and sociological presuppositions that undergird various authors' analyses. Strengths and weaknesses of placing primary or exclusive emphasis on one or the other model of power have been considered, and the case for an integrated appropriation of both advanced. Finally, building on insights drawn from our investigation of key secular and religious sources, directions for of a constructive, comprehensive approach to socio-political power in Christian ethics have been suggested.

It is in the nature of the subject matter and aims of this project that I have not provided a conclusive demonstration of my constructive thesis. Instead, the viability of the power-to and power-over typologies has been confirmed, the importance of setting a theory of power within a coherent presuppositional context has been shown, and groundwork for a comprehensive approach to power has been laid. Doing this, I hope, has contributed to the development of criteria for an adequate conception of socio-political power in Christian ethics.

Power understood in a comprehensive manner illumines features of the social and political landscape otherwise obscured, and lends the necessary starting point and context for a sophisticated Christian social and political ethics. In the end, the particular way of being comprehensive that a Christian ethicist embraces transfuses fundamental theological and anthropological convictions into the heart of ethical thinking about society and politics. For my own part, the evidence of scripture and Christian tradition, social analysis, and especially the historical testimony of peoples' struggles for empowerment and justice, converge in a concluding theological judgment. Most essentially, God's kingdom, God's power, and God's glory bespeak the shining forth not of dominion over the other, but of sheer, overflowing, efficacy of being, and being together. Divine efficacy, graciously reflected in the creative and collaborative features of human agency: here we find the most profound and truthful starting point, motive, and term for comprehending power in Christian social ethics.

SELECTED BIBLIOGRAPHY

Adams, James Luther. *Voluntary Associations*. J. Ronald Engel, Ed. Chicago: Exploration Press, 1986.

Alinsky, Saul. *Rules for Radicals*. New York: Harper Vintage Books, 1970.

Allard, Jean-Louis, Ed. *Jacques Maritain: philosophe dans la cité*. Ottawa, Canada: Editions de l'Université d'Ottawa, 1985.

Allen, Wayne. "Hannah Arendt and the Ideological Structure of Totalitarianism." *Man and World* 26 (1993): 115-129.

Anderson, Alan B. and George Pickering. *Confronting the Color Line: The Broken Promise of the Civil Rights Movement in Chicago*. Macon, GA: University of Georgia Press, 1987.

Andolsen, Barbara Hilkert. *Daughters of Bootblacks, Daughters of Jefferson: Racism and American Feminism*. Macon, GA: Mercer University Press, 1986.

Andolsen, Barbara Hilkert, Christine E. Gudorf, and Mary D. Pellauer, Eds. *Women's Consciousness, Women's Conscience: A Reader in Feminist Ethics*. Minneapolis: Seabury Books, Winston Press, 1985.

Ansbro, John J. *Martin Luther King, Jr.: The Making of a Mind*. Maryknoll, NY: Orbis Books, 1984.

Antonio, Robert J. & Ronald M. Glassman, Eds. *A Weber-Marx Dialogue*. Lawrence, KS: University of Kansas Press, 1985.

Arendt, Hannah. *Between Past and Future: Eight Exercises in Political Thought*. New York: Penguin Books, 1961.

___. "Collective Responsibility." In *Amor Mundi: Explorations in the Faith and Thought of Hannah Arendt*. James W. Bernauer, S.J., Ed. Boston: Martinus Nijhoff, Publishers, 1987.

Arendt, Hannah. *Crises of the Republic.* New York: Harcourt Brace Jovanovich, 1969.

___. *The Human Condition.* Chicago: The University of Chicago Press, 1958.

___. *The Origins of Totalitarianism.* Cleveland and New York: Meridian Books, The World Publishing Company, 1951.

___. *On Revolution.* New York: Penguin Books, 1963.

Aron, Raymond. *German Sociology.* Trans. Mary and Thomas Bottomore. Glencoe, IL: The Free Press, 1964.

Augustine of Hippo. *City of God.* Ed. David Knowles, trans. Henry Bettenson. New York: Penguin Books, 1972.

Bachrach, Peter, and Gordon Baratz. "Two Faces of Power." *American Political Science Review* 56 (1962): 947-52.

Balbus, Isaac D. *Marxism and Domination: A Neo-Hegelian, Feminist, Psychoanalytic Theory of Sexual, Political, and Technological Liberation.* Princeton, NJ: Princeton University Press, 1982.

Barth, Karl. *Church Dogmatics.* Edinburgh: T. & T. Clark, 1956-1974.

Beetham, David. *The Legitimation of Power.* Atlantic Highlands, NJ: Humanities Press, 1991.

Bellah, Robert, Richard Madsen, William M. Sullivan, Ann Swidler, and Steven M. Tipton. *Habits of the Heart: Individualism and Commitment in American Life.* New York: Harper and Row Paperback, 1985.

Benhabib, Seyla. "Hannah Arendt and the Redemptive Power of Narrative." *Social Research* 57/1 (Spring 1990): 188-96.

___ and Drucilla Cornell, Eds. *Feminism as Critique.* Minneapolis: University of Minnesota Press, 1987.

Bernauer, James W., S.J., Ed. *Amor Mundi: Explorations in the Faith and Thought of Hannah Arendt*. Boston: Martinus Nijhoff Publishers, 1987.

Bloch, Michael, Byran Heading, and Philip Lawrence. "Power in Social Theory: A Non-Relative View." *Philosophical Disputes in the Social Sciences*, 243-274. Ed. S. C. Brown. Sussex, NJ: Harvester and Humanities Press, 1979.

Boff, Leonardo. *Church: Charism and Power*. New York: Crossroad, 1983.

___ and Clodovis Boff. *Introducing Liberation Theology*. Paul Burns, trans. Maryknoll, NY: Orbis Books, 1987.

Borne, Etienne. "La philosphie politique de Jacques Maritain." *Jacques Maritain: philosophe dans la cité*. Ed. Jean-Louis Allard. Ottawa, Canada: Editions de l'université d'Ottawa, 1985, 247-62.

Boyte, Harry, ed. *The New Populism*. Philadelphia: Temple University Press, 1986.

Boulding, Kenneth. *Three Faces of Power*. Newbury Park, CA: Sage Publications, 1992.

Brackley, J. Dean. *Salvation and Social Transformation in the Theologies of Jacques Maritain and Gustavo Gutierrez*. Unpublished Ph.D. thesis. University of Chicago, 1981.

Braybrooke, David. "Ideology." *Encyclopedia of Philosophy*, vol. 4, 124-127. Ed. Paul Edwards. New York: Macmillan and The Free Press, 1967.

Burkitt, Ian. "Overcoming Metaphysics: Elias and Foucault on Power and Freedom." *Philosophy of the Social Sciences* 23/1: (March 1993): 50-72.

Cahill, Lisa Sowle. *Between the Sexes: Foundations for a Christian Ethics of Sexuality*. Philadelphia: Fortress Press, 1985.

Calhoun, Craig, Ed. *Habermas and the Public Sphere*. Cambridge, MA: MIT Press, 1993.

Cannon, Katie Geneva. *Black Womanist Ethics*. Atlanta, GA: Scholars Press, 1988.

Canovan, Margaret. *Hannah Arendt: A Reinterpretation of Her Political Thought*. New York: Cambridge University Press, 1992.

Caraway, Nancy. *Segregated Sisterhood: Racism and the Politics of American Feminism*. Knoxville, TN: University of Tennessee Press, 1991.

Card, Claudia, Ed. *Feminist Ethics*. Lawrence, KS: University of Kansas Press, 1991.

Carlsnaes, Walter. *The Concept of Ideology in Political Analysis*. Westport, CT: Greenwood Press, 1981.

Carr, Anne E. *Transforming Grace: Christian Tradition and Women's Experience*. San Francisco: Harper and Row, 1988.

Carver, Terrell, Ed. *The Cambridge Companion to Marx*. Cambridge: Cambridge University Press, 1991.

Case-Winters, Anna. *God's Power: Traditional Understandings and Contemporary Challenges*. Louisville, KY: Westminster/John Knox Press, 1990.

Chilcote, Ronald H. *Theories of Development and Underdevelopment*. Boulder, CO: Westview Press, 1984.

Chodorow, Nancy. *The Reproduction of Mothering*. Berkeley, CA: University of California Press, 1978.

Christ, Carol C. and Judith Plaskow, Eds. *Womanspirit Rising: A Feminist Reader in Religion*. New York: Harper and Row, 1979.

Chung, Hyun Kyung. *The Struggle to be the Sun Again: Introducing Asian Women's Theology*. Maryknoll, NY: Orbis Books, 1990.

Cobb, John B., Jr. *Process Theology as Political Theology*. Philadelphia: Westminster Press, 1982.

Cohen, Ira. "The Underemphasis on Democracy in Marx and Weber." *A Weber-Marx Dialogue*. Ed. Robert J. Antonio and Ronald M. Glassman. Lawrence, KS: University Press of Kansas, 1985, 274-299.

Coll, Regina, CSJ. "Power, Powerlessness and Empowerment." *Religious Education* 81:3 (Summer 1986): 412-423.

Collins, Patricia Hill. *Black Feminist Thought: Knowledge, Consciousness, and the Politics of Empowerment*. Boston: Unwin Hyman, 1990.

Comblin, José. *The Church and the National Security State*. Maryknoll, NY: Orbis Books, 1979.

Cone, James. *Black Theology and Black Power*. New York: Seabury Press, 1969.

___. *For My People: Black Theology and the Black Church*. Maryknoll, NY: Orbis Books, 1984.

___. *God of the Oppressed: A Black Theology of Liberation*. New York: Seabury, 1975.

Connolly, William. *The Terms of Political Discourse*. Lexington, MA: Heath Publishing Company, 1974.

Cooey, Paula. "The Power of Transformation and the Transformation of Power." *Journal of Feminist Studies in Religion* 1 (1985): 22-35.

Cooper, John W. *The Theology of Freedom: The Legacy of Jacques Maritain and Reinhold Niebuhr*. Macon, GA: Mercer University Press, 1985.

Couture, Pamela D. *Blessed are the Poor? Women's Poverty, Family Policy, and Practical Theology*. Nashville, TN: Abingdon, 1991.

Cox, Harvey. "Reply." *New York Review of Books* (Feb 9, 1986): 40.

Cropsey, Joseph. "Karl Marx." *History of Political Philosophy*, 697-723. Ed. Leo Strauss and Joseph Cropsey. Chicago: Rand McNally, 1969.

Dahl, Robert. *Who Governs? Democracy and Power in an American City.* New Haven, CT: Yale University Press, 1981.

Dallmayr, Fred R. "Agency and Structure." Review of *Central Problems in Social Theory*, by Anthony Giddens. In *Philosophy of the Social Sciences* 12 (December, 1982): 427-438.

Daly, Herman E. and John B. Cobb, Jr. *For the Common Good.* Boston: Beacon Press, 1989.

Daly, Mary. *Beyond God the Father.* Boston: Beacon Press, 1980.

Davaney, Sheila Greeve. *Divine Power.* Harvard Dissertations in Religion No. 19. Philadelphia: Fortress Press, 1986.

Davaney, Sheila Greeve, Ed. *Feminism and Process Thought.* The Harvard Divinity School/Claremont Center for Process Studies Symposium Papers. New York: E. Mellen Press, 1981.

D'Entreves, Maurizio Passerin. "Agency, Identity, and Culture: Hannah Arendt's Conception of Citizenship." *Praxis International* 9:1/2 (April & July 1989): 1-24.

Downey, Michael J., ed. *That They Might Live: Power, Empowerment, and Leadership in the Church.* New York: Crossroad, 1991.

Dreyfus, Hubert L. and Paul Rabinow, Eds. *Michel Foucault: Beyond Structuralism and Hermeneutics.* Chicago: The University of Chicago Press, 1982.

Duffé, Bruno-Marie. "Hannah Arendt, le 'religieux' dans le politique. *Revue de théologie et philosophie* 120 (1988): 161-178.

Duquesne, M. "La philosophie politique de Jacques Maritian." Louvain, *Centre d'archives Maurice Blondel, Journée d'études* 4 (November, 1974): 39-56.

Dussel, Enrique. *Ethics and Community*. Maryknoll, NY: Orbis Books, 1988.

Elshtain, Jean Bethke. *Public Man, Private Woman: Women in Social and Political Thought*. Princeton, NJ: Princeton University Press, 1981.

___. *Power Trips and Other Journeys: Essays in Feminism as Civic Discourse*. Madison, WI: University of Wisconsin Press, 1990.

___. *Women and War*. New York: Basic Books, 1987.

Evans, Sara M. and Harry C. Boyte. *Free Spaces: The Sources of Democratic Change in America*. Chicago: The University of Chicago Press, 1992.

Esquith, Stephen L. "Politics and Values in Marx and Weber." In *A Weber-Marx Dialogue*, ed. Robert J. Antonio and Ronald M. Glassman, 300-318. Lawrence, KS: University Press of Kansas, 1985.

Fabella, Virginia and Mercy Amba Oduyoye, Eds. *With Passion and Compassion: Third World Women Doing Theology*. Maryknoll, NY: Orbis Books, 1988.

Fanon, Frantz. *The Wretched of the Earth*. New York: Grove Publishing Co., 1963.

Farley, Wendy. *Tragic Vision and Divine Compassion*. Louisville, KY: Westminster Press, 1990.

Ferguson, Kathy E. *The Feminist Case Against Bureaucracy*. Philadelphia: Temple University Press, 1984.

___. *Self, Society, and Womankind: The Dialectic of Liberation*. Westbury, CT: Greenwood Press, 1980.

Fiorenza, Elisabeth Schüssler. *But She Said: Feminist Practices of Biblical Interpretation*. Boston: Beacon Press, 1992.

Fiorenza, Elisabeth Schüssler. "Claiming our Authority and Power." In *The Teaching Authority of the Believers*, ed. J-B. Metz and E. Schillebeeckx. Edinburgh: T. & T. Clark Ltd., 1985.

___. *Discipleship of Equals: A Critical Feminist Ekklesia-logy of Liberation*. New York: Crossroad, 1993.

Follett, Mary Parker. *Dynamic Administration: The Collected Papers of Mary Parker Follett*. Ed. Henry C. Metcalf and L. Urwick. New York: Harper Company, 1941.

Fornet-Betancourt, H. Becker, A. Gomez-Müller, interviewers. "The Ethic of Care for the Self as a Practice of Freedom: An Interview with Michel Foucault." J.D. Gauthier, S.J., trans. *Philosophy and Social Criticism* 12 (Summer, 1987), 112-31.

Foucault, Michel. *Discipline and Punish*. London: Allen Lane, 1977.

___. *The History of Sexuality, Vol. 1: An Introduction*. Trans. Robert Hurley. New York: Vintage Books, 1980.

___. *Power/Knowledge: Selected Interviews and Other Writings 1972-1977*. Ed. Colin Gordon. Trans. L. Marshall, J. Mepham, K. Soper. New York: Pantheon Books, 1980.

___. *Power, Truth, Strategy*. Sydney: Feral Publications, 1979.

___. "The Subject and Power." In Hubert L. Dreyfus and Paul Rabinow, *Michel Foucault: Beyond Structuralism and Hermeneutics*, 209-238. Chicago: The University of Chicago Press, 1982.

Fraser, Nancy. *Unruly Practices: Power, Discourse and Gender in Contemporary Social Theory*. Minneapolis: University of Minnesota Press, 1989.

French, Marilyn. *Beyond Power: Of Women, Men, and Morals*. New York: Summit Books, 1985.

Garner, Rueben, Ed. *The Realm of Humanitas: Responses to the Writings of Hannah Arendt.* American University Studies Series V, Vol. 83. New York: Peter Lang, 1990.

Geuss, Raymond. *The Idea of a Critical Theory: Habermas and the Frankfurt School.* Cambridge: Cambridge University Press, 1981.

Gibbons, William J., S.J., Ed. *Seven Great Encyclicals.* Paramus, NJ: Paulist Press, 1963.

Giddens, Anthony. *Capitalism and Modern Social Theory.* Cambridge: Cambridge University Press, 1971.

___. *Central Problems in Social Theory: Action, Structure, and Contradiction in Social Analysis.* Berkeley: University of California Press, 1979.

___. *A Contemporary Critique of Historical Materialism.* 2 vols. Berkeley: University of California Press, 1981, 1985.

___. *Profiles and Critiques in Social Theory.* Berkeley: University of California Press, 1982.

___. "On the Relation of Sociology to Philosophy." In Paul R. Secord, Ed. *Explaining Human Behavior: Consciousness, Human Action, and Social Structure.* Beverly Hills, CA: Sage Publications, 1982.

___. *Sociology: A Brief but Critical Introduction.* London: MacMillan, 1982.

___. *Studies in Social and Political Theory.* New York: Basic Books, 1977.

Gordon, Suzanne. "Anger, Power, and Women's Sense of Self." *Ms.* (July 1985): 42.

Gouldner, Alvin W. *The Two Marxisms.* New York: Oxford University Press, 1980.

Grigg, Richard. "The Experiential Center of Tillich's System." *Journal of the American Academy of Religion* 53:2 (Summer 1985): 251-58.

Gurian, Waldemar. "On Maritain's Political Philosophy." *The Thomist* 5 (1943): 15-31.

Gustafson, James M. *Ethics from a Theocentric Perspective.* 2 vols. Chicago: The University of Chicago Press, 1981, 1984.

____. *Protestant and Roman Catholic Ethics: Prospects for Rapprochement.* Chicago: The University of Chicago Press, 1978.

Gutierrez, Gustavo. *On Job: God-Talk and the Suffering of the Innocent.* Mary O'Connell, trans. Maryknoll, NY: Orbis Books, 1987.

____. *A Theology of Liberation: History, Politics, and Salvation.* Trans. and ed., Sister Caridad Inda and John Eagleson. Maryknoll, NY: Orbis Books, 1973.

Hampson, Daphne. "On Power and Gender." *Modern Theology* 4/2 (1988): 234-50.

Habermas, Jürgen. *The Philosophical Discourse of Modernity: Twelve Lectures.* Trans. Frederick Lawrence. Cambridge, MA: MIT Press, 1987.

____. *The Structural Transformation of the Public Sphere,* trans. T. Burger and F. Lawrence. Cambridge, MA: MIT Press, 1989).

____. *The Theory of Communicative Action* Cambridge, MA: MIT Press, 1987.

Hampson, Daphne. "On Power and Gender." *Modern Theology* 4:3 (1988): 234-250.

Harland, Gordon. *The Thought of Reinhold Niebuhr.* New York: Oxford Press, 1960.

Harrison, Beverly Wildung. *Making the Connections: Essays in Feminist Social Ethics.* Ed. Carol S. Robb. Boston: Beacon Press, 1985.

Harrison, Paul R. "Power, Culture, and the Interpretation of Democracy." *Praxis International* 11:3 (October 1991): 340-353.

Hartsock, Nancy C. M. *Money, Sex, and Power: Toward a Feminist Historical Materialism.* Boston: Northeastern University Press, 1985.

Haward. David W., Ed. *Power: Its Forms, Bases, Uses.* New York, NY: Harper and Row, 1979.

Held, David, and John B. Thompson, Eds. *Social Theory of Modern Societies: Anthony Giddens and His Critics.* Cambridge: Cambridge University Press, 1989.

Hewitt, Marcia. "The Politics of Empowerment: Ethical Paradigms in a Feminist Critique of Critical Social Theory." *Annual of the Society of Christian Ethics* (1991): 173-92.

Hiley, David R. "Foucault and the Analysis of Power: Political Engagement Without Liberal Hope or Comfort." *Praxis International* 4/2 (July 1984): 191-207.

Hinze, Christine Firer. "Christian Feminists, James Luther Adams, and the Search for a Radically Transformative Ethics." *Journal of Religious Ethics* (1993): 275-302.

___. "Power in Christian Ethics: Resources and Frontiers for Scholarly Exploration." *Annual of the Society of Christian Ethics* (1992): 277-90.

Hopkins, Dwight N. *Shoes That Fit Our Feet: Sources for a Constructive Black Theology.* Maryknoll, NY: Orbis, 1993.

Hoy, David Couzens, Ed. *Foucault: A Critical Reader.* Oxford: Basil Blackwell, 1986.

Isasi-Diaz, Ada Maria and Yolanda Tarango. *Hispanic Women: Prophetic Voice in the Church.* San Francisco: Harper and Row, 1988.

Jaggar, Allison M. *Feminist Politics and Human Nature.* Sussex, NJ: Rowman and Allenheld, Publishers, 1983.

Janeway, Elizabeth. *Powers of the Weak.* New York: Morrow Quill, 1980.

Johnson, Elizabeth. *She Who Is: The Mystery of God in Feminist Theological Discourse.* New York: Crossroad, 1993.

Kahn, Robbie Pfeufer. "The Problem of Power in Habermas." *Human Studies* 11 (1988): 361-387.

Kain, Philip J. "Marx, Housework, and Alienation." *Hypatia* 8:1 (Winter 1993): 121-143.

____. *Marx and Modern Political Theory.* Lanham, MD: Rowman & Littlefield, 1993.

Kalumba, Kibujjo M. "Maritain on 'The Common Good': Reflections on the Concept," *Laval theologique et philosophique* 49 (fevrier 1993): 93-104.

Kateb, George. *Hannah Arendt: Politics, Conscience, Evil.* Totowa, NJ: Rowman and Allenheld Publishers, 1984.

Kegley, Charles W., and Robert W. Bretall, Eds. *Reinhold Niebuhr: His Religious and Political Thought.* New York: MacMillan, 1956.

Keller, Catherine. *From a Broken Web: Separation, Sexism, and the Self.* Boston: Beacon Press, 1986.

Keller, Jack A., Jr. "Niebuhr, Tillich, and Whitehead on the Ethics of Power." *American Journal of Theology and Philosophy* 7:3 (September 1986): 132-48.

King, Martin Luther, Jr. "Beyond the Los Angeles Riots." *Saturday Review*, 35. November 13, 1965.

____. *Where Do We Go From Here: Chaos or Community?* Boston, Beacon Press, 1967.

____. "Who Is Their God?" *The Nation* 195 (Oct. 13, 1962): 210.

Krips, Henry. "Power and Resistance." *Philosophy of the Social Sciences* 20/2 (June 1990): 170-82.

Kristjansson, K. "'Constraining Freedom' and 'Exercising Power Over.'" *International Journal of Moral and Social Studies* 2 (Summer, 1992): 127-138.

Kreisberg, Seth. *Transforming Power: Domination, Empowerment, and Education.* Albany: State University of New York, 1992.

LaCugna, Catherine Mowry, Ed. *Freeing Theology: The Essentials of Theology in Feminist Perspective.* San Francisco: Harper, 1993.

Layder, Derek. "Power, Structure, and Agency." *Journal of the Theory of Social Behavior* 15 (July 1985): 131-150.

Lebacqz, Karen. *Justice in an Unjust World: Foundations for a Christian Approach to Justice.* Minneapolis, MN: Augsburg, 1987.

___. "Love Your Enemy: Sex, Power, and Christian Ethics." *Annual of the Society of Christian Ethics* (1990): 3-24.

Leidholdt, Dorchen and Janice G. Raymond, Eds. *The Sexual Liberals and the Attack on Feminism.* Elmsford, NY: Pergamon Press, 1990.

Levine, Donald N. "Rationality and Freedom: Weber and Beyond." *Sociological Inquiry* 51 (1983): 5-25.

Lerner, Gerda. *The Creation of Patriarchy.* Oxford: Oxford University Press, 1986.

Livesey, Lois Gehr. "Women, Power, and Politics: Feminist Theology in Process Perspective." *Process Studies* 17/2 (Summer 1988): 67-77.

Loomer, Bernard. "Two Kinds of Power." *Criterion* 15 (Winter 1976): 11-29.

Lonergan, Bernard J. F., S.J. "The Dialectic of Authority." *A Third Collection.* Ed. Frederick E. Crowe, S.J. New York, Mahwah: Paulist Press; London: Geoffrey Chapman, 1985, pp. 5-12.

Lorde, Audre. *Sister Outsider*. Trumansburg, NY: Crossing Press, 1984.

Löwith, Karl. *Max Weber and Karl Marx*. *Controversies in Sociology* 12. Ed. T. B. Bottomore and M. J. Mulkay. Trans. H. Fantel. London: George Allen and Unwin, 1982.

Lukes, Steven. *Essays in Social Theory*. New York: Columbia University Press, 1977.

____. "Power and Authority." *History of Sociological Analysis*, 633-676. Ed. T. Bottomore and R. Nisbet. New York: Basic Books, 1978.

____. *Power: A Radical View*. New York: MacMillan, 1974.

Maguire, John A. "Marx on Ideology, Power, and Force," *Theory and Decision* 7 (1976): 315-329.

Maritain, Jacques. *Freedom in the Modern World*. New York: Charles Scribner's Sons, 1936.

____. *Integral Humanism*. Trans. J. Evans. Notre Dame, IN: University of Notre Dame Press, 1968.

____. *Man and the State*. Chicago: The University of Chicago Press, 1951.

____. *On the Philosophy of History*. New York: Charles Scribner's Sons, 1957.

____. *The Person and the Common Good*. Notre Dame, IN: University of Notre Dame Press, 1946, 1966.

____. *The Rights of Man and Natural Law*. New York: Charles Scribner's Sons, 1943.

____. *Scholasticism and Politics*. Ed. Mortimer J. Adler. London: Geoffrey Bles, 1940, 3rd ed., 1954.

____. *The Social and Political Philosophy of Jacques Maritain: Selected Readings*. Ed. J. W. Evans and L. R. Ward. New York: Charles Scribner's Sons, 1955.

Maritain, Jacques. *The Things That Are Not Caesar's.* New York: Charles Scribner, 1930.

Marx, Karl. *The Poverty of Philosophy.* New York: International Publishers, 1967.

Marx, Karl and Friedrich Engels. *Marx and Engels: Basic Writings on Politics and Philosophy.* Ed. Lewis S. Feuer. Garden City, New York: Doubleday Anchor Books, 1959.

____. *The Marx Engels Reader.* 2nd ed. Ed. Robert C. Tucker. New York: W. W. Norton and Company, 1978.

McCann, Dennis. *Christian Realism and Liberation Theology: Practical Theologies in Creative Conflict.* Maryknoll, NY: Orbis Books, 1981.

McGill, Arthur C. *Suffering: A Test of Theological Method.* Philadelphia, Westminster Press, 1982.

Mead, George Herbert. *Mind, Self, and Society.* Chicago: The University of Chicago Press, 1934. Paperback edition, 1962.

Metcalf, H. C. and L. Urwick, Eds. *Dynamic Administration: The Collected Papers of Mary Parker Follett.* New York: Harper Brothers, 1941.

Miguez Bonino, José. *Christians and Marxists: The Mutual Challenge to Revolution.* Grand Rapids, MI: William G. Eerdmans Publishing Company, 1976.

____. *Toward a Christian Political Ethics.* Philadelphia: Fortress Press, 1983.

Miller, Alice. *For Your Own Good: Hidden Cruelty in Child-Rearing and the Roots of Violence.* New York: Farrar, Straus, Giroux, 1983.

Miller, Jean Baker. *Toward A New Psychology of Women.* Boston: Beacon Press, 1976, 2nd edition, 1986.

Miller-McLemore, Bonnie J. *Also A Mother: Work and Family as a Theological Dilemma.* Nashville, TN: Abingdon Press, 1994.

Mills, C. Wright. *The Power Elite.* New York: Oxford University Press, 1956.

Mommsen, Wolfgang J. *The Age of Bureaucracy: Perspectives on the Political Sociology of Max Weber.* Oxford: Basil Blackwell, 1974.

Moraga, Cherrie and Gloria Anzaldua, Eds. *This Bridge Called My Back: Writings By Radical Women of Color.* Watertown, MA: Persephone Press, 1981.

Morriss, Peter. *Power: A Philosophical Analysis.* Manchester: Manchester University Press, 1987.

Murray, John Courtney, S.J. *We Hold These Truths: Catholic Reflections on the American Proposition.* New York: Sheed and Ward, 1960.

Myers, Max A. "'Ideology' and 'Legitimation' as Necessary Concepts for Christian Ethics." *Journal of the American Academy of Religion* XLIX/2 (1981): 187-210.

Niebuhr, H. Richard. *Christ and Culture.* New York: Harper and Row, 1951. Harper Torchbook, 1956.

____. *The Responsible Self.* New York: Harper and Row, 1963.

Niebuhr, Reinhold. *The Children of Light and the Children of Darkness: A Vindication of Democracy and a Critique of its Traditional Defense.* New York: Charles Scribner's Sons, 1944.

____. *Christian Realism and Political Problems.* New York: Charles Scribner's Sons, 1953.

____. *Discerning the Signs of the Times: Sermons for Today and Tomorrow.* New York: Charles Scribner's Sons, 1946.

____. *Faith and History: A Comparison of Christian and Modern Views of History.* New York: Charles Scribner's Sons, 1949.

Niebuhr, Reinhold. *Faith and Politics*. Ed. R. H. Stone. New York: George Braziller, 1968.

___. "Force and Reason in Politics." *Nation* 150 (1940): 216.

___. "The Illusion of World Government." *Foreign Affairs* 27 (1949): 379-88.

___. *An Interpretation of Christian Ethics*. New York: Harper and Brothers, 1935.

___. *Love and Justice: Selections from the Shorter Writings of Reinhold Niebuhr*. Ed. D. B. Robertson. Philadelphia: Westminster Press, 1957.

___. *Moral Man and Immoral Society*. New York: Charles Scribner's Sons, 1932, 1960.

___. *The Nature and Destiny of Man: A Christian Interpretation*. 2 vols. New York: Charles Scribner's Sons, 1941, 1943.

___. *Reflections on the End of an Era*. New York: Charles Scribner, 1934.

___. *The Structure of Nations and Empires*. New York: Charles Scribner's Sons, 1959.

Nothwehr, Dawn M., O.S.F. "Mutuality: A Formal Norm for Christian Social Ethics." Unpublished Ph.D. Dissertation. Marquette University, 1995.

O'Connell, Timothy. E. *Principles for a Catholic Morality*, Revised Ed. San Francisco: Harper San Francisco, 1990.

Parsons, Talcott. *Politics and Social Structure*. New York: The Free Press, 1969.

___. *Sociological Theory in Modern Society*. New York: The Free Press, 1967.

Pasewark, Kyle A. *A Theology of Power: Being Beyond Domination.* Minneapolis: Fortress Press, 1993.

Patomäki, Heikki. Concepts of 'Action', 'Structure' and 'Power' in 'Critical Social Realism': A Positive and Reconstructive Critique." *Journal for the Theory of Social Behavior* 21/2 (1992): 221-250.

Petrovic, Gayo. "Alienation." *Encyclopedia of Philosophy* vol. 1, 76-81. Ed. Paul Edwards. New York: MacMillan and the Free Press, 1967.

Philp, Mark. "Foucault on Power: A Problem in Radical Translation?" *Political Theory* 11 (Feb 1983): 29-52.

Proceedings of the Catholic Theological Society of America 37 (1982). Ed. Luke Salm, F.S.C. Theme: "Power as an Issue in Theology."

Quelquejeu, Bernard. "K. Marx a-t-il constitué une theorie du pouvoir d'Etât?" *Revue des sciences philosophiques et théologiques* 63 (1979). I. 17-60; II. 203-240; III. 365-418.

Rabuzzi, Kathryn Allen. "The Socialist Feminist Vision of Rosemary Radford Ruether." *Religious Studies Review* 15/1 (January 1989): 15-18.

Rahner, Karl. "The Theology of Power." *Theological Investigations* vol 4, 391-410. Trans. Kevin Smyth. New York: Crossroad, 1982.

Redpath, Peter A., Ed. *From Twilight to Dawn: The Cultural Vision of Jacques Maritain.* Mishawaka, IN: American Maritain Association, 1990.

Ross, Stephen David. "Foucault's Radical Politics." *Praxis International* 5/2 (July 1985): 131-43.

Ross, Susan A. "'He has Pulled Down the Mighty from their Thrones and has Exalted the Lowly': A Feminist Reflection on Empowerment." In Michael Downey, Ed., *That They Might Live: Power, Empowerment, and Leadership in the Church.* New York: Crossroad, 1991, 145-159.

Ruddick, Sara. *Maternal Thinking.* Boston: Beacon Press, 1989.

Russell, Letty M. *Household of Freedom: Authority in Feminist Theology.* Philadelphia: Westminster Press, 1987.

Scarry, Elaine. *The Body in Pain: The Making and Unmaking of the World.* New York: Oxford University Press, 1985.

Schneck, Stephen Frederick. "Michel Foucault on Power/Discourse, Theory and Practice." *Human Studies* 10 (1987): 15-33.

Schubeck, Thomas L., S.J. *Liberation Ethics: Sources, Models, Norms.* Minneapolis: Fortress Press, 1993.

Scott, James C. *Domination and the Arts of Resistance.* New Haven, CT: Yale University Press, 1990.

Seigfried, Charlene Haddock. "Shared Communities of Interest: Feminism and Pragmatism." *Hypatia* 8/2 (Spring 1993): 1-14.

Sharp, Gene. *The Politics of Non-Violent Action, Part One: Power and Struggle.* Boston: Porter-Sargent, 1973.

Springborg, Patricia. "Arendt, Republicanism, and Patriarchalism." *History of Political Thought* 10/3 (Autumn, 1989): 499-523.

____. "Hannah Arendt and the Classical Republican Tradition." In Gisela T. Kaplan and Clive S. Kessler, Eds. *Hannah Arendt: Thinking, Judging, and Freedom.* Sydney: Allen & Unwin, 1989, 9-17.

Starhawk (Miriam Simos). *Truth or Dare: Encounters with Power, Authority, and Mystery.* San Francisco: Harper and Row, 1987.

Sturm, Douglas. "Praxis and Promise: On the Ethics of Political Theology." *Ethics* 92 (July 1982): 733-750.

Tillich, Paul. *The Interpretation of History.* New York: Charles Scribner's Sons, 1936.

____. *Love, Power, and Justice: Ontological Analyses and Ethical Applications.* London: Oxford University Press, 1954.

Tillich, Paul. *Political Expectation*. Ed. James Luther Adams. New York: Harper and Row, 1971; Macon, GA: Mercer University Press, 1981.

____. *Systematic Theology*. 3 vols. Chicago:The University of Chicago Press, 1951, 1957, 1963.

Tirrell, Lynn. "Definition and Power: Toward Authority Without Privilege." *Hypatia* 8/4 (Fall 1993): 1-34.

Tolle, Gordon. *Human Nature Under Fire: The Political Philosophy of Hannah Arendt*. Washington, D.C.: University Press of America, 1982.

Townes, Emily, Ed. *A Troubling in My Soul: Womanist Perspectives on Evil and Suffering*. Maryknoll, NY: Orbis Books, 1993.

Tracy, David. *Analogical Imagination*. New York: Crossroad, 1981.

____. *Blessed Rage for Order: The New Pluralism in Theology*. New York: Seabury, 1975.

Walzer, Michael. *Spheres of Justice: A Defense of Pluralism and Equality*. New York: Basic Books, 1983.

Wapner, Paul. "What's Left: Marx, Foucault, and Contemporary Problems of Social Change." *Praxis International* 9: 1/2 (April & July 1989): 88-111.

Wartenberg, Thomas E. "The Concept of Power in Feminist Theory." *Praxis International* 8 (October 1988): 301-316.

____. *The Forms of Power: From Domination to Transformation*. Philadelphia: Temple University Press, 1990.

Weber, Max. *Economy and Society*. 2 vols. Ed. Guenther Roth and Claus Wittich. Berkeley: University of California Press, 1968.

____. *From Max Weber: Essays in Sociology*. Ed. Trans., introduction by H. H. Gerth and C. Wright Mills. New York: Oxford University Press, 1946. Paperback edition, 1958.

Weber, Max. "The Interpretive Understanding of Social Action." *Readings in the Philosophy of Science*, 19-33. Ed. H. Feigl and M. Brodbeck. New York: Appleton-Century-Crofts, 1953.

___. *The Methodology of the Social Sciences*. Ed. and trans. E. A. Shils and H. A. Finch. New York: The Free Press, 1949.

___. *The Protestant Ethic and the Spirit of Capitalism*. Trans. Talcott Parsons. New York: Charles Scribner's Sons, 1958.

___. *The Sociology of Religion*. Ed. and introduced Talcott Parsons. Boston: Beacon Press, 1964.

___. *Weber: Selections in Translation*. Ed. W. G. Runciman. Cambridge: Cambridge University Press, 1978.

Webster's Ninth New Collegiate Dictionary. Springfield, MA: Merriam-Webster, Inc., 1983.

Welch, Sharon. *Communities of Resistance and Solidarity: A Feminist Theology of Liberation*. Maryknoll, NY: Orbis Books, 1985.

___. *A Feminist Ethic of Risk*. Minneapolis: Fortress Press, 1990.

West, Cornel. *Prophesy Deliverance!: An Afro-American Revolutionary Christianity*. Philadelphia: Westminster Press, 1982.

Whitbeck, Carolyn. "A Different Reality: Feminist Ontology." Carol C. Gould, Ed. *Beyond Domination: New Perspectives on Women and Philosophy*, 64-88. Totowa, NJ: Rowman and Allanheld, Publishers, 1983.

Whitehead, Albert North. *Adventures of Ideas*. New York: The Free Press, 1933.

Wiley, Norbert, Ed. *The Marx-Weber Debate*. Key Issues in Sociological Theory, vol. 2. Newbury Park, CA: Sage Publications, 1987.

Wilmore, Gayraud S. and James H. Cone, Eds. *Black Theology: A Documentary History, 1966-1979*. Maryknoll, NY: Orbis Books, 1979.

Wolin, Sheldon. "Contract and Birthright." *Political Theory* 14/2: 1986: 179-93.

Wrong, Dennis. *Power: Its Forms, Bases, and Uses.* New York: Harper and Row, 1979.

Young, Iris Marion. "Humanism, Gynocentrism and Feminist Politics." *Women's Studies International Forum* 8:1 (1985) 173-183.

Young, Pamela Dickey. *Feminist Theology/Christian Theology: In Search of A Method.* Minneapolis, MN: Fortress Press, 1990.